Joseph Emerson

Lectures and sermons on subjects connected with Christian liberal education

Joseph Emerson

Lectures and sermons on subjects connected with Christian liberal education

ISBN/EAN: 9783337265274

Printed in Europe, USA, Canada, Australia, Japan

Cover: Foto ©Lupo / pixelio.de

More available books at **www.hansebooks.com**

LECTURES AND SERMONS

ON

SUBJECTS CONNECTED WITH CHRISTIAN LIBERAL EDUCATION.

BY

JOSEPH EMERSON, D.D.

PROFESSOR OF GREEK IN BELOIT COLLEGE.

CHICAGO

P. F. PETTIBONE & CO.

1897

TO MY WIFE AND MY PUPILS,

THE COMPANIONS OF MY STUDIES,

THESE FRAGMENTS OF THEIR RESULTS

ARE GRATEFULLY INSCRIBED.

INTRODUCTION.

These Lectures and Sermons are given to the press in compliance with the solicitation of friends, and in part, also, in a desire to endeavor something still in the work of Christian Liberal Education, a work which has been the privilege of the author's life during such a half century as that now closing.

It has been a further privilege to have, in such an education, the Department of Greek, not merely the language, but the life of which the language was the voice. The harmonious zeal and thought, which produced such minds and souls as Homer, Æschylus and Socrates, and in turn were moulded by them, created and developed a nation, whose intellectual and moral life had pervaded the world when the Savior came, preparing mind to receive the word of life, as well as language to express it.

It has been a still further privilege to "unroll the books of the ancients" with the young men of a nation, itself as young as were the Greeks themselves who thought and felt and spoke and lived with Solon or Demosthenes. A young college, a young state, a young nation, and a great crisis in that nation's life, brought young men to a communion with ever young forces of truth and of life, which could not but tell upon the communicants.

If it was inspiring to study the heroisms of the old time with the young spirits of the new time, it has been grand to see the kindling and the proving of the new heroism, which has gone from that study, as the call has come, to some to die and to others to live for God, for Man and for Truth.

The opportunity for such study has been mainly in the intercourse of the class-room or individual association and conversation. The class-room, however, or various platforms have given occasion for lectures or addresses, and the College chapel and various pulpits have called for sermons, all of which belong to a Christian Liberal Education, and from which a few have been detached for this volume.

As faith and thought were made to live together, and our time, at least, cannot afford their divorce, it has seemed right to publish lectures and sermons in the same volume, and that religious thought should not be excluded from the one or practical thought from the other.

The crisis of our time has led all our people through a course of high Christian and Liberal Education, from which we ought to come out larger and better men. The impressions of that education should not pass from our minds or be erased from our writings or our lives. Let them go with us into the coming time. So may we pass on from this into another, and, as we hope, an "ever better age."

It is good to think that the struggles, the sufferings, the martyrdoms of all the past and the present shall not be lost. To minds stayed by such a faith, the depth and the length of the sorrow is the measure of the height and the duration of the deliverance. The trials and the triumphs which we have seen may assure our hope, if they confirm our devotion. To contribute to such faith and hope and work, the true fruit of Christian Education, has been an aim of these essays. They are presented to the thought, rather than the criticism, of those who would love the light that they may do the truth.

CONTENTS.

LECTURES.

SERMONS.

I.

HOMER AND THE INFANCY OF GREECE.

History is biography.   Races and nations are individuals. Civilization is the education by which persons become citizens, making and sharing the commonwealth.

Races and nations succeed one another, by families and genealogies of races and nations, leaving their wisdom and their wealth to their heirs.

Our own civilization, the intellectual and spiritual movement and life which have come to us, was born in ancient Greece.   It drew its nurture from much older nations, from Egypt and the East; but its own young life was a new life, which has been continuous in many ages and lands from then until now.

We do not ignore the older wisdom of Egypt; nor the Phoenician enterprise, which brought that teaching to the new-born child; nor the Roman law or the Hebrew faith, which trained him afterward; nor the Teutonic vigor, which, still later, took that education as the soul of its own great might.   But we hold that the common life, in which we live, was born when the power, which had grown for ages in northern mountains, came down to the capes and isles of Greece, and there met the thought, which studious ages had matured on the southern shores of the great Mediterranean.

Let us look back, so far as we can, to the infancy of that life, which is our own.

Of the commencement of Greek civilization, we, of course, know nothing, and of its early progress but very little, historically.   A nation is like a child in this, as in other respects, that its early thoughts are without articulate expression or permanent impression upon its own memory; yet in those forgotten years are the springing of traits which make up the character of the man, and it may be that a single word or look of kindness may call to the infant's eye a light gleam of love—a first opening to sunlight of a fountain of affection, which will thenceforth continue to flow, a well-spring of benevolence, throughout the life of the man. And by tracing back the currents of prevalent thought and feeling, we may divine what were the influences which surrounded the infancy of a man, a people, or a race.

In seeking the sources of Greek civilization we are not left merely to such inferences. For the mind of the nation has gratefully cherished in memory the lessons by which it was formed.

The child is a poet child. The father of history tells us that the epic poetry, which is daily read in our schools as a class exercise, was sung in Greece four hundred years before his time. We can only say of it, that it was composed in ages before the Greeks had any prose literature or permanent chronicles; that the days in which it was sung are separated from historic times by a gulf which no antiquarian scholar can bridge with events. But there we hear it, clearly echoing the manners of its own age, while it celebrates the deeds of a former one, of what was to it, antiquity.

After those poems were composed we know but little of the course of things in Greece; the brave that lived after Agamemnon sleep forgotten like those that lived before him.

But we know that the old songs were still chanted to the lyre, and that by them the admiring mind and soul of the nation were filled with high thoughts and heroic emotions, until they became mature enough for a new kind of exercise; to enter upon that active and self-conscious life which records itself in history, which thinks and writes and speaks, with and for the mind, as well as feels, and plays and sings, in and to the soul.

The great peculiarity, then, of Greek civilization throughout, is that it is continually led and guided by music.

In the times when Hellas was an infant, for it was never other than a singing child, the music and song is of heroes, the epic, which is to a nation of minds strengthened by years and experience of strong, rude impulses, but not matured by philosophic thought, what the nursery ballad is to the unschooled child. As Hellas grew older and more thoughtful and self-conscious, its youthful development, like that of lad or maiden, is marked by the song of love and of hope; and so there follows next in Greece the age of lyric poetry. Then as, under this perennial childhood, there grew the strength of manhood, like the unconquerable heart of the live oak under its evergreen foliage, and the Persian invaders came, like a tornado of the tropics upon the same oak; the music that ever played about it assumed strains fitted to the mind and soul of man, bracing itself with high thoughts for strife and suffering, and unbending itself in rude hilarity; and they that struggled and prevailed at Marathon and Salamis, wrote and acted, and heard at their festivals, from daybreak until nightfall, tragedies and comedies.

And as the maturity of green and hale age comes on, its philosophical thought is still harmonious and musical, not in vocal measure, but in the beautiful, melodious, active vibrations of mind and spirit. Socrates, walking the streets of Athens and conversing in the market, seems not so much like a profound philosopher as like an inspired minstrel, gifted to touch the cords of the human heart and to draw from it that wondrous and celestial music of true and holy thoughts and feelings, which alone can give us some idea of what may be meant by the music of "harpers harping with their harps," which one hath told us that he heard round about the throne on high. And, if Socrates was thus the Aoidos—the original bard of philosophy—Plato follows him as its Rhapsodist, the singer to transmit to future times in permanent forms, those strains by which men should learn " the numbers and measures of a true life,"

" Numerosque modosque verae ediscere vitae."

But with declining years and strength, trouble came to Hellas, and the voice, grown mellow and canorous, but not less flexible by age, must learn the persuasivenesss of the plea and the protest, and so in the din of the rude Macedonian arms we hear the tuneful eloquence of Demosthenes, and the scene closes, but suddenly it opens again and reveals Greece as mistress of all Asia.

So Hellenic national life is continually led and guided by music; its childhood is stimulated and trained by the epic; its youth is charmed by the lyric; its manhood is moved by the drama; its age is instructed by harmonious philosophy; and its departing spirit persuaded to linger yet longer about the Acropolis by eloquence.

Now let us go back and observe more particularly the earlier ages of Greek civilization. Apollo and the Muses presided over it. Its instruments were music, and those customs and tendencies and exercises which music may fitly accompany.

This agency of music in the early development of Hellenic culture is fully recognized by the ancients themselves. Horace expresses their opinion in his well-known lines, which we may freely translate, as follows:

Orpheus, as a sacred voice of the gods, called the forest-roving men from the life of slaughter and vile food; therefore it was said that he soothed tigers and fierce lions. And Amphion, too, founder of Thebes, was said to move rocks and lead them where he would by the soft persuasiveness of his lyre. This was their wisdom of old, to distinguish the public

from the private, the sacred from the common, to withhold from promiscu-
ous love, to give rights of marriage, to make common works for defense,
to grave laws in wood. So came to bards the respect and the name of divine. After these, glorious Homer and Tyrtaeus incited masculine hearts
to war by their songs; oracles were spoken in verse, and men were pointed
the way to live.

So far Horace. Indeed, all the early tradition of Greece
is as much pervaded by music as that of Rome is by stern
hardihood. The listening for divine melody is co-extensive
with the Greek race. In all Northern Greece "the
Muses haunt clear spring and shady grove and sunny hill."
Pieria, in Macedonia, was their native home; their presence
pervaded the grand ranges of Pindus, which border Thessaly,
and the cliffs of Parnassus in Phocis and Helicon in Beotia.
Their influence was over the fountains of Hippocrene and
Aganippe. In the Peloponnesus was Cyllene, where Mercury
invented the lyre, and the mountain ranges which Apollo and
the Muses frequented with dance and song. The hills and
forests of Arcadia were resonant with the musical reeds of
Pan. In their foreign settlements and voyages the world
was still for them full of music. It mingled strangely with
the rude and fearful imaginings with which they peopled the
borders of the world. They associated the minstrelsy of
Orpheus with the cruel savageness of Thrace and located
Sirens upon a fearful coast in the dim west of the Mediterranean.

All these fables express the tone of mind of the Hellenic
people in their early rudeness, and they would be of themselves sufficient to point to the natural history of their marvelous culture.

But, as we have already said, we have now in our hands
poems which reveal to us life in Greece ages before Greece
came to be historical. The revelations are principally of
two periods, that of the minstrels themselves and that of the
heroes whom they sang.

The poems which pass under the name of Homer came into being so long before history that we have no means of assigning to them any certain date. They are supposed to have been sung about eight hundred years before the Christian era. This would be three hundred years before Tragedy, three hundred and fifty before history was written by Herodotus, and fifty years before the reputed founding of Rome.

Greece as revealed to us then was in many particulars like the Greece of historic times. It was a nation, not by unity of government, but by common language, institutions and sympathies. The general meetings of Greece were not judicial or legislative as among our nations, but for common sacrifices and exhibitions.

The representatives of Hellenic unity, and, indeed, the ministers of Greek society were the priests and minstrels, quite as much as the kings.

It is a little difficult for us, with our machinery of government, to understand the constitution of society in the primitive times. Each man then was the vindicator of his own rights, according to certain principles of common law, which were recognized by the common consent of men. His appeal was not to a regular judiciary, but to the old men of the city, sitting " in a sacred circle," either at the city gate, or in the market place, and forming a court of arbitration, sustained by the public opinion of the community.

For instruction in those principles of natural and traditional right by which the intercourse of man with man was to be governed, as well as in their relations and duties to their gods, the early Greeks depended, like all other nations, upon their educated lass. And, in the absence of books and prose literature, who were the educated class of Greece? Who led the thinking of the people? The priests and the bards, to whom also the respect of the people attached not a little of sacredness of character. And of these two classes, while the priests, especially those of the oracles, might have spoken with more authority, the traveling minstrels must, on the other hand, have exerted a more general influence upon the forming thoughts and sentiments of the people. For, traveling from place to place, they came continually in contact with the people at large, and everywhere finding ready entertainment and eager listeners, they supplied almost the entire intellectual and spiritual incitement of the people. They exercised upon a people of quick and trustful mind the influence at once of the sermon, the code of laws, the common school, the public lecture, the newspaper, and the whole body of literature. The impressions which the bard made were not carelessly received and soon effaced; but when he came to a village and sung of the virtue of Penelope, the wisdom of Nestor, or of the endurance of Ulysses, he left material for thought and for character with the men and the women, the maidens and the youth who heard him.

But the minstrel was in his glory in the common festivals of Greece. Common games and common sacrifices were almost the only formal union known among the Greek states, and in times somewhat later than those of which we are now speaking, the national games, particularly the Olympic games, constituted such a general reunion of the whole Hellenic family.

But in the times of the Aoidoi, Panhellenic unity was mainly expressed by a common reverence for the oracle at Delphi, and by the common language and sentiments diffused by wandering bards and somewhat by commercial connections. There were, however, festivals which brought together neighboring or kindred states in various parts of the Greek world. These were generally connected with the worship of some deity who was the patron of the confederacy.

Perhaps we can in no way get a better view of the influence of the bards, or of the civilization of Greece in their day, than by trying to realize the scene of one of these "panegyries." Let us go then to the May Day of Ionia,

THE FESTIVAL AT DELOS.

In the midst of the Aegean Sea lies a little island, hardly three miles in length and less than one mile in breadth, which the ancients called Delos. It is surrounded by the beautiful group of the Cyclades, many of which are much larger than itself, but they all, in the estimation of the Greeks, were honored in being members of its court.

For Delos was the birthplace of Apollo and Diana. According to their legend the island itself was once a goddess of heaven, Asteria, who fled from the sky to escape the passion of Jove, and became an island floating in the sea, until after long wanderings it was at last fixed, in order that Latona, sister of Asteria, who was wandering, rejected by every land as she was about to become a mother, might find a resting place and give birth to the new divinities. It was fastened by four columns of adamant to the solid foundations of the earth, so that earthquakes could not shake it, and mortals named it Delos, but the gods in Olympus called it the far-famed star of the earth.

In the earliest times of which we have record, the Ionic Greeks used to assemble at Delos, with their wives and their children, to celebrate an annual festival in honor of their patron deity, Apollo, probably choosing for the purpose the reputed birthday of the god, which fell on the sixth of Thargelion, about our first of May.

In the gray of the morning we will ascend Mount Cynthus, the rugged mass of granite which rises five hundred feet high in the midst of the island. We climb by stone steps which lead up the western slope, and passing under a portal of huge rough stones, which shall bear witness ages hence that there were mighty men in these days of old, we find ourselves in the Acropolis, upon the summit.

Beneath us sleeps the sea, and all around stand the Cyclades, solemnly guarding the sacred island. But the repose is not long. Already in the first thin light of dawn boats are putting off from every harbor and beach, and they come more and more thickly until the sea is alive with them. The sun rises. Its light falls first upon the wild ridges of Naxos to the south, where Bacchus and his train used to revel; then it glistens upon the marble peaks of Paros, and soon Syros and Rheneia and Olearos and all the Cyclades are bathed in light.

The level beams, as they strike the sea, flash in the spray of a thousand oars in the straits toward the northeast and the east and they are reflected from the southwest, the west and the northwest by a cloud of sails, swollen by the zephyr, and every oar and every sail is hurrying to Delos.

So the Ionians come, little boats from many islands in the south, the fleets of Samos and Miletus from the east, from the northeast barges of Chios, and from the north thronging boats coming out from the shadows of the grave mountains of Andros and Tenos. But we cannot stay here longer, for there in the northwest the sacred galley of Athens is already in view from the summit.

Athens is the mother city of all the Ionians. In all their cities there is a sacred hearth upon which is continually burning a fire, originally kindled from the sacred hearth of the "Prytaneion" of Athens.

As we come to the shore we find a busy scene. For this is a great mart, as well as a festival. All the Greek commerce and art of the day is represented, and there are great Phoenician ships at the beach, which have visited lands of which the Greeks almost dread to hear. These have brought, not only their own choice manufactures of cloth and their unrivalled purple, but tin from Britain, gold from Spain, ivory and precious woods from Africa, amber from the shores of the Baltic, silks and gems from India and China.

Our attention is suddenly called away from the fair by the cry of "Homer!" "Homer!" A Chian vessel has touched the strand and a blind old man is led from it by a boy, who bears a harp. We shall hear that harp before the day is done.

Hardly is the poet on shore, when the Athenian galley appears, rounding the point of the adjoining island, Rheneia. It is the same vessel in which Theseus went to Crete when he slew the Minotaur, and he instituted this festival on his return. It is the law at Athens that this same vessel shall always be sent upon this "Theoria," and so they continually replace its decayed timbers, preparing for the philosophers of future centuries their curious question, whether after the repairs of a thousand years the "Theoris" is, or is not, still the old galley of Theseus. It is moved not by sails, but by thirty long oars, all keeping perfect time to the clear song of the "Keleustes."

Before it left Athens, the priest of Apollo adorned the barge with garlands of bay branches and a solemn sacrifice was offered at Marathon for its safe voyage. While it is gone no man may suffer the penalty of death at Athens, a law destined, many generations later, to secure to the world the last lessons of the wisdom of Socrates.

The barge is brought to the shore, and its landing is the signal for forming the grand procession. It moves to the sound of music, and is led by the "Architheoros" of Athens in gorgeous attire, followed by the rest of his "theoria," all with garlands of bay, and after them, state by state, follow the other Ionians in long and brilliant festal robes. They proceed to the sacred enclosure of the temple of Apollo, where, after the sacrifices, they present their gifts, which consist of such possessions as are esteemed most valuable and most worthy to be given to a god—tripods and caldrons of bronze, or more valuable ones of "much labored" iron, or even of silver and costly gold, and all the choice works of their rude art and treasures from distant lands.

Next they gather round a famous altar, one of the wonders of the world, made entirely of the horns of wild beasts, so interlaced as, without other fastening, to constitute a firm and symmetrical structure. They said that Apollo made it from the horns of beasts slain by his huntress sister.

About this altar they dance a sacred dance, instituted by Theseus on his return from Crete. It is the same of which we have a description from Homer himself, which we give in a literal version, without venturing to refine the simplicity of the master:

> The dance, which once in broad Cnossus
> Daedalus contrived for fair-haired Ariadne.
> There youth and maids, whom lovers must buy with many oxen,
> Danced, each with his hand upon the wrist of his partner.
> And the maids had delicate linen veils, and the youth wore
> Tunics well woven, and softly shining with olive oil.
> And the maids bore beautiful garlands, while the boys
> Had glittering daggers in silver belts.
> And now they flitted with knowing feet
> Right easily, as when a wheel, well fitted in his hands,
> A potter sits and tries if it will run.
> And again they danced in rows opposed one to another,
> And a multitude stand around the charming dance
> Delighted; and among them played a divine bard
> Upon his lyre, while in the very midst of the dancers
> Two tumblers were whirling wildly, but in perfect time to the music.

The strain is one which Olen, the Lycian, taught at Delos in the former days. The dancers accompanied it with a song, singing first of Apollo, then of Latona and of Artemis, lover of arrows and of heroes and heroines of old.

The auditory, charmed with this song, are next amused with a medley imitating to the life, with the voice and with the castanets, the languages and music and manners of all the nations of the earth.

After the dances the hosts of spectators are seated to witness games of skill and prowess. The prizes for victors are brought forth. They are "kettles and tripods, horses and mules and strong oxen, and fair girdled women and gray iron." The chiefs and men of renown from all Greece come forward to strive for them, for to be an athlete has not yet become a trade. The games are boxing, wrestling, the foot and chariot race, combats of spearmen, pitching the quoit, archery and hurling stones.

These contests have their interest, but let us refresh our minds with quieter scenes for a little while.

Here are palm trees, the sacred tree of Delos. They do not grow in Greece proper. There our guide shows us the identical one beneath which Apollo was born. This little stream, the Inopus, they say, is a branch of the Nile, which has flowed to Delos under the sea. Now come to the Artemisium, or temple of Diana. As we enter the enclosure, here upon the left is a green mound with an olive tree upon it. There were buried Hyperoche and Laodice, two maidens who came long ago bringing gifts to Diana from the Hyperboreans, a people living in perpetual peace and blessedness, free from sickness, toil or battle, in a happy clime, beyond the birthplace of the north wind. But the maidens never returned home from their pious embassy, and from that time their nation has wrapped their gifts in wheaten straw and commended them to the piety of all the intervening nations to transmit them to Delos. The strangers, however, were not forgotten by the people among whom they died. They rest here in the holy ground, and the maids of Delos, before they are married, cut off a braid of hair and wind it round a spindle and lay it on their tomb, and the Delian youth wreathe a lock of their hair about a young green twig, and they, too, put it upon the mound of the Hyperborean maidens.

We return to the great assembly just in time for the contest for the palm branch, which is to be the prize for the poets. In the midst of the concourse, but most closely surrounded by a throng of those maids of Delos who have been in the dance which we have seen, sits that blind bard from Chios. He sings, as was fit, the praises of Apollo, not forgetting, as was also fit, more earthly objects of poetical adoration. We give, as before, in a literal translation, the conclusion of his song:

> " All peaks are dear and jutting headlands
> Of lofty mountains,and rivers that roll to the sea,
> But Delos, thou shining one, is most the joy of thy heart;
> There for thee, in their flowing robes, the Ionians gather,
> With their children and their honored wives.
> When they form their assembly they remember thee
> And gladden thee with boxing and dance and song.
> He that should come then, when the Ionians were gathered,
> Would say that they were free from death and age forever,
> For he would see the grace of all and be glad in his soul,
> As he looked on men and fair-zoned women,
> And swift ships and their manifold treasures,
> And this great wonder, too, whose fame shall never die,
> The maids of Delos, hand maidens of the archer god;
> But now may Apollo be kind and Diana,
> And fare ye all well, and so henceforth
> Remember, when any one of earth-dwelling men,
> A way-faring stranger that may come, shall ask:
> ' Maidens, what man is to you sweetest of bards
> That come hither, and in whom do ye delight most?'
> Then right well do ye answer all in kindness:
> 'A blind man, and he dwells in craggy Chios;
> His songs henceforth all bear the palm,'
> And we will carry your fame wheresoever over the earth
> We go about to fair cities of men,
> And they will believe our report, for it is true."

So he ceases and they give him the palm. The assembly is broken up and night comes on, a night of rest and pleasant dreams. On the morrow the Ionians are away for their homes. But they go richer than they came, for they go with new thoughts and emotions; germs that shall be throughout the year maturing into the civilization of Greece.

This scene is not one of mere amusement. It is the education of Greece and the preparation of our own civilization. These Greeks at Delos are a rude race. The Phoenicians trading there despise them. They come to these isles of Javan to bring the wares of older nations in exchange for "persons of men and vessels of brass." (Ezekiel 27, 13.) And many a tale of wonder and of fear have these Tyrian sailors and merchants told the simple natives respecting the lands from which these wonderful things have come, stories inspired by that Oriental imagination which pervades the Arabian Nights, stimulated by the eagerness of the auditors and tinged by a crafty disposition to terrify them from entering into a rivalry with them in their commerce.

The Phoenicians had, moreover, the wonder of letters, and the Greeks learned from them their alphabet, that column of strange characters, which, according to all our conceptions, leads the van of all education.

We talk of literature and of letters as essential conditions and definitions of human knowledge and thought. But literature is not a Greek word or a Greek thought. Education with them was not by letters, but by music. And so when Cadmus and other Phoenicians brought them letters they did not need them as conditions of thought or of memory, but only for such use as they saw the Phoenicians make of them, for numerical calculations. For their thought and history they had a more living expression, which they never learned of the Phoenicians. For the Muses, daughters of Memory, were born upon their own soil, and from them the Greeks had learned rhythm, by which their spoken words assumed a stable form and made thought abiding. Those forms of rhythmic thought, which formed the nation, were prepared by their poets, like this Homer, whom we have seen and heard. Content with this education, they seem not to have used the "Phoenician marks" as alphabetic letters till long after they used them as numerical figures.

And Homer has gone! But he does not go as he came. A new palm branch is in his hand, a new garland is about his temples. But, more than these, a new poem is forming in his mind. During the sports which his blind eyes could not behold, he has been sitting by a Phoenician ship, just from Tarshish, hearing a Sidonian sailor, who has served many long years in the navy of King Hiram, tell of the wonders he has seen in distant lands and waters. The sailor is of that Oriental race whose imaginations indited the Arabian Nights. His name might be Sinbad, and, seeing the enthusiasm of the bard, he goes on to tell him not only of Egyptian Thebes, with its hundred gates, but to clothe all the far-off islands and coasts of the great sea with fabulous attractions and fabulous terrors. The bard has heard him silently. And when the last great shout from the arena told him that the games of the athletes were done, he took his harp and sung the song whose conclusion we have heard. But when the festival is over his mind reverts to the strange things which he has heard. His mind is the mind of a Greek poet, and those fables cannot remain in it, that chaos of "Gorgons, Hydras and Chimæras dire," which they were, as they came from the Canaanite.

A poet is a maker, a creator, and in his mind is a living principle of order and law, of rhythm, which is the forming principle of civilization. It is a part of that image of God in which He made man. And so the spirit of the poet moving over that chaos of imaginations called out of it a poem.

His eye, secluded as it is by his physical infirmity from the distractions of the visible world, follows a hero, a Greek, Ulysses, the most sagacious chief of those who fought at

Troy, as he is driven by adverse winds round these fearful coasts of which the sailor told, and borne through them all by the blessing of the gods upon the struggle and endurance of a ready mind, a stout heart and a God-fearing spirit.

So as the poet passes from island to island in the Grecian sea, and from valley to valley among the Greek mountains, the successive scenes of that Greek Pilgrim's Progress, which we call the Odyssey, are composed and set to music in his mind. Whenever he comes to a village the young and the old gather around him and he sings to them the song that is in his heart, and its burden ever is the victory of the hero soul, especially as a victory of self-command and loyalty; the hero, whom the excitement of victory can not carry away, whom not the sweet lotus fruit, nor the wiles of Circe, the song of the Sirens, or the blandishments of Calypso, divine goddess, who besought him to remain in her lovely island and become immortal, could tempt to forget his home. Famine could not drive him to touch the sacred kine of the sun god. Fear could not unman him, even in the horrid cave of the Cyclops, or as he looked down into the seething abyss of Charybdis, or saw the six heads of Scylla bear his companions aloft, or on the misty shore of the land of ghosts. Cast alone and destitute upon a strange land, he proves himself a hero hardly more by his achievements than by his modesty. At last he arrives at home, and here, too, he is great in his single-handed victory over the host of suitors, but if possible even greater in that self-command which could bear in a beggar's garb their jeers, abuse and violence. So he presents his picture of the man who is every inch a king, and his royalty is a throne of self-command in his own heart, so that he is a king when all alone, or in the form of a beggar or of a suppliant, as well as when fawned upon by men. So we welcome him home after his twenty years of war and wandering to rocky Ithaca and to his own true wife again.　For Penelope, too, is the hero woman and her heroism also is the heroism of inward truth.

The story, wherever sung, has not been an idle song, but it has left materials for thought and character with the men and women, the maidens and the youth, who have heard it.

So the bards went everywhere winning hearts and stirring spirits and feeding minds, and thus forming the nation for its greatness.

The subjects of the songs were as various as the thoughts of active though unreflecting minds, for all the life and thought of Greece was tuneful, the deeds of heroes, the wars of Thebes and Troy, the labors of Hercules and the honors of their gods;—and others sung of love, and instilled the sentiments of old Greek chivalry; and others again, like Hesiod, struck a more thoughtful vein, telling of the works by which the husbandman must thrive, and anon leading them to a higher and deeper contemplation by singing of the golden age, that had been, and which might perhaps in some distant time come again, the days of Kronos, when

> Men lived as gods with hearts free from care,
> Far away from toil and sorrow; and timorous age
> Fell not upon them; but ever with hands and feet alike
> They rejoiced in festivity away from all ills,
> Rich in flocks and dear to the blessed gods.
> And they died as subdued by sleep, and noble things all
> Were theirs;—the corn-bearing field bore them fruits
> Of its own motion, plenteous and unbegrudged, and at free
> Ease they did their works with many noble mates.
> But now that earth had hidden this stock beneath it,
> By the counsel of great Jove they are noble spirits,
> Dwellers still of earth, watchers of mortal men,
> That watch their justice and their deeds of wrong;
> That go clad in mist all over the earth,
> Givers of good.　This kingly honor had they.

By such songs was the mind of young Greece nurtured through centuries until Athens became possible.　The measure of them all was the Dactylic hexameter, a measure not well suited to a monosyllabic language like our own, but admirably accordant with the constitution of the Greek tongue, with its host of sonorous polysyllables, and with the constitution of the young Greek soul with its tides of harmonious enthusiasm. Lucian calls them ''men full of blood.'' They were hearty out-door men, that breathed oxygen and enjoyed poetry with their hearts rather than with their tastes, and with whom poetry was large enough to cover all their life. And so the full swell and roll of the hexameter, with its capacity to express both the rapture and the heavy sorrow of a great heart, answered their wants. It is a measure preëminently capable of expressing all generous emotion and sublime thought and straightforward truth, and singularly incapable of expressing anything mean or narrow, or merely fantastical.

Under this tuition Greece continued for an indefinite series of generations. We have remains of these poems dating centuries back of any known author of any other species of composition, and the earliest poets tell of singers in the days which were antiquity to them, and even in the day of those earlier bards the art would seem to have been already developed and in its ascendancy, so that when it arose no man can tell. But this we know, that it was thus moving over the surface of the Greek mind for centuries before Pisistratus, tyrant of Athens, caused the poems of Homer to be collected and arranged.

Then we come to the age of Greek literature; then the Iliad came to be a literary work; till then it had been in its relation to the people generally an oral song. Then, too, poetry lost its entire command over the spiritual exercise of man, and as it withdrew to the more refined parts of human nature, losing, of course, more in losing the wholeness of the soul than it could gain by retiring to its choice faculties, it left the comprehensive hexameter for other measures, which express the poet who is only the noblest and most refined part of a man, rather than the poet who is the fully developed man in all the nobleness of his complete humanity —the image of God; and so the name of bard, with the divinity which attaches to it, goes out with the epic age and the heroic verse.

After this come other ages of Greek culture, the lyric, the tragic, the artistic, the philosophic and the rhetorical.

This early poetry delighted chiefly in the presentation of the hero man, that model which the Greeks loved to look upon, that they might be changed to the same image.

There was the story of Jason bidden to bring the golden fleece from Colchis. It was a fearful enterprise, like that of Christopher Columbus, but his brave heart assayed it. Athena taught him to build his ship, the " Argo," and to put in it a speaking beam to tell the way. He gathered the braves of Greece and sailed away from the known to the unknown seas. The Symplegades rocks, by continual dashing, forbade their way. Trusting in the divine word and their own brave hearts, they dared the passage, and the rocks just grazed their ship as they gnashed together for the last time; for their courage had done what God-fearing courage does—had vanquished the danger and fixed the rocks forever; and that courage and help divine bore them on through perils and victories till they brought home the golden fleece.

Then there was Hercules, with his great heavy-laden heart, wandering over many lands, quelling monsters; and the wars of Thebes and Troy; and that Pilgrim's Progress of Greece, the Odyssey, of which we have spoken. It was not to them a mere Crusoe story, though who shall tell how much Robinson Crusoe has done for English-speaking boys? It nursed the heroism of patience in all Greek history. Horace tells us how to the Romans Homer was wiser than Platonist or Stoic.

The story of Ulysses and Telemachus inspired the French sage, Fenelon, and his work again found its way to the backwoods of America, and when there a child of destiny was born, he was named, in memory of the ancient hero, Ulysses Grant.

If Homer's Achilles was the model which inspired the career of Alexander the Great, how much may we owe to that picture of versatile sagacity, unflinching courage, clear self-reliance and invincible endurance, which he gave in his Ulysses and which we have seen reproduced in our own? So the honor and the influence of these old bards still remain in the new as in the old world and time.

What shall we say of the Iliad? It is the epic, heroic poem of the world; heroic, because its subject is the hero; epic, because its material is, not the cold stone or the dead letter, but the living, the " winged word;"—a poem, because its author is a poet, a creator. He is Phidias and Angelo, making of his living words statues of heroes and of gods, and setting them in the gallery of the mind of every Greek who was enough a Greek to receive them. Again, he is a Sophocles and a Shakespeare, making his gods and heroes to move in a great drama, which, fixed in memory by its rhythm, would pass before the mind's eye of that Greek, even at his daily labor.

Still again, he is an Aeschylus, a Milton, and a Bunyan. We call his work an Iliad. He did not call it so. His title was, " The Ruinous Wrath of Achilles," and, as the Odyssey is a Pilgrim's Progress, so the subject of the Iliad is not so much the Siege of Troy as the "Holy War of Law and Order Against Passion and Anarchy for the Possession of the Town of Mansoul." This theme runs through it, not only in the strife in the hearts of Achilles and Agamemnon, but in the oppositions of god and god, and of hero and hero, and especially in the continual contrast of the orderly Greek host and the Trojan mob. The "winged word" could wing its way to every Greek, and he, having no dime novel or daily paper to distract his digestion, lived upon it, and it formed a nation full of the instinct of loyalty and law, which showed itself as a forming principle in all Greek thought and life, and as a force in all the long-drawn conflicts of Europe with Asia, standing like Ajax at Thermopylae, and charging like Achilles at Marathon, Salamis and Cynaxa, until for its crowning achievement it tamed the wild spirit of the new Achilles, Alexander of Macedon, who, making himself leader of Greece, extended her laws from the Adriatic to the Indus; a rule soon to be extended, by her moral conquest of her Roman victor, to the Atlantic; and now it has found and annexed the New World and is encircling the globe. A grand token of it is the collection of antique statuary which Greece sent to the Columbian Exposition, and which is now the prized possession of our own College. Those forms are the mute counterpart of those Homeric heroes, who, though "the earth hath hidden their stock beneath it," still live in our minds.

May we without impiety so vary Hesiod as to say, that " by the counsel of the great Jehovah, they go clad in mist all over the earth;" that Homer's " winged words," going wheresoever the sunlight goes, are a part of the healing in the wings of the Son of Righteousness?

Upon the wall of my own class-room is a bust of old Homer, with those of Socrates, Plato and Demosthenes, which are to us memorials of the hour when our own young men were in the war for liberty and law and the country's cause.

Homer looks down upon us all the day long in a quiet serenity and dignity of wisdom; but as the beaming of the declining sun creeps up the wall, and begins to gild the features, they gather glory. I gaze with a pleased interest, then with wonder, admiration, awe, as the ancient wisdom seems to live again, yet not to open the eyes to wonder at the novelties of these later days, but rather to wake to communion with that all-seeing sun, which alone of all things here had known him in that morning of civilization, when in old Greece he struck the key-note to which the mind of man is still vibrating. So I sit a hushed spectator, and feel that mute wisdom, until the sun is gone and the illusion fades in twilight. But the impression is a lasting one. I return to the work of the present with a more cheerful joy, for that view of the wisdom of the past, glorified by the hopes of the future.

Those features, carved by some old artist, express what Homer was to the men of old time. To us he is a poet, and poetry is an embellishment and a luxury. To them he was the wise man, and his wisdom was a fountain of life.

In their view it was his voice which waked the Greek nation, and his word which falling upon that barbarous mind was like the echo of that potent word, which spake in chaos, "Let there be light, and there was light!"

And then it was the harmony, at once of his verse and of his thought, which formed that Greek mind to those harmonies which made Greece the teacher of the world.

II.

FINE ART.

We meet this evening to commence a course of lectures whose aim is the intellectual improvement and the refinement of the community. Such occasions naturally suggest to the mind the general head under which such efforts are to be classed, namely, the Fine Arts. Why I classify them thus, I shall endeavor to show as we proceed.

Art and nature are correlative terms. The one expresses the toilsome effort of man to embody his conception; the other is the body which the free volition of Deity hath prepared for His thought. Art is the work of the hands of man; nature is the handiwork of God.

Art, like nature, has a division into two kinds, corresponding to the double nature of man. We have what we call "the Arts," whose aim is to meet the exigencies and practical necessities of life, or to contribute to its comfort or convenience. And, again, we have another sphere of effort, in which the aim is not to satisfy man's wants, but to gratify his taste and to realize his ideals—to this we apply the singular, "Art," or the term, "Fine Arts."

It is to the character, the sphere, and the worth of art in this latter sense that I wish now to invite the attention of this audience. And, first of all, let us fix definitely in mind what it is that we mean when we speak of Fine Arts.

The distinction between fine and practical art, lies not in the effects produced, but in the attitude of the mind exercising itself in the one or in the other. The aim of the practical arts is to attain an end; the action of mind in them is contrivance.   The aim of the fine arts is to represent a model or to embody a conception.   The mental act is imitation or creation.

The Maker of this Universe was, in forming it, continually embodying conceptions of beauty, and of grandeur, and of rectitude, which fill His own soul—and so His work is the reflection of His own mind—and as such it is a work analogous to fine art.   The Greeks called it "Kosmos," "beauty." Again, in building that same world, He adapted it to ends, with a sovereign skill; and therein His work is analogous to useful art, and the Greeks again called the Creator, Demiourgos, "the Artificer."   In each of these He bespeaks Himself God. Socrates and Dr. Paley, tracing the adaptation which fills the creation, have come to the just conclusion that this sovereign skill manifests to us a mind no less than divine.   Thus the intellect feels after Deity and finds Him.   But there is another way, whereby the soul, finding itself in the midst of this Kosmos, sees God in its beauty, hears Him in its music, and feels Him in its blessedness, and so a more transcendental mind than Dr. Paley's declares that "God hath not left himself without witness, in that He giveth us rain from heaven and fruitful seasons, filling our hearts with food and gladness."   For he recognized that Deity, in thus making His works the representation of His own soul to our souls, immediately, without the intervention of the intellect, has given us a higher assurance of His being than logic could afford—the assurance, not of the logician's conclusion, but of his major-premise.

We, then, in our practical art, imitate Deity in His work of contrivance, and, in our fine art, we follow the exercise of His mind in embodying or expressing His thought and feeling.   We take such modes of expression as we have, and seek to embody our ideas as He did with His.   Art continually follows and models after nature—but the work of art is not to copy nature. It is, through the suggestions which nature affords, to repeat, as well as we may, those processes of the Perfect Mind which nature expresses, and to realize to ourselves, under some form, the conceptions which our minds, through the suggestions of nature, create.

Remember then that fine art has not to do with the mere results of effort, but with the character of the effort which produces the result. For example, portrait painting is a fine art, because the painter applies his powers consciously to the transference, first to his own mind and then to his canvas, of the lineaments of the countenance before him. But daguerreotyping is not a fine art, for the reason that the man who takes your picture, though he may be in soul a true artist, a Washington Allston in refinement, and the rival of Milton himself in poetry, when he is taking your daguerreotype, does nothing but mechanically put together certain materials which shall, by a way that he cannot explain, produce the perfect likeness. There is a sovereign artist there, but it is not the man who puts the plate in the camera. No machine can practice fine art.

And, lest any should think it lost time or perhaps unmanly to be dwelling upon these embellishments of life, let us consider a little further the respective relations of useful and fine art to the being of man.

It is written, "man shall not live by bread alone." As we have said, the twofold character of art corresponds to the twofold character of man. Man is mortal and he is immortal. He is material and he is spiritual. As a mortal, he has certain present wants, and appetites to indicate them, and arts of contrivance to provide for them. As an immortal, he has certain intellectual and spiritual wants, and he has aspirations to indicate them, and the struggle for the realization of these aspirations is that exercise of his being which we denominate fine art. "This is the victory which overcometh the world even our faith"—faith, a habit of mind which keeps constantly before itself the conception and realization of certain ideals, that is, of things more beautiful and nobler and better than any which it has seen as yet, and toward which it strives with an inexpressible and a victorious longing. In such making faith " the substance of things hoped for and the evidence of things not seen " lies the true range of fine art.

And here let us guard against an impression which may be somewhat general, that the fine arts, the "polite" arts, are for those who consider themselves as moving in the higher circles of life, while the mechanic arts are for ordinary men. I should be ashamed to stand here, or anywhere, as the advocate of occupations, whose aim is to amuse luxurious idleness. If any will not work, neither should he eat. That is God's verdict, and if it is God's verdict then it is law. None but a hard working man is worthy of the enjoyment of fine art; nor is he capable of it; the law executes itself. Sometimes we classify men as artists and artisans—the workers at some handicraft, and those who work at a craft of taste. This is a correct distinction of employments, but, as a classification of men, we must protest against it. Every man ought to be at once an artisan and an artist. He ought in all his occupations to seek at once that which is useful and that which is comely. The earnestness of practical life is necessary to the healthful and vigorous development of the most sentimental spirit, and, again, the refinement of art is needful to the comeliness of character of the hardest worker. The man that despises taste will be nothing more than a bungler, even at rolling a wheelbarrow. And on the other hand, he that scorns to be an artisan, true art shall scorn him. Without honest and earnest desire for usefulness, art may have brilliancy, but it will not be the glow of life but rather the phosphorescence of decay.

Every man, then, should always be both artisan and artist, always aiming at that which is useful, and never forgetting that which, in work and speech and act and thought, is lovely and noble, becoming and true.

The fine arts and the practical arts run through life parallel in general the one to the other, as the lark, with the same wing, skims the ground in quest of food and soars to sing at heaven's gate. They blend one with another, and we denominate one art useful, and another ornamental, according as the one or the other idea is most prominent in them. Thus prose belongs to practical art, because it aims chiefly through the intervention of words to attain some ulterior end; still, it may also have something of fine art, consisting in the taseful embodiment of inward thought in sensible language. Poetry is a fine art, because in it the main aim is the setting forth in its perfectness of the conception of the mind; yet poetry may also aim at a practical end and so become in part a practical art.

In almost all the various spheres of human effort we have, side by side, a practical art and a fine art. Thus, architecture provides shelter for the body, and at the same time enables genius to express majestic or graceful conceptions. Again, we have the power of variation of sound, giving us the practical art of speech and the fine art of music.

The practical art proceeds by coining words, which shall be its arbitrary signs of ideas, which, singly, shall be its tools, and which, taken together, shall be its machines for carrying on the intercourse required in its operations. These words are in general but cold interpreters of thought. We must learn what men have agreed that they shall mean, before we can use them or understand them. That is speech—the practical art. And against it is a fine art of sound. It rests upon this fact, that we have not only a mortal body, with transient wants, in the supplying of which such coarse and temporary contrivances as arbitrary words are well enough, but that we also have an enduring spirit with lasting emotions, and that these emotions, which belong to the nature of spirit, have specific sounds which are their natural expressions. And here arises music, the eldest, if not the divinest, of fine arts.

The province of music is the relation of audible sound to inward emotion. Its aim is to find such vocal expression as shall so embody the feeling of one mind as to convey it, warm and without the intervention of any arbitrary symbol, to another mind. With us, so dull are our senses, and so indistinct are the emotions which we wish to convey, it is in general needful that the melody and rhythm be accompanied by words which shall express, according to the rules of practical art, the thought which fills the mind. These are needful to us, as an interpreter is to our understanding a foreign orator; but they must, like an interpreter, be an impediment to our reception of the living thought or emotion intended to be conveyed. Some of the coarser distinctions of emotion are marked by utterances which we can all use and understand. Such are weeping and laughter, the voice of scorn or of pity; and to more refined tastes a nicer and nicer discrimination becomes practicable. How far we may hope that in this or any other state of being the ideal of music may be realized, I know not. But I suppose that idea to be this: That every emotion of the immortal spirit has its appropriate intonation of sound, or of that which, in another world, may take the place of sound; and that these intonations are the elements of music, and, further, that the harmonious flow and succession of emotions, in a pure spirit, should express itself in a like harmony of sound, rising of itself, like the unconscious voice of the harp of the winds, or of falling waters, so that it may be that, in a better land the emotions of pure spirits,

> "Voluntary move
> Harmonious numbers,"

and so the spirit goes spontaneously singing a perfect Æolian strain in its blessedness.

But on the other hand, if there is a perfection of harmony expressing the perfect life, so may there be also utterances of the diseased soul combining in a perfection of discord.

The proper sphere of music then, being the expressing of right and harmonious emotion, it continually suggests to man the perfectness of the pure spirit and calls him to seek it. Longfellow's blacksmith

> "Hears his daughter's voice
> Singing in the village choir;
> And it makes his heart rejoice,
> It sounds to him like her mother's voice
> Singing in Paradise."

That is the office of music, that it may

> "To our high raised fantasy present
> That undisturbed song of pure concent,"

when, not in Hebrew nor in Greek nor in our Saxon vernacular, but in such voice as the feeling shall, as it rises, find for itself, pure spirits shall pour their emotions into the ear of spirit.

Again, the relation of practical and fine art may be seen in the language of visible symbols. For our ordinary expression of thought, we contrive letters of the alphabet, arbitrary signs of sounds, with which we represent these arbitrary words which we had before, and it gives us a good enough language to buy and sell with.

But delineation has another and a more appropriate office; and here, against the practical art of writing we have the fine art of painting, by which, as in sound, the image before one mind is conveyed to another by a natural instead of an arbitrary symbol. And this expression, too, is open to the corrupt as well as to the pure mind. It begins with the copying of visible objects, but its tendency is to lead the mind, having found its power to produce such expression, to form and represent also ideals of perfection. Its specific relation seems to be to the representation of broad and comprehensive scenes and actions, as that of music is to emotion, and of statuary to individual and fixed character. It is an art of great and manifest capacity for influence. But I dwell the less upon it, partly from a suspicion that it is yet to find the sphere and style of action by which it is to do most for the world. Perhaps it may become less imitative and more suggestive than it has been; may copy less and create more.

Another form of visible expression, statuary, has perhaps entered with more success upon its proper field, though that field may be narrower, and its influence less than may be in store for painting. It rose to its eminence in ancient Greece, and was favored by the fact that, when it turned from the representation of actual men to enter the ideal world, it found in the Greek mythology exactly the themes which it desired. Working with rigid materials it is not adapted to the representation of varying action, nor well to that of composite emotion. It naturally seeks for some simple and strongly marked character, and then presents a form and countenance most expressive of those traits. It is rare to find among men a character at once great enough and consistent enough and supported by a personal aspect sufficiently in accordance with it to meet the demands of the sculptor. Perhaps George Washington's statue would have been a work to delight the chisel of Phidias himself. And here let me say, that there are few things which I would more desire for the boys of these United States than that each of them should have distinctly imprinted upon his mind that look and bearing of magnanimity which distinguishes the representations of the Father of our Country from those of any other man. But ordinarily the characters of men are not high enough nor have unity enough for the sculptor. Therefore it was fortunate for the art that it sprung up amid a polytheism which distributes the attributes of Deity, so that the artist could embody his conception of every phase of character under the form of some mythological being, which, so far as his material and his skill would allow, he could then present in marble. His ideal of art or wisdom, for example, he could represent in Athene, the Goddess of Wisdom; that of sovereign dignity and command in Jove; and Venus was his expression for beauty and melting tenderness; and so through the whole range of his ideals.

The arts of which we have spoken are adapted severally to the expression of some particular phases of human thought or feeling. The mind has, however, a means of almost universal expression in language, which seems to be constituted as the body of thought. In the use of language, we have a new class of arts, covering all man's activity. Its great divisions are the practical art of prose, and the fine art of rhythm or poetry.

Prose stands ready for all the exigencies of man's practical life, to express for him the thoughts which he has to express merely for the accomplishment of his ends. It is his obedient servant.

Poetry, on the other hand is ready with comely expression, with sympathetic rhythm of word and of thought, for his emotions and ideals, to embody and to clothe for him those thoughts which he loves for their own sake and desires to present in fitting form and attire. It is his bosom companion.

This fine art of language has modes of expression by formal and regular rhythms, which we call verse, and this is extensive enough to correspond to the entire field of art which we have thus far surveyed. Music has its counterpart in lyric poetry, painting in descriptive and in epic poetry, and statuary, which presents the forms of heroes, in tragedy, which presents their acts.

Again the fine art of language has forms of expression by unconstrained rhythms, rising and falling and changing freely with the eddyings of emotion or the heavings of thought.

These rhythms are the material of choral measures, of anthems and of oratory.

With these forms of expression, the fine art of language seeks for beautiful conceptions and noble thoughts, uniting in harmonious combinations or rhythms of thought, by virtue of which verse becomes poetry, and oratory, eloquence. The ideal perfection sought in each case is such an expression as shall fully convey the blended thought and emotion which fill the mind. If man could perfectly acquire the art of language, he would find the due rhythm for his thought, with no more artistic effort than is involved in changing the expressions of the countenance, as feelings change. Some approach to this in unmeasured rhythms we have in the highest bursts of eloquence. And there may have been the same in sustained and regular rhythm before the soul lost its tune by sin, so that in Eden our first parents voiced their emotions to their Maker with unstudied yet perfect and accordant harmony of verse and voice.

Again, man not only utters sound, and delineates and expresses thought by language; no, he acts, and here too the arts attend him. And here too we have a practical art of action, which we call prudence, or a little more bluntly or harshly—selfishness. And we have a fine art of action, to which belong magnanimity, heroism, honor, sincerity, generosity, kindness.

This is characterized as a fine art by the constant differentia or distinguishing element of fine art, namely, this: that its aim is to conform its work to some ideal of excellence, and not to attain a practical end. Jesuitism, as Protestants understand it, that is, the doctrine that the end sanctifies the means, is the extreme expression of the practical without the fine art of life, while the Christian tenet that no gain can pay for doing wrong is the principle of the fine art. The lives of Aristides, of Phocion, of Cato, of Milton, of Chief Justice Marshall, are examples of this art. In a great crisis of Greek history, after Xerxes was driven back, there is a story that Themistocles, the great practical contriver, told the Athenians that he had a stroke of policy to propose which must be kept secret. They deputed Aristides, the just, to hear it. Aristides reported back to them that nothing could be more gainful or more unjust, and so they rejected it. We have an illustrious utterance of the same art by that great and gallant spirit which was so long the ornament of our own national councils: "I would rather be right than be President." And so, too, our Washington, of whom I have spoken as one of the most perfect earthly models for the statuary, was also one of the noblest artists in this fine art of action.

I have yet to bring forward a higher view of the whole subject of art. But first let us clear the ground of an impression which may be somewhat prevalent, namely, that there is inherent in the very nature of art something of falsehood and deception. I think that the reverse is the fact, and that art is really fine art, only just so far as it is true. Its first canon is that it must be true to its model. The statuary carves his marble to the most perfect likeness of life that he can attain. If the likeness is so perfect that you do at first think that it is a living form, your mistake is a proof of the success of the work; but such deception was not the object of the art. That object is not attained until your mistake is corrected and you are made to see that this likeness of life is after all nothing but cold stone. Phidias wrought of ivory and gold a colossal statue of Athene, which was placed upon the Acropolis of Athens. He intended to embody his ideal of the goddess. But he did not intend to make men believe that the work was the goddess herself. The spiritual reality which spectators were to see in that form, was not that a spirit occupied it, but this, that there is a severe, serene, dignified grace in wisdom, which is true, and also this, that a noble conception of that majestic grace had been formed and existed in the mind of the artist, which was also true. The Athenians could not honor Phidias for his matchless Athene and Jove, except as they believed that those statues represented glorious images which had risen and been admired in his own mind before he wrought the gold and ivory, and that each line of majesty or grace told them truly of a vivid thought that filled his own mind as he carved it. And so it is with all art. Its power rests upon its truth. The orator has little sway unless he can show his hearers that he feels the sentiments which he utters. The poet moves none who do not believe that the rapture which he expresses is his own. And music, when we know that there is no music in the soul, is repulsive. The final triumph is the creation in the soul of the auditor or of the spectator of such an image as was in the soul of the artist, and that his soul be purified and en-nobled by that vision; an image of that exaltation whereby "we, beholding as in a glass the glory of the Lord, shall be changed into the same image from glory to glory, even as by the spirit of the Lord."

And now we are ready for the question which practical art may be pressing. What after all is the use of this fine art? We answer: Practical art has its use, and it is an important one, in the sustaining of the physical being of mortal man. Fine art has its use in the nurturing and the moulding of the spiritual being of immortal man.

Here then is a serious end for fine art. It is not a matter of mere embellishment. It is not intended to be the minister of practical life, to smooth its rugged ways and cheer its hardships. Practical art becomes its minister; its hewer of wood and drawer of water, while it is engaged in doing earnestly the real work of life. Bear with me then, while I endeavor to lead your minds in forming the idea of the Art of Arts. It is The Art of Spiritual Statuary.

Its material is the human nature. Its studio is in the chambers of the brain and heart. The ideal which it would fashion is the perfect man. Its model is the character of God. Its artist is each individual free moral agent for himself. Its means are all the faculties of man and all the surrounding influences which he can call in to aid him.

This is the art which every man may and should practice, laboring continually to make more comely his own nature and, as he may be able, that of other men.

The work is to take the plastic character of man and mould it to the likeness of the character of God. Like every other sphere of human art it has its limitations, in which it acquiesces. The sculptor cannot give to his cold, hard marble the soft, warm life of man, but he does what he can. He carves it to the likeness of the most perfect form of humanity of which he can conceive, and then he leaves it—preëminent among the works of man as its original was preëminent among the works of God. So the work of the spiritual sculptor must at best be finite in its dimensions, and certain perfections he cannot approach or even conceive. Yet as the marble, which could not be endowed with life, might still be pure as innocence itself; so, man may not be wise as God is wise, yet he may be merciful even as his Father which is in heaven is merciful.

To this art all other arts are merely subsidiary. They are only of worth as they minister to it. And here let me say again that all art which does not terminate in this art is counterfeit art. That only is true art in the highest sense whose ideals of perfectness exist and take effect in the inner heart of the artist. A vicious artist is a monster. Artistic skill or discernment that resides only in the eye or the voice or the ear is a hollow mockery of art. Be it understood, then, that in speaking of the relations of external art to the inward art we are only speaking of those artists who are artists in heart as well as in expression. Our position, then, is this, that all fine arts are or should be merely processes or outward phenomena, manifestations or echoes of a real artist work that is going on in the secret studio. If the sculptor is a true artist he is continually laboring not only to form his image of excellence in marble, but at the same time to grave those same lineaments upon the inner man. The painter's work is a diagram of beauty by which his mind is making distinct to itself that perfect grace to which itself would attain. Thus, as the great musician, Mozart, drew near his end, a stranger came and employed him to compose a requiem. He accepted the duty and received his hundred ducats, his artisan hire for the work, and the stranger departed. After some months Mozart commenced his work, feeling that death, which he was to treat, was near to himself. As he composed his life ebbed; the work was taken from him, and he regained his strength. He returned to it again, but before it was done he was gone. When he was dead the stranger came and received the unfinished work. The ducats Mozart had earned as an artisan. As an artist of sensible external art, he had wrought out so far his impression of the sublimity of death and sorrow. But he had all the while been engaged upon a greater work of art, the forming of his own soul to the rhythm of that contemplation of death and eternity. The music that he left was only the echo of a song that was rising within, the tuning of his soul as of a noble instrument which was to be heard elsewhere. And so always with the true art. The ravishing music that we hear is not the ultimate fruit of the art, it is merely the attuning in the earthly manufactory of the organ that is to peal in the heavenly temple.

But there are other ways of pursuing this spiritual art, beside the practice of what are technically called the fine arts. Great artists themselves must pursue it in their lives as well as in their art. John Milton is an illustrious example. He applied himself to the fullest training. His classical education embraced the perusal of the entire remains of classic literature. For he had a great end in view. He was "meditating", as he wrote to his friend in the modest pride of young genius, "by the help of heaven an immortality of fame." But his life was cast upon the stirring times of Cromwell, and as a practical man he devoted to the good of those times the intellectual strength and accomplishment which he had gathered from all time, even freely sacrificing to liberty's defense that eyesight to which he owed his accomplishment. Yet, even in his practical employments, he was always an artist, choosing and cleaving to nothing but that which is noble and honest and free. At length, when he was blind and the evil days came, when he could no longer serve the state, he returned to his artistic pursuits and gave ten years to the composition of the Paradise Lost. And here perhaps appear in fair proportion the relative worth of artisan and artistic effort. When his book was done he sold it to "Samuel Symons, printer," and received five pounds upon the spot, and five pounds more two years after, and in eleven years more Elizabeth Milton, his widow, received eight pounds. That was his artisan pay for his ten years' work, and he needed it to buy him bread in his blindness and poverty. For his artist labor he gained that "immortality of fame" which he was so long before meditating, and perhaps what he had done in the inward art was a third proportional to these two, as much surpassing his immortal fame as that fame was better than the eighteen pounds. But it was not only in his public life that Milton was an artist.

> "His soul was like a star and dwelt apart;
> He had a voice whose sound was like the sea;
> Pure as the naked heavens, majestic, free,
> So did he travel on life's common way,
> In cheerful goodliness; and yet his heart
> The lowliest duties on herself did lay."

Nor need a man be a Milton in order to aspire to this true art. We cannot all carve marble nor write poetry, nor even sing nor paint, but we may all attain toward this right moulding of soul. Every man may do it, as every man may be an artist without leaving his ordinary craft, for there is no honest work that a man can do which he may not do handsomely, and every work handsomely done is, so far, a work of taste—a work of art. A good shoemaker has a right to call himself an artist, a better right than some painters and musicians. Comeliness of appearance and attire and propriety of manners belong to fine art. He that is scrupulously honest in his dealings for honesty's sake is following true fine art. He is cultivating the character of an honest man, and it will stand him in good stead at a certain coming exhibition of these works of art. Magnanimity, generosity, honor, kindness are accomplishments within the reach of all, yet even in fine art they are of more permanent value than the painter's eye or the sculptor's hand.

While we live, then, by means of practical art, let us devote ourselves to the fine art of making ourselves and others as noble and fully developed men as we can. The first condition of this, as of any other art, is the careful and distinct forming of our ideal and study of our model. They that have produced surpassing statues or pictures, or poems or musical compositions, have fixed their minds intently and long upon the ideal which they essayed to develop. It has been with them in their meditation and their solitary walk by day and haunted the dream by night, so that whenever the mind might be in a happier mood or a gleam of light might cross it, some new or more perfect lineament of that ideal might be formed or traced; and then it was a cheerful patience which gave its months and years to the minute elaboration of the work which was to perpetuate that delicate offspring of the mind so long as the rock should endure.

By just such diligent contemplation is the ideal of the perfect man to be formed. We must familiarize ourselves with the best specimens of human character and action. Seek out in history the examples of truly great and noble deeds.

Single out for companions the noblest men you know, and in each individual who comes under observation seek out the noble traits. Do not be always looking under for some meanness. If meanness is forced upon your notice, get away from it and forget it. It is not wholesome to be thinking of meanness. Be in the habit of seeking and contemplating whatever is fair and comely, in art, in nature, and in action, and let the taste thus cultivated apply itself to add more graces to your forming ideal of man. Dwell much upon characters like Washington and John Jay, or like Howard the philanthropist, or Wilberforce, especially upon the perfect model, the God-man.

The very forming of this ideal of the true man is very much toward its realization; for this is not an art which must depend upon mechanical contrivance. When Raphael had formed in his mind the idea of the picture which he was to present, he must go into his studio and mingle his paints and handle his tools like a common craftsman. The will of the artist must laboriously direct material arrangements which are the condition of the embodiment of his conception. But in this higher art the studio itself is in the recesses of the mind, and the very act of forming the ideal and the very longing for assimilation to that beautiful likeness are acts in the perfecting of the work. Yet there will still be much to be done by patient toil. The taste is to be formed, the intellect is to be furnished and invigorated, the thought and life are to be purified and ennobled. There must be a wakeful watchfulness hour by hour; for every hour gives opportunity for the exercise of magnanimity or the indulgence of selfishness. Every employment enables us to ennoble ourselves by an honest endeavor to do our best, or to belittle ourselves by a disgraceful and lazy thought that an imperfect or even slovenly performance will do well enough for this time. And then, too, we may always bear a kind and cheerful or a sour temper and visage. The most exquisite art has not yet been able to produce anything so beautiful as a smile and an eye full of kindness coming from the heart. Every act of our lives, every work of our hands should be a chisel stroke in the elaboration of that statue. Everything that we can do like our Maker does so much to make us like our Maker.

We may do much toward exalting our own character by cultivating a ready and full sympathy with the best feeling with which we meet. Choose the noble and high-minded side of every question. If you see another man getting credit worthily do not envy him, but be proud of him as a brother man. Rejoice with them that do rejoice and weep with them that weep.

Our times promise to be rich in these means of spiritual culture, in suggestive men and inspiring movement. An open eye and ear, an open mind and an open heart will of themselves drink in the inspiration. Men like Milton have been on earth "like stars dwelling apart," but henceforward nations are to think and great subjects are coming before them, and we may expect that those "mute, inglorious Miltons," who have hitherto been unknown, will be brought forward, and great men will multiply among us as the stars multiply when mist disperses.

I have sought to lay before you a fine art of such a character that when, as the doors of the studio were opened to reveal the work of the sculptor, so the walls of this earthly house shall fall asunder, there shall be revealed within a work of art which even the Divine artist can approve. Let me close by naming again the definitions of this art:

Its material is the human mind and soul; its studio is the human heart and mind; its means are human faculties and opportunities; its ideal is the perfect man; its aim is to take the plastic being of man and fashion it to the image of God.

III.

ANCIENT CIVILIZATIONS.

Ancient culture was simple in its structure, but divided into many diverse civilizations. Modern life is most complex, but all its elements are growing together into one common wealth of mankind.

Civilization is the culture of man. The very form of the word assumes that man is not an individual but a citizen. Its aim is to form every man to the most complete manhood and to the best fitness, both of will and of skill, for that man's place in the community; and to form all together into the most fully developed and fully equipped total of humanity.

Wherever, then, there is a common bond, uniting men for common culture and for common good, there is a civilization. The trite saying, that in old times the individual existed for the state, but now the state for the individual, contains two-thirds of the fact, and, stopping there, inverts the truth. Old communities took the barbarous man and brought him by will or by force into the mass of the state. Modern culture takes the citizen and trains him toward that perfectness, which will of itself fit into that crystallization of mankind, whose conditions and whose unwritten law it is also perfecting. We may think of old states as the academies; of modern Christendom as the college. Neither is complete without the universitas, the millennium, or "the good time coming." The line between ancient and modern times is drawn by the advent of Christianity, which is the principle of union. The law of the old world was separation; the new

brings together.   And each nation enters into the new, when
it becomes, and in proportion as it becomes, a Christian
nation.

The whole world was built for such a history.   The
mountains and seas, and especially the deserts, which divided
the old nations, compelled their secluded culture; and no less
conspicuously do the modern victories over space and time
and toil fuse men together in a whole, in which the
wisest is the chiefest, the common interest is the interest of
every man, and every man's good is part of the commonwealth.

The world, when built, was divided by oceans into two
hemispheres, of which one was reserved for that reconstruction
of civilization of which we are a part; while the other was
divided into two most unequal sections by a mountain wall,
running from the mouth of the Indus or of the Ganges to
that of the Rhone or the Rhine.   All the great regions to the
north of this wall were also reserved, nursing populations
who were preparing physical strength and rudiments of
manhood, which were to come to great use when their time
should come, but who were not yet at school.   The greater
portion of the remainder, including all southern Europe and
Central Asia, consists of the southern slopes, ranges and
spurs of the mountains, and is all occupied by tribes kindred
to one another and to us, all except the spur of Lebanon and
Sinai, a line most peculiar in its geographical and in its historical relations, the pivot of the world.

We have left a small circle in the center of the hemisphere, bounded by the Mediterranean Sea, Mounts Taurus
and Zagros, the Indian Ocean and the desert of Sahara.   Of
this the greater part is desert, and as such almost out of the
history of civilization.   It was wisely said, in this region
itself, that " wisdom rejoiceth in the habitable parts of the
earth," which would here be Mesopotamia, Arabia Felix and

the scattered oases of Arabia, and the valley and Delta of the Nile. It is a rainless region, under the power of the sun, which makes the uplands deserts, but covers the lowlands, which drink waters flowing from other climes, with a teeming life, thus preparing them for the hot-beds of a precocious civilization. This they were to pass on to their neighbors on the mountains, and these to those beyond the ridge, and they to the new world across the sea. The education of ancient nations was organized into two or three great classes of tribes, the Egyptians, Arabs, Chaldeans and Assyrians on the plains; and the Persians, Medes, Armenians, Phrygians, Greeks and Romans on the mountains, with the Phoenicians and Hebrews between them.

In each of these three departments we find in national culture the two phases which we, in modern times, have in the education of individuals. One man is educated by secluded study for professional life; another is trained for and thrown into business. So some nations formed their culture in seclusion, like the Arabs, Egyptians, Hebrews, Persians, Athenians, Spartans, Romans; others in thoroughfares of nations, like Babylon, Nineveh, Media, Phoenicia, Ionia, Corinth, Sicily. Each is necessary; for the closet is always the source of power, but power must always work in public life.

We have already been struck by the great reserves of power by which regions and races which were to be ruling agents in the history of culture, are kept back till their time should come; we shall also discern a corresponding plan in the use of the natural instrumentalities of education.

We have two teachers, the eye and the ear, which have two assistants, the hand and the tongue. To each of these teachers is assigned a department in the earliest education of mankind—to the eye the sunny plains, and to the ear the breezy mountains. For a thousand years Egypt and Chaldea were building monuments or writing in hieroglyphic or cuneiform, while Persia and Greece were singing songs of war or work or worship. Let us see the working of the systems. Egypt and Chaldea, then, are sent to school in their earliest childhood, to the college of letters on the Nile and the commercial college on the Euphrates, while the mountain boys are left to play and sing for a thousand years more.

It seems not unlikely that picture-writing was invented in Arabia and brought thence to Chaldea and to Egypt. In Chaldea the writing material was clay, on which impressions were made with the edges of a stick, making wedge-shaped indentations, which were combined into pictures which soon lost all likeness to any object and became characters in which the learned could effectually conceal their knowledge, as they did. Various systems of cuneiform were formed for the tribes of that quarter of Asia, all crude and obscure enough to defy the wit of common men and to exhaust that of the learned. It served some purpose, invaluable indeed to us, as a laborious record of scientific observations and of historic facts, but must have been a very lame help to study. Its chief labor was with its own grammar.

But, in Egypt, the new culture bore great fruit. It was a secluded land, guarded by the desert and the sea. The teeming soil bore and fed an immense population. Great quarries gave material for building, while the surfaces of stone favored the use of either the pencil or the chisel, while the dreamy quietness of the secluded realm bred in ruling minds, thoughts and plans, and sought visible expression for them all. So Egypt is the land of monuments. Every thought, as well as every man, must be embalmed. The fields are dotted and the hills are honeycombed with obelisks, temples and tombs, and every temple and sarcophagus and burial case is covered, within and without, with inscriptions, and voluminous rolls of papyrus are buried with the dead. But all this literature gives only a kind of nebulous idea of the intense instinct for visible representation which possessed the people. The temples and tombs and obelisks are themselves, as it were, gigantic inscriptions or reliefs, and so are the sphinxes and the pyramids. All this gives us the idea of a very mature people and we say, how old must Egypt have been before she built a pyramid? We are judging others by ourselves. We are of a slow-maturing race of men. It is but a little time since our fathers began to read and write. But these Egyptians were never young. They would seem placed in their Eden, like Adam, in full maturity. We do not find a series of crude preparatory works. The Sphinx and the Great Pyramid are the oldest works of Egypt, and they are the greatest and the most perfect. Modern science is now discovering in the dimensions, the position, the passages, and the lines of the Pyramid of Cheops the mute record of scientific facts, like the place of the pole, the latitude of Memphis, the ratio of the diameter to the circumference of the circle, such as, if they are really there, as they seem to prove, were worthy to have a pyramid for their record. From the pyramid downward, Egypt seems to shrink gradually to second childhood; like the Nile which is never so great again as when it leaves the cataracts. The Nile had grown great in the unknown heart of Africa, and perhaps this wisdom of the oldest Egypt is the legacy of antediluvian lore. If not, it is the precocity of a race which was never a child and whose only work is its own tomb. The Pyramid itself, compact as it may have been with scientific thought, was a tomb; and the thoughts, as well as the monarch which it incased, seem to have been hidden, when its passages were closed and its surface smoothed, to wait their three thousand years for the resurrection; four thousand years it is now that they are coming forth.

What was the effect of letters upon Egypt? They found Egypt wise, did they make her wiser? Perhaps we ought not to expect that they would do so. It is a clime for quick

maturity rather than for perennial growth. Yet, with such a
beginning, and with such an auxiliary as visible forms are,
especially to scientific inquiry, it does seem strange that we
are not able to distinguish some great progress, at least in
science, as consequent upon their introduction. The apparent want of intellectual movement in Egypt during all this
literary activity,—or at least busy-ness,—almost raises the
question whether a thought written be not, at least for him
who writes it, a thought embalmed, and whether it be best
that a man write anything till he have occasion to write his
will. Certainly such a conclusion would be most unjust, the
simple fact respecting Egypt being that, even at that time, it
was time for her to write her testament. It may be that she
would have made somewhat more progress if she had not so
soon entered upon her scholastic age, but the world would
not now have been the richer for it.

A thought reduced to visible form, either in written
word or picture or statue or edifice, if it be not a step for
further progress becomes a limit to thought. And, as every
expression is inferior to the thought, it may even dwarf the
idea of the mind. This is especially true in religious
thought, and perhaps we are to understand the second command given upon Sinai as a divine comment upon the religious
influence of the Egyptian hieroglyphic system. The Sphinx
itself, the lion body with the human head, carved from the
native rock, colossal in size, majestic and solemn in aspect,
looking over fruitful Egypt toward the sunrise, as it may be
the oldest of human monuments, is, to-day, one of the most
impressive embodiments of human thought. But here their
form of expression led their people on to the worship of images,
growing ever more gross and grotesque, and of four-footed
beasts and creeping things! Visible forms may be a great
help to science, but they may destroy the life of religion.
We do not know that Jesus wrote a word except in the sand.

We shall find the same association of idolatry with the language of visible symbols elsewhere. Babylon and Nineveh were full of inscriptions and of idols. According to Herodotus, the Greeks received the names of the gods, as well as of the letters, from their neighbors across the Mediterranean, and the Persians had not image or temple or writing, till they learned them from the valley of the Tigris. Even Hindoostan seems not to have worshiped idols in the old Vedic ages.

Yet the immense and intense religious thought of Egypt was far from lost to the world. Their view of human life as seen in the light of judgment after death, as unfolded in their Book of the Dead, is a legacy worthy of their toil and thought. But we ought not to emphasize the question of the results obtained by the Egyptians, or by the Chaldeans, through the use of letters. The alphabet would be in itself a sufficient legacy and monument of a nation's wisdom, even if it were not accompanied by evidence of other achievements of thought brought forth in that same morning hour which lies just below our horizon. That is the law of life in those plains of the south; a century of tense life and a thousand years of rest; one man of vigor enough to move to great works a million of passive men, who, "seeing that rest is good and the land that it is pleasant, bow their shoulders to bear and become servants to tribute." For inertness, there, is not the sturdy and stubborn laziness of the north. It is a passiveness, which finds it less trouble to toil than to resist command.

We wish we could look just a little over the rolling world and see the young genius of Egypt in its fervent work from Menes to Cheops; those keen and eager minds at work upon problems of art, science, and life, resolute monarchs supporting their thoughts, and obedient populations embodying them in great works. We may compare it with the century which invented printing, or with that which has learned to write with the lightning; but we must admit that neither the telegraph nor the type shows a genius or an inspiration like that which invented or developed the alphabet. And, in the light of such a token of the genius of that age, it becomes easier to ascribe the culture which appears suddenly with the pyramids to the enthusiasm of one generation, than to the droning of an hundred.

The art of printing seems to be, and it is, the natural development of that of writing, and yet the two are in their operations as unlike as the worm and the butterfly. Printing is the most democratic writing is the most aristocratic of institutions, as it enables those who possess it to make and keep advances in science which leave the rest of men hopelessly behind. So in the literary nations of antiquity were castes, the Egyptian priests, the Hebrew scribes, the Chaldeans, the Magi, the Brahmins; and on the other hand, now, it is the leaden type and not the bullet which sweeps away the barriers of privilege. Writing makes knowledge the prerogative of the few; printing makes it the common wealth of all.

Perhaps it is not unfortunate that the Egyptian priests were not inclined to teach the world all their science. In many things half is more than all, and the greater part of secret things the world is wiser not to know. The Egyptians did business with the Phoenicians who, as business men, did not care to learn all the obscurities of the hieroglyphics, but they could see the value of a table of characters for elementary sounds, and for numbers, and so they formed an alphabet, rich in what it took from Egypt and almost equally fortunate in what it left behind. From them the alphabet has spread to the Asiatic and to the American shore of the Pacific.

The Phoenicians carried the alphabet to the Greeks, the people who were destined to make the most of it. But for centuries they found no market for it there.

The Greeks represented the mountain races, who were forming a civilization which was not yet ready to be stereotyped. From the Himalayas to the Alps kindred tribes had been forming culture for a thousand years before Cadmus; and for hundreds of years after him they used his figures only as they had occasion to count with a Sidonian trader the price of a kettle, a garment, or a slave. For the rest, their thoughts refused the bonds of the written word. "The letter killeth, the spirit giveth life," and the natural utterance of a live thought is by the living breath.

It seems to us impossible to advance or record the progress of man without letters as a help to memory. But the Greeks had nine Muses, all daughters of Memory, but none of them is a Muse of letters. They and the other northern nations had found another way of communicating and recording thought which pleased them better. They gave it a body, not to the eye by letters, but to the ear by rhythms.

The method did not favor a very thorough culture of science, but it was not without its advantages for the culture of man.

We may say that it was so, even for his early scientific culture; for what he did elaborate must be wrought out by pure power of thought and must be held by the grasp of his own mind, and must be told so plainly that another mind may take and keep it without notes; and in that process the other mind is also trained to a clear and vigorous apprehension, and when the other has the fact, he has it not in a note-book but in his mind. Still the main training in illiterate nations must have been in elements of character rather than of knowledge.

Literary culture is in prose, while oral culture was in poetry. The former deals naturally in facts; the latter in enthusiasms.

Which is of more value may depend upon the question whether we are to regard man as a thinking mind or as a living soul; or whether we ask what the man knows, or what the man is; whether a nurture is to be judged by the amount of food, or by the amount of health, which it gives. Enthusiasm is life and inertness is death. If the grand enthusiasm which produced letters and so many other arts in Egypt could have continued, we cannot tell what a Babel they would have builded. It may have been as well for them to rest, and leave their work to be used by other men, who were at the same time preparing a greater manhood.

We might perhaps suppose that a people whose education is committed to bards, rather than to scribes, will be more liable to superstitions and extravagances. Does not such a conclusion forget that health is itself the greatest of all purifying agencies, and that it is death which works corruption?

The Hindoos, for a thousand or more years before Alexander the Great came with the alphabet, had chanted their sacred songs, as they made their way through the gigantic mountains which stand between Bactria and the Ganges. The serene or tempestuous aspects of nature around them filled them with a loving reverence for the god of day and an awe in the presence of the spirit of the storm. They were full of deep religious feeling covering this life and looking on into the future. From that time has come down to us a poetic literature, larger than the Iliad, which proves the activity of their minds and souls; but it speaks a simple and manly faith. The superstitions and idolatries of Brahmanism seem to have come in with the idea of letters and of visible forms as an aid to devotion and religious thought, coöperating, of course, with many other demoralizing influences.

During the same ages, a kindred tribe were wandering along the Hindoo Koosh and the Zagros from Bactria to the mountains of Persia. They were impressed with a conflict above the wars of the elements and above their own struggles for life; with a great warfare filling the universe between the powers of good and of ill, a war which concerns man and in which man may and must bear a part; a war between the truth and "the lie." It was a great idea, fit to take possession of a soul and to make it great. It took possession of the soul of Persia and made it great. Persian boys went to school to learn—not letters—but these three things, "to draw the bow, to ride the horse, to speak the truth." The teachers spent the day in teaching principles of justice as illustrated in the every-day life of boys as well as men. Was that not a training for which we might exchange very much of the objective truth which we study in our schools? Such an education in civil life, harmonizing with the religious chants in which they honored Ormuzd, the god of truth, trained a nation of true men, who, of course, were conquerors when they came down to the plain. When letters and science and the craft of the Chaldeans came, their kings and nobles were apt scholars, so that the last days of Persia show examples of falseness such as only an apostate from truth could achieve, but the Persian commons showed their breeding when they threw themselves in hopeless devotion upon the Grecian spears at Thermopylae and Plataea, at Issus and Arbela.

They were able to conquer and to govern the literary nations, and the stability of their power and the stanchness of their host proves that they were not a horde of barbarians, nor Cyrus a savage chief, but a nation and a king, educated to as good manhood as Chaldean numbers or Memphian letters could have given. Still their culture was not broad enough to consummate the work of the old civilizations. The same was true of the Romans, who, during the same centuries, were working out in the far West their portion of the common problem of the Indo-European family. For all these tribes, the want of letters was supplied by an instinct of order, which wrought out a civilization which produced in India the solemn measure of their hymns and movement of their processions, and later their castes and laws of Menu; in Persia their religious chants, their principles of equity and the "Laws of the Medes and Persians," in Rome it organized the Republic and the legion, and was victorious over Carthage, the representative of lettered culture, not so much by elements of barbaric strength as by those of disciplined power.

Every old nation that had a character, like every man of character, ancient or modern, prepared that character in seclusion; and then it came forth to its work in the world, as a living seed cannot be hidden in the earth. So Egypt had given letters, Babylon astronomy, Nineveh the vigor of empire, Persia the organization of power; Rome was forging the iron links which should hold the elements of the world together, that it might be pervaded by the fear and love of the one God which Judea had cherished. But it must be first brought into something like one system of thought.

The education of the Greek nation to be the mediator and ultimately the choir-leader of the old civilizations is one of the chief wonders of history; a wonder which is continued by the natural adaptation of Europe to continue the work of Greece and that of America to succeed to that of Europe.

Greece is a peninsula full of little valleys, and a sea full of little islands. Into these valleys and islands were brought a people kindred to the Hindoos, Persians, Romans and ourselves. Every family of them had worked its way along all the mountain road from Bactria, and here every man must wrest his living, every day, from the rough land or the rough sea. There are no great rich plains here, where the many can do the work and let the few do the thinking. Kind step-motherly nature will make a man of every one of them. Their toil is full of health and their land is full of inspiration. Their land forbids great cities, but it requires villages. In these they gather when the day is done, or at their festivals. Of course they sing, and the full throbbing of their hearts forms the measure—not the laboring iambic, with which their kinsmen are climbing the Himalayas, but the exuberant dactylic hexameter, which is able to meet all the various moods of a generous soul.

In this measure their enthusiasm and their wisdom were enshrined. It was better, far better for them than letters. It reached every man. It filled the mind and the soul of every man with thoughts and sentiments which were with him at his work and in his rest. It educated every man. It called out what was in every man and made it the common property of all.

Among these islands and harbors came Phoenician ships, with the wares and thought of Egypt and the East. There sprung up the half oriental civilization of the heroic times. The Greeks then learned the alphabet and used its characters for numbers, and might soon have learned them as letters, had not their own enterprise crowded the Phoenicians from their seas, and the old Heracleid Greeks overthrown the institutions of the Pelopidae. So Greece took three centuries to prepare from foreign elements and nature its proper civilization. No people ever equaled them in the most decisive test of vitality, in that power of digestion or assimilation which is able to convert foreign matter into its own life. When their own commerce reached Egypt again, they were mature enough to take the alphabet and the papyrus and add a prose literature to the poetry which had formed the nation, but in all their wisdom they always felt that Homer was "the wise." They felt that his verse struck the keynote of a life full of sympathy and full of thought and of harmony.

Such a mind was ready to receive the results of the study of the older nations and form with them a literature which is now continually inspiring our civilization, as their own was inspired by Homer.

But if some old nations could do good work without letters, what is that to us? We cannot go back to the infancy of time if we would. Certainly not, and we would not if we could. It is better to live now than then; and one reason why it is better is, that the free and general culture of the old Greek life is so largely and so richly reproduced for us. Writing, when it came, was an aristocratic institution. It made knowledge the property of the few. But printing as we have said, makes it the wealth of the many, and so is for us what the song of Homer was, a popular education of manhood, as well as of childhood, bringing to every man the thought of all the past—as the electrician brings that of all the present; and all the development of the powers of man and of nature knit again the muscles and the nerves, by which, if we have soul enough for it, we may come into the full throb of our larger life, the fellowship of mankind.

Thus the various civilizations of old time, bound together, by Roman law, blended together by Greek art and inspired by Christian faith, come to us as the one culture which we are to receive and develop into the one civilization of the United States of Mankind.

Swifter than a weaver's shuttle these days are weaving the curtains of the Tabernacle of that Congregation.

It is good to be living now.

IV.

THE GOLDEN AGE.

THE GOLDEN AGE.

Do we think that the Golden Age is poetry, while real life is prose? Is that so? Or is it rather true that real life is poetry, and that mere prose is mere death?

Poetry is the enthusiasm which sends through this world of dumb matter the throb of life. It is not just "the accomplishment of verse." It is the soul, that makes the verse and all the while is doing greater things than that.

Every just thought, every generous act or word, every thing done as well as you can do it, for the love of doing it so, is part of that harmony which is the true life of man.

Prose, mere prose, drudges through what it has to do in the old rut; but touch the soul with life and it does what its hand finds to do with all its heart, every time as well as it can, and every next time a little better.

Such a life is a poem and it writes itself in its works.

What a poem is your farm, for even the wayfaring man to read! Its fences and its furrows are works of art; its fields are pictures, and as he looks over its pastures, it comes to him as a psalm telling how "our Lord hath set his glory above the heavens, in making man little lower than angels and crowning him with glory and honor and giving him dominion over the works of his hands, all sheep and oxen, the beasts of the field, the fowl of the air and the fish of the sea." Such a picture, such a poem, if we have poetry enough in us to read it as the angels do, is the farmer life of man, God's vicegerent on the earth.

Shall we come to your palace and find the Queen in the shining kitchen, and see the work of her royal hands; the meat which she giveth to her household, the golden butter and honey which the young princes eat, that they may know to refuse the evil and choose the good, that even it may be a part of that hallowed knowledge of good and evil which is to reverse the doom of Eden, and which may bring back the lost Paradise and the days of " Immanuel—God with us."

That dream of the good time coming is part of the soul of man, and it is what makes life worth living, and it is a dream which is working its own fulfillment, for even so runs the promise, " Your young men shall see visions and your old men shall dream dreams."

And now, as we stand where the dream of the old is already becoming the vision of the new, it will be good and meet for us to take a little thought of that vision and of that hope which we may realize. The dream is as old and as wide as the history of man. It is just that deathless hope, implanted by Him who made man, by reason of which he does not give up under his bondage of corruption, but bears up in the assurance of a Paradise which he has known and which he is to know again; and everywhere it is a dream of country life and of man's presidency over the animal world, and the ministry of earth and its inhabitants to him. He is placed in Eden " to dress it and to keep it," and he names its beasts.

The Paradise of the Hebrew is the Golden Age of the Greek and the Roman, the time of peace and plenty and perpetual spring when, as Hesiod, almost the oldest Greek poet, sings,

" Men lived like gods."

And Virgil, the farmer and dairyman poet of Rome, sings, even in the court of the Caesars, of the Golden Age, whose fading image was still upon the recollections of his boyhood upon the farm; of "The rest free from care, and the life that knew no guile, rich in varied wealth, and of the sacred worship of the gods, and reverence for parents."

This farm life, he says, "Golden Saturn passed upon the earth," and "among them were the last footsteps of the goddess, Justice, as she left the earth."

So he recalls the sigh of old Hesiod:

> "Then to Olympus from the broad ways of earth,
> Veiling with white mantles their beautiful color,
> To the race of immortals, forsaking men,
> Pass Reverence and Conscience."

So,

> "Many a sacred hymn comes stealing
> Down from the Eden aisles,"

and they bring cheer though we are laboring through thorns and thistles, for, sweet as is the dream of infancy and of perennial spring, we believe in manhood and in work, and we feel that the thorns and the thistles are good for us, and that the best promise for man is that of winter as well as summer, of night as well as day; and yet the beauty of the hard work of life is the glory, shining through it, of the Sabbath that lies beyond, that "promise that remaineth" that we shall enter into the rest of the Maker of the world.

Glorious, as well as horrible, has been the Brazen Age of War, which we hope that we are leaving behind. Grand is this Age of Iron, in which we live, perfecting the machinery and the equipments of the new Golden Age, of the good time coming. But the world feels that when that age comes men "shall learn war no more," nor will the best of life of that day be in the mine, or the workshop, or in the city, but in the open country. That hope man never would give up, long and bitterly as it has been mocked.

Nor should we forget the honor which is due to the Silver Age of Money. We must have business men, and most noble qualities and characters have been bred in the counting room, but yet we feel that in city bank or on country farm "the man 's the gold for a' that," and true manhood, that "pure gold like unto transparent glass," is the material for the Age of Gold.

The world has waited long for that manhood to appear,—for those "Sons of God." Thousands of years ago the poet that sung of the Golden Age cried, " Oh that I had not lived in this Age of Iron, but had died before, or lived after it." We do not feel so now. We seem to feel the morning air and to see the morning light. But are we wiser than all the men before us, whose eyes have glowed with that hope and been disappointed ?

In the days of Augustus Caesar, the Roman poet, Virgil, sang almost in the words of Isaiah, of the child to be born in that same year, with whom the Golden Age was to come again. It did not come, but, instead of it, came Ages of Misery. What was the matter? It was the oppression and the ignorance of the cultivators of the soil; the same cause which, for all these ages, has kept that hope of mankind, as unable to live as it was, by its own nature, unable to die, and so it has been flitting like a soul on the banks of the Styx, waiting for its time to pass on to Elysium.

How should that wandering soul of man be delivered? It never could locate its Elysium except upon the farm, and it never could realize it there because the tillers of the soil were not the owners of the soil, and because they had not the culture of mind and refinement of soul without which neither land or man can be fit for Paradise.

Have you seen that criticism of a noted picture of " The Sower " by J. F. Millet? It was said of the sower: " That man looks like a convict," and the answer was: " He is a convict; he has been chained and manacled to the soil for generations."

So Virgil, the Latin poet, who sings with such ecstasy of farm life, still says that, for himself, he would rather be a student and know something.

Let that artist or that poet look in the face of this audience, or let him know how in America the leading positions in the counting-room, at the bar, the pulpit and the senate, are held by the men who have been born and bred upon the farm. Perhaps he may think that the new Age of Gold began to be when the Pilgrims founded a free state in a new world.

If Oliver Cromwell had been allowed to come with them, instead of remaining to liberate England and to subjugate Ireland, it probably would have made very little difference here, but it might have changed the problem with which England has to deal to-day.

Two hundred and sixty-six years have not brought England on so far in history as sixty-four days brought the Mayflower. Doomsday Book and primogeniture and entails and the peers were left behind. A state substantially free arose and a man was able in America to be a man, to have his own home and his own farm, to educate his children, to be a free citizen of a free state. And yet New England was rather an education for the new paradise than the inauguration of it, or shall we say rather its vestibule and the commencement of its preparation; for it is to come by education.

All this education must begin and end with man. Your farm, your tools, your crops, your stock wait for your motion. If you do your best they will do their best, and when the year is done, if you have done your thinking and working wisely and well, the balance-sheet will show it by showing that your farm is a better farm, your equipments better equipments, your stock better stock, your products better products, but especially if it shall show that you yourself are a better man, able for the next year to enter upon a higher grade of education.

The men who began two hundred and sixty years ago that American experiment in the education of earth and man were themselves the finest product of the previous education, the best and the best developed bodies, minds and souls which the world had thus far produced. And they were released from the trammels of the old world and set upon a new soil with will and with wit to make the most of their opportunity. And not only had they release from old fetters; they had the girding of new difficulties, the savage foe, the rigorous winter, the granite mountain, the tangled forest. They made their clearings in the wilderness. They planted the corn, the tree, the home, the school, the college, the church, the commonwealth—the commonwealth they called it, and every Thanksgiving Proclamation closed with the prayer, "God save the commonwealth of Massachusetts." It is a thanksgiving and a prayer for us. This Beloit of ours is in the heart of that Massachusetts, which, by the charter of King James, runs across the continent, on a line from three miles north of the Merrimac to three miles south of the Charles river, from the Atlantic Ocean to the South Sea. Beside it stretch other like lines, and here, in these free fields of the great Interior, they commingle, as heirs of the same promise, sharers in that same commonwealth. That is a good word— the commonwealth—that community of good which is worth so much more to every man than is anything which he can call his own peculiar property, which is worth so much more to every man than it would be if it were not shared by every other man. A man used to think himself rich if he had a hundred slaves. What think you of the wealth of the man who has a hundred thousand fellow citizens, each of them a free man, and all joined to him and he to them in one commonwealth?

If the commonwealth itself is the greatest of the riches it brings, it is also full of other wealth. It has gone on from the Atlantic to the Western ocean, taking possession of its domain in obedience to that urgent command which has been driving the sons of men for four thousand years, and all the way from Bactria to Dakotah: "Go West, young man." At the same time the other young man heard the call, "Go East," and now they have met. So the young man has gone till he can go no further; the round world is rounded, and has he found the West? Has he been chasing a rainbow, or has he been pursuing a manifest destiny? He must at least say, "Here or nowhere is what I am seeking." The tide which seeks the West has met that setting toward the East. The movement which began in the center of the Eastern hemisphere is at a pause in the center of the Western, and what has it found? What is this Northwest which is here to-day? As the young man and the young commonwealth found it, it was a great plain, bounded north and east by great lakes, south by great prairies and west by huge mountains; embraced by the mighty arms and caressed by the fingers of great rivers and purling streams, bearing flowers while it waited for the crops; coursed over by buffalo and deer and Indian while waiting for the herd and the dairyman. Now it is a great field, bounded on the north by copper and iron and wheat, on the south by coal and corn, east by great waters and great orchards, and west by mountains of silver and gold; its brow and its girdle of lake and river set with busy cities, and its strong streams gladly turning from their ages of play to the higher joy of sharing the fervent and fruitful work of man. Its oak openings are changed to orchards, its flowery prairies to fields of waving grain, and especially its herds from buffalo to kine, its flocks from deer to sheep, its wigwams to homes, schools and churches.

We have to do now with that dairy industry, which is coming so largely and so hopefully to the front as the occupation of this region, and to ask how that will bear upon the realization of the Paradise in search of which the "young man" has been so long "going west." We note that in the old days, when the young man was young, he used to worship the cow. It was so in old India and it was so in old Egypt. Do you remember how it was said that when the English brought their Hindoo sepoys to their Egyptian war, they fell down and worshiped the image of a cow in an old Egyptian temple? We can hardly wonder at their act if the image was that heifer in black stone which was carved in the days of Cephrenes, the builder of the second pyramid, and which now stands in the museum at Ghizeh, expressing wondrously that ideal of serene gentleness, of meekness worthy to inherit the earth, which satisfied the soul of the mild Egyptian and Hindoo, as the bulls with eagle wing and human face stand at the portals of old Nineveh, to express the divine might worshiped by the men who went forth from those doors to shake the earth.

Then there were the golden calves which Aaron and Jeroboam made to represent the God of Israel. If we call all these heathen idols, perhaps we may accept the Scripture symbols, the oxen which bore the laver of purification, and the bovine cherub forms which adorned the Tabernacle of Moses and the Temple of Solomon, and the ox which, with lion, eagle and man, bore the throne in the vision of Ezekiel, as not unfit suggestions, even for us, of the mighty, the gentle, the pure, the holy, the loving might and wisdom and grace and bounty which sits above, and which hath made man His almoner, to take from His hand the bounty with which He satisfieth the desire of every living thing. So, if we do not worship the ox that eateth grass, we will at least regard him as a fellow citizen of that commonwealth of which the presidency is committed to us.

For what is its charter? "I will remember my covenant which is between me and you and every living creature of all flesh, * * * and the bow shall be in the cloud and I will look upon it, that I may remember the everlasting covenant between God and every living creature of all flesh that is upon the earth."

Such is the covenant and the seal, and the promise is, "While earth remaineth, seed-time and harvest, and cold and heat, and summer and winter, and day and night shall not cease."

That is a good constitution for an adult world. We would not ask for the infantile Paradise of the Roman poet Ovid, when "no sail stirred the sea, nor plow the soil, but content with food that grew without care, they gathered the fruits of the trees and the berries of the mountain and the acorns that dropped from the oaks. Spring was eternal, and gentle zephyrs with tepid breath soothed flowers born without seed, and soon the unplowed earth was bearing fruits and the untilled field was white with corn. Rivers of milk and of nectar flowed, and amber honey dropped from the green oaks." That is all very sweet and blessed, but we would rather work for our living. "The Father worketh hitherto" and we would work.

We take the promise as giving conditions of the best vigor of manhood. We accept our office, and will discharge it, as we can, in justice to our wards as well as ourselves. And what are our wards? Are there others as well as ourselves for whom we are responsible? That is the question which the first farmer asked: "Am I my brother's keeper?"

We will try to answer it more wisely and truly than he did. First, there is our duty to the soil itself, to this our mother earth, sacred, like the duty we owe to our own mothers. Let her not be impoverished by wasteful tillage or by desolating crops, or starved for want of needful food. Let her be richer every year, and better dressed and younger. How rich and how beautiful was this virgin Northwest as we found her, waving with grass, blooming with flowers; and how comely, again, in the glory of those teeming early crops. But the willing soil grew faint with giving much and receiving no return.

But what could be done? We wanted the springs and little streams by which the prairie farms could keep the herds and flocks which were needful that the strength might return to the soil. There was abundant water below, but how to bring it to the surface? There was on our frontier a mission-ary* caring for the physical as well as the spiritual well-being of the earlier tenants of our soil. Disabled for a season from his ministry, he matured a thought which, in later years, he, and now his sons, have developed into those engines with which the winds of heaven are lifting those deep-lying waters, not only for our fields and cattle but for others all across our land and in far-away islands and continents, making waters to break out in the wilderness and streams in the desert. Is it not noble to be able, in such ways, by our own thought and care, to bring back to our mother earth blessings of heaven above and of the deep that lieth under, through which she shall be able to put on every year a younger and more fruitful life, preparing the home of our children in the good time coming?

We have to cultivate also the fruits of the earth. It is pretty to think of the children of the Golden Age gathering the acorns under the oaks, and with their good digestion and sweet content they might have made a cheery life in those native oak orchards which used to dot our prairies. But think of the orchards and the fields which are to replace them in the days of our children.

We have a duty also to what we call our dumb animals, though if we could understand their voice as well as they

---

* Rev. L. H. Wheeler, missionary to the Ojibwa Indians, and inventor of the Eclipse wind engine.

earn to understand ours, perhaps we should not call them so, nd who knows what communications we may yet learn to old with these our partners in that covenant of which the ainbow is the seal? At least we cannot say that a " brute " as no rights which a man is bound to respect. Make them our friends, give them your wise and tender care. Meet hat appealing home-feeling of the ox that "knoweth his wner," by giving him what shall be for him a home. I annot show you the aspect of that heifer image from Memhis of which I spoke, but you, that have cared for your erd with that kind interest which has made you acquainted rith them and them with you, have looked into many an ye which has made you understand how the Greeks should ave ascribed that eye to their queen of the gods, the " oxyed Juno." Give them such care and it will repay you not ess richly as a matter of business than as a matter of morals. They will be profitable members of our common wealth in arge proportion to the dividend which you give to them rom the income of that commonwealth.

Next comes the care of the products which your quadrued helpers bring to be wrought by the aptness of your ninds and hands. This theme will be so well treated by so nany experts that I have only to speak of the satisfaction rith which the remaining community see the phenomenal riumphs of the past and anticipate those of the future of the Northwestern Dairymen.

How we enjoyed to see you in your last convention eviewing the awards of the New Orleans Exposition—Wisonsin rejoicing in her cheeses, and in more prizes for dairy roducts than all the rest of the world, and rejoicing in her laughters, Iowa and Minnesota, in the glow of their contenion over their butter, in which they, equal with each other, ad distanced all other competitors, and, with all their strife, vere as proud of one another, as the mother, Wisconsin, was of both. And well they might be, for what in art can be more perfect than the product of an Iowa or Minnesota creamery or of a Wisconsin dairy that I wot of?

It is more in order for an outsider to speak of your occupation in its relation to the higher range of culture, that of manhood and womanhood, of the home, the family, the community, the state.

It has always been recognized that farm life was the most healthful life, morally as well as physically.

The difficulty has been that the rural population was too sparse to allow the facilities for education or the intellectual stimulus, by means of which the farmers' boys and girls could keep up with their city cousins. Another difficulty has been the necessity of long and hard work for a mere living, leaving little time or vigor for the culture of the mind; and another, a desolating one in a large part of the world and of history, has been that the tillers of the soil were not the owners of the soil. The policy of our nation and the instinct of our people are occupying our country with small farms, each of which is the empire of the working farmer.

The improvements in culture and care of land will enable the soil to support a dense population, especially in the interior, where all the land is susceptible of cultivation, so that the school-house and the church may be in the vicinity of every home. The improvements in machinery and methods of culture, and quality of animals, and in the intelligence and morality of the community will all give time and taste and means of mental culture.

Will give! Do we say? We have almost been speaking as if the farming population of America had been deficient in that regard. Let us rather say that all these things will enable that community, here in this heart of the continent, to carry on, to a higher perfection that culture which has been growing in this land from the first. Its history has been a demonstration that an intelligent, educated and Christian farming community is a safe reliance for the present and for the future of the country and of man.

There must be cities, commercial and manufacturing; but their citizens could not live except by nurture and air and water, continually coming in from the free and pure country. And our history is proving that, in a true system, the moral and even intellectual and business life of the city needs to be continually recruited from the country. There is no more interesting feature in American life than the healthful circulation incident to the absence of caste and the prevalence of education and freedom of communication. Pass along any respectable business street of the city and you shall find that its business men come from the farms. You will find the same if you call the roll of Congress, or of any profession. And, on the other hand, you will find in our minor cities and villages and on our farms the men who have been in city life. And the health of the whole is in the prevalence, on the whole, of the farming community, both by virtue of its numbers and its health, physical, intellectual and moral. The farmers of America have made their country free, and they have vindicated liberty for all the inhabitants of the land. They are going on, in the solid movement of the phalanx of their conviction, against the vices that still fortify themselves in cities.

We believe that year by year and day by day this population is growing in intelligence, wealth, morality and power, and in the intent to use its power for the well-being of the land and of mankind.

They will be the ruling force of the coming time, and it is because such an association as yours is an efficient means of bringing on that good coming time that we all rejoice in its work. For henceforth the home of the farmer is the nucleus of the commonwealth of man, and what those homes are to be is to be largely determined by the inspiration and suggestion of such occasions as this. You will go to your home minded to make a better year than you have ever made before, and with new ideas as to how you will do it, and that purpose and those thoughts will be so much effective manhood in you.

Your cattle will feel it, your family will feel it, your children will do better work at school for the impulse which your quickened spirit will give them at home. As the season opens, your farms will feel it and your neighbors' farms. It will appear in the plans of your year, in the first furrows of the spring and in the last sheaf of your harvest-home, in the equipments, the stock and the products of your farm, and in your own home.

In the mingling of what has been the secluded life of the farmer, with the tides of the outside world the farmer gains much and gives more. Style is gained and dignity is given. Good taste comes to the kitchen and is more than repaid by good sense in the parlor. Good manners come from the city; good morals from the country. Intercourse sharpens the steel, but manhood is the steel, and manhood grows upon the farm, and, as we said at the beginning, manhood is the chief product of the farm.

The farmers of America have reason to be proud of the prizes they have won for the products of their fields and their dairies. They are honored also in the prizes won by such farmers' sons as Horace Greeley, James G. Blaine, James A. Garfield, Abraham Lincoln and Daniel Webster.

But these are merely specimens of the truth and worth of the strong, sound health of body, mind and soul, of the salvation, which is continually, and more and more continually, springing up on the farm and going into all the life of the commonwealth.

Now this is a matter of which I wish to say a word just here and just to you who are studying this question of farm products. We note marked differences between different localities as to this as well as other results. Some small farming communities have become memorable for the number and the quality of the men whom they have contributed to the public life of the commonwealth, and generally it is traceable to the influence of some man, who is a man, or of some true woman, in that community, who has had the public spirit and the intelligence to devise and realize plans for the common education of the community, adults as well as children, to discern the boys and girls that should have special education, not so much for themselves as for the service they may do for their kind. What has been the record of your town? What will it be hereafter?

This at least every man may do. He may be himself an educator, by being the best man he is able to be, doing his duty every time, to his farm, to his cattle, to his home, to his community, his state, his nation, to man and to God, and so he will have done a man's part to bring again the Golden Age.

V.

EMPIRE.

"Vanity of vanities," saith the Preacher, "all is vanity;" and other men, ever since the Preacher's day, who have been, like him, "shadows pursuing shadows" all over the world, have echoed his words—change, change, change, vanity of vanities. But did you ever mark that the Preacher became wiser, that he discovered that there was reality, and such reality as God and God's commandment and God's fear and God's judgment, and that in these was the whole of man ? So this is his conclusion of the whole matter, Reality of Realities, all is Reality and that Reality is God.

So say we, Vanity of Vanities? Vanity of Vanities? Naught is Vanity. Reality, substantial, eternal, fearful reality pervades and imprisons or glorifies all.

Nowhere has this continual song of Vanity been sung more continually than in the department of thought which we consider this evening, Empire. History reads like the continual obituary of dead empires. The world's poetry is their dirge. The soil of the earth is a cemetery of empires. Old mounds in Asia cover ruins of gorgeous palaces. The king who built the largest pyramid of Egypt is only recognized by a chalk mark, casually left upon a stone by one of his workmen. In ancient Etruria and in the primitive forests of America alike, are stupendous ruins of powers unknown to us. Is it not true, then, that the empires of the world are vanity?

Certainly there is no more imposing fact in history, none which more illustrates the godlikeness of man, than this of empire: that a word spoken in Shushan, the palace, shall carry trembling or joy over a hundred and seven and twenty provinces; that a stroke of the pen in London shall be followed by cannonading upon the Baltic, the Black, or the China Sea, shall be obeyed at Canton, at Calcutta, at the Cape of Good Hope, at Gibraltar, at Belize, at Quebec, at Vancouver's Island, in New Zealand and Australia. This ubiquity of man's will, is it vanity? Does it rise and pervade and search the earth with dominion like the sun's light, only to pass away and leave darkness?

No! Not so! Neither sunlight nor empire passes away and is lost in mere night. No day that God has made—no empire, that is by legitimate right an empire, ever passed or can pass away in mere defeat or vanity. But each before it left the earth has united itself with works that never shall die. It lives still in influences permanent, ever advancing and victorious.

Rome fell. But the influence of old Rome is broader to-day than in the days of Trajan. Roman law is more a law to more men, than it was when Roman lictors carried the axes before the Consul.

Oliver Cromwell died and Richard Cromwell, his son, succeeded him in the title of Lord Protector of England. The government went on for a time under the system of the father. But when it was found that the hands of the hero no longer held the reins, England was no longer protected. Anarchy and royalty came in again. Now while the protectorate continued after the death of its founder, who was the true protector of England, was it Richard in the office, or was it still Oliver in his grave?

The essence of empire, then, is actual command, real power. In the theory of the thing, the title or the ensign is nothing. The emperor—imperator, commander—is he whose efficient will and thought commands and it is done. No man is truly an emperor except by virtue of some command, which

is in him by the prerogative of nature. He has some
thought in him, which by its own truth will command the
minds of other men, or which so possesses his own soul as to
give it a greatness and force which human souls, not magni-
fied and fortified by like living thoughts, have no power to
withstand.

The same is true of imperial nations. Whatever people
has enjoyed true empire has gained, and holds it by virtue of
some individuality of its own, some forming thought or
principle, which was in it a source of organization and of power.
And so long and so far as that thought or that principle
continues and extends its power, proceeding from that impulse, so long and so far extends the empire of the man or
the nation which proclaimed that command.

Philosophically, then, and truly, he only is an emperor,
who has a command to give. And empire is only the
dominion of an idea or principle, the obedience to the command which the emperor, man, or race has given. And so
long as that command rules mankind the empire continues,
though the lips or the city from which it went forth be buried
beneath the soil of centuries. That Cyrus or Nineveh are
gone is a matter of sentimental pathos. If the work they
did in reclaiming man from anarchy had perished, that would
be a cause of solid concern. Those oriental monarchies have
passed, but their law continues. Men traveling in those
countries now, wonder at the stable forms of society there.
Probably if we knew how to dig beneath the surface of
national mind, as Layard could dig into the mounds at
Nimrood, we would find, upon the foundations of that society,
as he found on the alabaster walls of the Assyrian kings, in
arrow-head characters, the laws of the old conquering race of
Nimrod. When another empire succeeded them, their work
and so their true empire was not destroyed, but only another
came to build upon it.

Whatever, then, of truth and principle was in those ancient eastern monarchies is still in being and in force. What that truth was we may know better when more arrow-head inscriptions have been deciphered. We may however assume this: That no great range of ideas could be expected from a race who expressed themselves in action and in literature with heads of arrows. One idea seems appropriate to them—that of command and its correlative, submission. And these seem to have been so well impressed upon those regions that the obsequiousness of the servant or the armed independence of the spearman seem to be the only conditions of man there. The nations have only changed dynasties ever since. From Belshazzar to Cyrus or from Darius to Alexander was not more of a change for them than in England from a Tudor to a Stuart. The mastership of the arrow king, of force, is still dominant there.

Perhaps those nations, unable as they are to live without a king, are a great example of the permanence of empire in this way. Nimrod and his successors commanded them to obey, and now they have so learned obedience that they must have a ruler. The throne stands in their souls, even when no monarch can be found to take it.

If indeed the mummy of Nebuchadnezzar has been raised from his grave by the modern searchers of ruins, he comes up among a people who have not forgotten his law.

But it is time to turn from him and his people and analyze our own civilization and see whether our liberty has thrown off all empire.

We shall find that we live under a concatenation of sovereignties—that we are all encompassed in a chain-mail of command, and indeed that such subjection is a necessary condition of our liberty, such as it is, and that the extension of such subjection to the yet unrhythmized parts of our being is the necessary means for our further emancipation.

I say, then, that every one of us is to day a subject of many empires; for empires may co-exist. Every several strand in this glorious robe of civilization which covers us, is a commanding word that has been uttered by some man— and its power, as a strand in that mantle, is empire.

For, if the essence of empire is command, power over man, it is manifest that the term is applicable to all the range of human thought, action and character, not only political, but also intellectual, social, religious.

Let us think a little of the national empires which are our bonds, and then of some of our individual emperors.

That we are under the Roman empire has already been said. That authoritative spirit of law, which walks the earth here more than in Italy, is clad in the toga of the Eternal City.

We are under the Greek empire. This spread over the world before and simultaneously with that of Rome, ruling minds as Rome ruled bodies, and so it does now. In thought, and in intellectual taste, in art, and in quick life, we still obey the canons of Athens.

When these were both in their widest extent and power the Christian element came in from Judea to claim dominion over the souls of men. And its sway was acknowledged.

Thus at length, under Constantine and in the central focus at Byzantium, Constantinople, the three great principles of empire which had held separate sway for so many centuries were united, and that union, so effected, announced what was true before, that the work of each was done. The Jewish Theocracy, the Greek Philosophy and Roman Authority had borne their distinct fruits and it was time for a new system of development, in which these should still have their sway in the form of principles lying in the foundations of all government and society, but no longer on the surface, fighting for a foothold.

Add to these that we are still under the British empire. How great a proportion of our laws, our maxims, our beliefs, our thoughts and our whole system of life came and is coming every day across the ocean! And how rich we are in it all! In many things we ought to own and to boast our allegiance to British thought. We have declared our independence, but in nothing have we shown ourselves more thoroughly Britons to the heart's core, than in our Declaration of Independence,— an act conceived in the very spirit of King John's barons and King Charles' Parliaments and carried out with the very heart of Cromwell and Russell. We are free from the outer rule of England simply by the inner law of Englishmen.

> " We must be free or die, who speak the tongue
> That Shakespeare spoke;—the faith and morals hold
> That Milton held."

We find ourselves, then, willing subjects of Jerusalem, of Greece, of Rome, of England. Many forgotten as well as known nations have reached us by principles which they hewed out with toil or wrote with their blood. We obey the law of many empires.

Now let us see some of our Emperors.

For the fountain head of all human power is, and needs must be, in some individual mind. In its first springing, it is the dim rising of a single thought in such a mind, which grows in that mind, and pervades it, and fills it, and makes it great, and gives it might and goes forth from it, first as influence over a few, then as a guidance to more, then, if it be great enough, as government to many, till finally it stands forth as law to man—law reaching on toward universality and eternity, in proportion as it is a true law for man's nature.

Politically, there are now in Europe three states which bear the name of empires: the Russia of the Czar and the Austria and Germany of the Kaisers.

But what is this "Kaiser" which names the powers? "Kaiser" is Cæsar, and Cæsar is the proper name of no Hapsburg, of no German sovereign, of no man who inherited royalty, but of that Caius Julius Cæsar, whose commentaries boys read in school—a Roman citizen, senator, and general, of the age before our era: the victor of five hundred battles, taker of a thousand cities, slayer in Gaul alone of a million of men, and conqueror finally of his own country, Rome itself, and so master of the world. But he was no mere conqueror. He was a man of letters and science, an orator, and a statesman. In a brief and troubled ascendency, he found time to initiate the organization of a great chaotic empire, in the same spirit of true command in which he regulated the calendar, and gave us what our almanacs even now call the "Julian" year.

He was a man who had capacity to gain command, and, when he had gained it, he had a command to give, and so, though he refused the old title of Rex, King, and took only the Roman title of Imperator, general or commander, he made his own name of Cæsar synonymous with rule over nations, and his title of Imperator lives now in our word, Emperor, so that not only Francis Joseph of Austria, but we, in our theme of this evening, are but " rendering to Cæsar the things that are Cæsar's."

In the achievements of Napoleon Bonaparte, we have had, in our own century, the rise of a true empire; a command gained and discharged by a mind and spirit competent to do it; the compeer of Cyrus or of Julius Cæsar in manifold capacities of body, mind and spirit, organizing command, or, perhaps we may say, developing itself in empire. The effect, as we see it, is amazing; but, when we study the cause, that effect appears simply necessary. I need not speak of the traits which won that command, the military genius, the power over men, the ambition, the energy, the will, the endurance; and I have not time to speak of the higher imperial qualities which displayed themselves in the exercise, organization and administration of the empire.

The man, overwhelmed by strength, was borne like Prometheus by Might and Force to a rock of the ocean. But his empire was fixed in the soul of France; and it stood and in wonderful strength, against the two mightiest things in the world—against the spirit of loyalty and the spirit of liberty—an unnatural position and one which must fall. But while that has in large measure fallen, there is still left a permanent empire of Napoleon in sentiments and principles governing men.

But we have other kings than Cæsar, many that we know, and many that we do not know, whose laws nevertheless are living stones in our structure of social order. Dimly and vaguely discerned in the mist of antique fable and yet secure upon thrones forever, sit Minos, the old sea-king of Crete, who with Aeacus of Ægina and Rhadamanthus of the Cyclades were named by Greek mythology as judges in the "Land of the Hereafter," because in their day they were lawgivers and just judges of men. Beside them sit Saturnus and old Janus, who ruled the golden age of Italy; and Hercules stands by with mace and lion's hide—champion of afflicted right in a savage age. Then there is Odin or Woden, the old chief of our northern ancestors, and we may well believe that his law has come down to us, when his name comes again every Wednesday.

So we come down to Numa and King Arthur, to Solon and King Alfred, to Roman Decemvirs and William the Conqueror, and so many more, who in earlier or in later times, from the throne, the tribune, or the bench, have first pronounced laws which have become fixed rules of our lives. And with them should be classed in honor, for they are with them in command, those men like Demosthenes and Milton, who have by

their voice or pen urged upon the general mind of men principles of nobleness or of human right and fixed them as convictions, and so as laws for men.

In a real crisis of our Union stood Daniel Webster in the
Senate of the United States to defend the Constitution against
the assault of nullification, which in that generation, who
knew not Washington, was a real danger. When he stood
forth, its friends were in dismay; as he spoke, they grew
strong, for they felt, as his words went forth, the walls
that had been shaken growing firm, becoming rock, becoming
adamant. He sat down in a victory than which the world
has never seen one more momentous, not at Marathon, not at
Waterloo, for that speech had made the Union strong again.
His words "Liberty and Union, now and forever, one and
inseparable," were words which he had made true. His
deep voice ceased in that hall. The assemblage recovered
from the overpowering impression and dispersed. But the
power of his words was but beginning; they are now the
strength of these pillars in which we confide. We tread
upon his ashes—and sometimes we may have said "Ichabod."
But let us remember that his ashes are the firmness of the
soil upon which we tread; that it is by the power which his
words have given that our republic has that stability which
enabled it to do the truth when the crisis came in which
the orator himself quailed. If Seward and Sumner
and Lincoln and Grant were our leaders to a yet higher
national nobleness, let us remember, with thankfulness to
God, that their leadership was possible only upon the basis
of his. Daniel Webster has an empire to endure while
America endures, that is, we hope, while time endures.

We may come now to a brief summary of the Principles
of Empire.

The foundation of Empire is laid by the Creator in the
nature of man. So it was at first, when man was made full of

want but surrounded by wealth, full of weakness yet full of capacity, needing guidance to take that wealth and to develop that capacity. It is more so now that man is fallen, so that he needs to be extricated from his new as well as his original disabilities.

Every man's humanity is a greater part of his being than his individuality, and his individuality becomes great in proportion as it drinks in, and unites itself with the greatness of humanity.

Mankind, then, commencing life with this being made up of wants and capacities and thus social in nature, must either remain forever feeblest of the feeble and poorest of the poor, or men must rise together toward the greatness of being set before them; and this rising must be by mutual help and mutual guidance; and all help implies service and all guidance involves command.

Liberty, Equality, Fraternity, are words which express great truths. But liberty which knows no law, equality which knows no leadership, fraternity which knows no elder brothers, are nihilism and chaos.

In this mutual dependence of man, then, and in our common wants, is the foundation of empire. We said that help and guidance are essential conditions of common progress. Guidance is leadership, and leadership is the radical idea of empire. Let us illustrate in its simplest form the nature and true spirit of empire.

In travelling alone I come to the border of a wide prairie, not knowing how to find my way over it, and I find a man who knows the landmarks and induce him to guide me. He guides me, and so is my commander; he helps me, and so is my servant, and we go on in pleasant human fellowship in our mutual dependence, in human liberty, equality and fraternity. But by and by a spirit of independence arises, and I say to my guide, "I will not be led by you!" and he retorts, "I will not be your servant!" and there we stand—he with his useless knowledge, and I with my useless money—but each independent, and useless and helpless.

A whole man will go on, doing duty to God and man, seeking first the favor of God and second that of man, and after that there will not be much room for the consulting of any merely individual conceit. If he opposes men, it is in love to humanity and to God and not in love to himself.

Taking, then, mutual dependence as the law of the progress of our race, and the frank recognition of that dependence as entirely honorable and only human, we find in that law the basis of empire. All advance into the unknown future, toward the better country, lies through unexplored regions of thought and truth, and we need guides. There is, however, this difference between the guide of an individual upon the prairie and the guide of mankind into new truth. The guide of mankind represents humanity as a whole, and so is clothed with some of that authority which mankind has over individual man. Here are three parties. First; the great community of mankind, of which each individual is a member, as the hand is of the body. Second; the leader set forth by this community as the organ of its authority. Third; the individual, who owes to this leader the same obedience, within the proper sphere of his action, which he owes to the community. It is just the temporary authority of the general of an army, the dictator of a state, the pilot of a ship.

Authority, then, of ruler or of state, of teacher or of sect, is binding so far and only so far as it speaks the voice of God or the voice of mankind. Ultimately always the voice of God, for "Vox populi Vox Dei." Whatever right humanity has over the individual rests upon the laws of Him who made man. "The powers that be are ordained of God," and their charter is written in the nature of man. The object of them is the progress, the improvement of man, **not** the mere keeping of order. A ship at anchor needs no pilot, much less does it need a pilot when it merely lies in timber about a shipyard; so barbarism needs little government, except for the purpose of rising from barbarism, but all development of man, individual or collective, requires law, and law implies a law-giver.

Every legitimate empire, social or intellectual, is legitimate by virtue of its maintenance of some true principle which is valuable to mankind, and every new empire is new in that it brings some principle, not before in force, but adapted to give new strength and development to man. Lycurgus in Sparta found a people of no special note among other Dorians, and he gave them a military organization, through which they became the strongest state in Greece. Mohammed rose among the Arabs, a vigorous race, but a race who, in their old Ishmaelite independence, had never been a power in the earth, and he gave them a strong common thought, religious and political: "There is no God but God, and Mahomet is the prophet of God," and they were suddenly the only living might then in the world. The power which was there was the power given by the truth, by the great thought of the one God as our God,—that which was the power of the Hebrew state, of the Christian religion, of Luther and the Puritans,—the thought in its nature most victorious, because most fundamental and mighty of all human thought, but one which man's depravity is always effacing, and so weakening and belittling man until some new proclamation of it shall awaken him again.

But there are many principles which may have such power over man as to become principles of civilization and of empire. The strength of the empire of old Rome was in the principle of martial law imbedded in the old Roman mind, and when the state became degenerate, so that individual Romans ceased to apply such law to their own characters,

Julius Cæsar arrested the dissolution by substituting martial law, personified in his cohorts, for the martial law which had before had its throne in the public heart, and so his was in form an imperium, a military command.

Now see the Greek principle of empire and the Greek emperor. Who was the man that gave direction to the common national development of Greece ?

The Greek emperor is Homer.

He led the nation as David led his flocks, by the harp. That rhythm, continually resounding in hall and in hut, in market-place and harvest-field, in solemn pæan and in merry vintage song, became a law of common development. That was a thoroughly free empire, the best human example of a "Royal law of liberty," a common movement in obedience to a law which every man spontaneously follows, and thus a genial human law, calling out and not repressing the powers of the mind and man, and so its fruits were developed in individual greatness, blending in national greatness. We see its power in contrast with that developed by the oriental civilization, that arrow-head civilization which brought together armies of millions and scourged them into battle, in the wreck of the great Persian invasions at Marathon and Salamis, and in the fall of the whole Persian empire before the little army of Alexander, "the king of Grecia;" and it was the same power that developed itself in all the art, literature and philosophy of Athens, though Phidias and Socrates and many more who developed new truths and art, were emperors too, but all of the dynasty of Homer.

Nor indeed was Homer the founder of the empire. That honor would belong to whoever may have first incited that national spirit of song. Yet Homer is a true emperor for the Greeks by this title, that by his genius in the direction of the nation's want and desire, he made himself the leader of all their chorus, of voice, of thought, and even of religious belief.

He was elected by the vote of men's instincts, expressed in song following his rhythm, as Cyrus by the vote of men's wills, expressed by spears, and George Washington by the vote of men's hearts, expressed by ballot. Each holds his power by some popular election, and bears his appropriate insignia and sanction. In Homer's empire the rewards were garlands; the penalties, hisses and neglect. In that of Cyrus they were satrapy and crucifixion. In that of Washington they are freemen's shares in a free commonwealth.

In the whole subject we discern these principles: Empire is founded upon some want of which man is conscious—and the emperor is he who can lead to the supply of that want. His title is his ability. His election is the recognition of his leadership. What we generally term the duration of an empire is merely the period while its principle is struggling for ascendency. Its real empire begins when the victory is sealed, the army disbanded, the watchmen discharged, because the law is written in the hearts of men. And so the field is open for the struggle of a new principle.

It is time now to show the relations of the idea of empire to those of Liberty, Equality and Fraternity.

To Liberty, it stands in the relation of the necessary means.

Humanity at the outset was in bondage—thoroughly unable, by reason primarily of its ignorance, of its weakness, of its want of development, and after that still more fatally by its selfishness. This is the substance of the bondage under which the creation groans, and all the history of empire is the history of the warfare of humanity for deliverance from that bondage. Every true emperor was the captain in some enterprise toward that deliverance. He helped man to establish some law by which his nature could be redeemed from its chaos. He brought forward some truth, a word of God made to give strength to mind, or taught some sentiment to raise the nature from the ground. Leadership, so long and so far as it leads man to truth and strengthens and organizes his nature, manifestly leads him toward liberty. When it does this no longer its work is done. If it restrain his advance it becomes tyranny. In either case it is time for a change. And, as before the right of the king was divine inasmuch as he was doing the work of God, so now the right of revolution is divine, doing the work of God. Each in its place is a stage or a step in man's advance toward true liberty, deliverance from his disabilities.

How does the idea of empire stand related to that of Equality?

The truth which lies under the doctrine of equality is this: that every man who has a mind and a soul has, in the fact of his manhood, a worth which renders insignificant the difference between any one man and any other man, and so he has a claim to an equal dividend of the common good of human society. The poorest man is entitled to the same protection of the law as is the President of the United States. The equality of man, then, is something far deeper, both in its ground and in its rights, than the accidents of talent or wealth. We call a king high in station and a servant low, but which of these is the emperor? The title of leadership lies simply in the fact of greater service. The command is simply a duty done for the time, for the general good, and not a prerogative or private good taken by one from the common stock. The pilot of a ship has a right to require the work of the ship's boy, and so has the ship's boy a right to require the skill of the pilot, and each has an equal right to be borne in the ship and brought safe to land. The guiding the helm is not so much the prerogative as the duty of the pilot. And so in all life. The man who has the knowledge, or the thought, or the capacity by which he might guide and benefit other men is false to his duty of service, if he does not bring it forward for the good of those who have the same right to help and to salvation as he. Herein then is that saying fulfilled, "Whosoever will be chief among you let him be your servant."

This brings us to human Brotherhood as manifested in empire. What brotherhood would that be, in which one should refuse to guide another when he might, for the good of the fraternity, saying, "Am I my brother's keeper?" This sharing of advice and direction, of thought and defense and development, is most peculiarly the province of brotherhood. And he who renders it most is most our brother. All imperial influence necessarily involves, on the part of him who acquires and holds it, the giving of himself to the service of the whole; and in proportion as he loses himself in the whole, or in the truth which is to help the whole, is his legitimate command. It is when a great soul goes forth and unites itself freely with the soul of mankind, that human souls flow back to it. And this confidence in mutual sympathy is the necessary condition of all real and just empire. The Czar is the father of his people and their love and honor for him is that of children. The great illustration of the necessity of the idea of brotherhood in true captaincy is one which I have not hitherto dwelt upon. It is the purest example of all principles of perfect rule. Our Maker himself, when he would be the Captain of our salvation, took our own nature and in all things was made like unto his brethern, and so He died for us, and "therefore, is divided to him a portion with the great."

Now let us glance back and see what Empire is and what it is for.

An emperor, an imperator, is not a civil but a military authority, and empire is an organization of martial law, a dictatorship, holding men together until they can grow together in that living whole which is the greater self, that so we may pass from the savage to the civilized life; from the law of will to the law of good will. It begins with Nimrod, hunting and ruling men by his spear. Then springs some rudiment of law, especially with the northern races; and the Persians, the Spartans, the Romans form peerages or senates which are themselves little republics, but domineer with empire over subject populations, tribes or nations. So grew Rome until her Senate ruled the world. When that Senate was no longer able to hold the empire, up rose Julius Cæsar and grasped the reins, which have passed down from his hands to those of the Czar Nicholas and the Kaiser William.

He did well to refuse the name of king and take that of emperor. For as soon as his empire made peace throughout the world the King was born in Bethlehem of Judea. Other preparations for the Kingdom had been going on before. We have spoken of the power and dominion of great thoughts. That greatest of thoughts, the one God, hàd been spoken on Sinai, and made the Hebrew nation the power which it is even to-day. It was spoken again by Mohammed and what an empire it holds in the East! and again by Luther and Calvin and with what a might it is encircling the earth! We have called Homer an emperor, but long before Homer was born, when Jove thundered from Olympus, Greek fable brings the song of the Muses from Pieria at the foot of those ancient mountains, beginning that strain of harmony which was to unite with the Hebrew awe and the Roman law in the moral bond which was to hold the nations in the better time.

To-day the armaments of Europe perpetuate the legions of Cæsar. To-day America presents a commonwealth with scarce a soldier. What shall be on the morrow? If our hopes shall be fulfilled in the Commonwealth of Mankind, let us not forget what Empire has done for the world.

VI.

SOCRATES AS A TEACHER.

We study this evening a teacher, who began to teach more than two thousand years ago, and who is teaching still. His school is larger to-day than ever before, and it must increase so long as the fellowship of men that know and love the truth shall go on toward embracing all mankind.

Socrates was born near Athens about 469 B. C. His early and middle life were in the glory of the age of Pericles, when Athens was the center of the life of the world, of its wealth and especially of its intellectual activity; and his later years were at the time of the struggle and fall of Athens in the Peloponnesian war and her rising again from that fall. He was not in public life; nor did he establish any great institution of learning. He simply went about the streets, conversing. The Athenians were the quickest wits of all the world, and all the rest of the wit of the world came into the same vortex, and every wit was at its wittiest there. Athens lived in the open air, and along its streets and public places might be seen throngs all intent to tell or hear some new thing. Among them was rising that architecture which crowned the Acropolis and spread a robe of beauty over all Athens. They first saw the statues of Phidias, and heard the tragedies of Aeschylus and Sophocles and Euripides, laughed at the comedy of Aristophanes, and listened to the eloquence and felt the statesmanship of Pericles.

Athens, too, was full of young men, brilliant, high-born and bred, wealthy, and ready for any influence which might bear them to greatness or to ruin. Greece, far and wide, had been for a century developing rhetoricians and philosophers, and now they all thronged to the center of thought, to vend their accomplishment. They were the sophists, the *teachers* of the age. Coming to a vain generation, they taught vain accomplishments, whose vanity is kept in memory by our definition of the word sophist. But there were among them splendid orators, with magnificent adorning of person as well as of words. And they sold their wisdom at high rates. Among them appeared another; a man grotesque in his aspect and appearance, plain, if not careless, in his attire, going about and questioning everybody, always so humble and respectful that no one could refuse him an answer, and one simple question would lead to another, until, before he knew it, the wisest man was helplessly beyond his depth. So that examiner went to statesmen and orators and philosophers, and to all men of pretence, and he turned them inside out, to the infinite amusement of the attentive crowd. Under it all there was a conviction and a moral purpose, which was taking hold of some choice spirits, but, necessarily, many influential men were greatly offended. Meanwhile the sophists, against whom he protested, had educated a corruption and infidelity, which wealth and ease had begotten in the higher classes, which alarmed the orthodoxy of Athens, and Aristophanes, the comic poet, held them up to the laughter and indignation of the people. Unfortunately it fitted his purpose of ridicule to introduce as their representative the grotesque figure of Socrates and his face, which represented in real life the comic mask of Silenus, the drunken comrade, the Jack Falstaff, of their god of wine, Dionysus. Aristophanes may only have intended sport, but the result seems to have been that the people laid upon Socrates all the sins of the age. He was accused of impiety and of corrupting the young, and, refusing to defend himself by the arts of Attic courts, was condemned and died, in the refined Attic way by a draught of poison, at the age of 70, in 399 B. C.

So he died by judgment of his fellow-citizens, after seventy years of life, on conviction for perverting the young, for malpractice as a teacher. And yet his fame as a teacher has lived and come to us.

His pupils appealed from the verdict, and ask us to judge whether he was competent to make his companions better men.

If we are not merely to prove Socrates not worthy to die, but to justify the honor which the world renders him, we must find some cogent reason which escaped the discernment of his judges.

The world has known one other, who, living in private life, and speaking words of truth and love which convicted men of sin, of righteousness and of judgment, had died the death of a malefactor but has been justified by the conscience of mankind and is being exalted as a Prince and a Savior. Does the case of Socrates bear any distant analogy to that, in its causes as well as in its phenomena?

The " teacher of Israel" came to the teacher of mankind and said: "Rabbi, we know that thou art a teacher come from God." Jesus answered: "Except a man be born again, he cannot see the kingdom of God."

Is not that the key to the teaching of Socrates, as well as to that of Jesus Christ?

The teacher is the messenger of God. The aim of his teaching is the reformation of character; the prize of that reformation is the kingdom of God.

It will be no presumptuous thought to suppose that he, Socrates, may have been one of those who received "the Word," which was in the world before it was made flesh, and of those to whom "he gave the privilege to become children of God," as "believing in his name," as receiving into soul and mind the name of God, our Father and our Friend, as it is written on all the world and in all the soul, and, so receiving, believing "with all the heart." For "in every nation he that feareth God and worketh righteousness is accepted with him."

If we would understand Socrates, as teacher or as man, we must not so much listen to the wit with which he demolished the conceits of men and gained the sentence of an unbeliever and the cup of poison, as study the faith by which he was the most believing man of his time, and by which he laid hold on eternal life. He believed in God. He believed in man. He believed in truth, and, so believing, he must speak the truth, for the saving of man and the service of God. Teaching, with him, was not a trade. He would not take money for it. It was not even a profession. He made no promises. It was a mission. Standing before the judges and considering whether, to save his life, he would consent to cease his teaching, he tells them, "Men of Athens, I honor and love you, but I shall obey God rather than you, and while I have life and strength I shall never cease from the practice and teaching of philosophy, exhorting every one whom I meet after my manner, and convincing him, saying, 'O my friend, why do you, who are a citizen of the great and mighty and wise city of Athens, care so much about laying up the greatest amount of money and honor and reputation, and so little about wisdom and truth and the greatest improvement of the soul, which you never regard or heed at all? Are you not ashamed of this?' * * * And this I should say to every one whom I meet, young and old, citizen and alien, but especially to the citizens, inasmuch as they are my brethren. For this is the command of God, as I would have you know. And I believe that to this day no greater good has ever happened to the state than my service to the God. For I do nothing but go about persuading you all, old and young alike, not to take thought for your persons or your properties, but first and chiefly to care about the greatest improvement of the soul. * * * This is my teaching."

This, then, was to him a mission, a commission given of God, to teach virtue, true manhood, "to care for the soul, that it may be the best." In fulfilling his mission he came first to the general public of Athens; secondly, and more especially, to those individuals who put themselves under his influence and became his pupils. This last was his proper work, and it is that with which we have most to do as teachers. It is also, like the work of Christ with his disciples, that which has taken hold upon the life and history of mankind. But his public life and death was, like that of Christ, the more conspicuous in history, and seems to have been intended in the original plan of history as a life and a martyrdom auxiliary to that of him who was "to be lifted up that he might draw all men unto him." So it is a permanent and a fruitful lesson to the world, and we cannot do justice to Socrates as a teacher without some study of

THE PUBLIC LIFE OF SOCRATES.

We say the public life of Socrates, because his life was his teaching. While it could be said of him, more than perhaps of any other mere man, that "never man spake like this man," his life was more convincing than his words. To an age more used to words than to deeds, the praises of continence, of fortitude, of loyalty to country and to God were an admiration; but it was an education, to see him indifferent to the most alluring temptations, or walking barefoot on Thracian ice, or meeting the rage of the people when, as moderator, he refused to put an illegal vote, with the same composure with which he marched in the midst of their panic at Delium; or, finally, to see that calm and resolute allegiance to the law of right in which he, without wavering and without bluster, "went to his house" instead of obeying the mandate of the thirty tyrants, and lovingly told his democratic judges that he must obey God rather than them, while at the same time he was so loyal to the state that he would not accept an offered deliverance, when the court had sentenced him to die.

The physical, the intellectual, the spiritual composure of the man was something marvelous, especially in the midst of a people that had learned everything else. Based as it was on a deep loyalty to God, to man and to truth, it made him a kind of permanent moderator in the midst of the Athenian people in all the fever of their life, as well as in that day of frenzy when they were clamoring for the death of their generals. It did not avail to save the lives of those generals, nor in the first end to save his own life, but we will believe that in the final end it did save his life eternal as well as his honor in all history.

His method as teacher of the people was, like that of the Great Teacher, not by public sermon, lecture, or harangue, nor by literature, but by simple conversation. He was to be found in market or gymnasium, or at any hour of the day in what was for that hour the most frequented resort. He was continually conversing and it was free for whosoever would, to hear. The conversation, starting with the most common things, and using the homeliest illustrations, would go to the depths of the soul, to the breadth of life, to the height of heaven.

If we come upon him as he is teaching we shall be struck first with his personal appearance. And we must pause to notice it, for it may have been a factor of his power. Hector in the Iliad taunts his weaker brother on his beauty of person. Paris meekly replies: "We must not refuse the glorious gifts of the gods." But those gifts may come in diverse forms. The magnificent presence of George Washington, may have helped in bringing his young nation to a position of honor among the powers of the world. And yet the very homeliness of Abraham Lincoln may have fitted him for a leader in making his country a true home for its humblest child, or the poorest stranger.

Beauty was the passion of Athens, and the young aristocrats of Athens were by nature and by culture the finest figures and aspects of mankind. Socrates was the living image of Silenus, the comic ideal of grotesque ugliness. And yet those young aristocrats were the men who gathered round him and fell in love with him. Let Xenophon bring us into a feast given by Callias, the richest man in Athens, in honor of an athletic victory of a beautiful favorite of his, that we may get not only the presence of our teacher, but his manifold good-nature. Here among the gorgeous guests is Socrates, with his old cloak and all his homeliness upon him, and they are telling upon what each prided himself most. Critobulus rests his claim on his beauty of person. "How now," said Socrates "do you pretend that you are handsomer than I!" "Yes, indeed, or I should be uglier than all the Silenuses in farces,   *   *   but tell us why you claim to be more beautiful than I." "Well, why do we call anything beautiful—horse, ox, shield, sword, spear?" "Everything is beautiful according to its fitness for its use." "Then do you know what we want eyes for?" "To see, of course." "Then my [bulging] eyes are finer than yours [deep-set eyes]." "How so?" "Because yours can only see straight forward, but mine can see sidewise because they are bulging." "Do you say then that the crab has the finest eyes of all creatures?" "Certainly, because they are the best eyes for practical use." "Well, but which is the finest nose?" "I think, mine—that is, if the gods gave us noses to smell with? For your nostrils look to the ground, but mine open up, so as to catch odors from every quarter." "But how is your flat nose finer than a straight one?" "Because it is not in the way, but lets my eyes see at once what they want. But a high nose intrudes a wall between the eyes." "As to the mouth," said Critobulus, "I give it up, for if it is made for biting off, you could bite off much more than I." "But do not you not think my kiss is softer because my lips are thick? I seem according to your reckoning to have an uglier mouth than a donkey. But don't you think it proves that I am handsomer than you if the naiads, who are goddesses, bear Silens more like me than like you?" So he closes his case, and while the jurors cast their secret ballots he holds the lamp to the face of his handsome antagonist. All the votes are against Socrates, which he charges to the corruption of the jury.

So he came, as a son of man, eating and drinking, but never forgetting his mission, and he closes the conversation on love at this banquet of wine, with this address to his host Callias, who was, as we have said, the wealthiest man of Athens, and who was fond of Autolycus, who had just been proclaimed victor in the Pancratium at the great Pan-Athenaic festival. He says, in substance, "The love of the person is transient. The love of the soul is immortal. He that loves the noble should himself learn nobility. You are fortunate in loving one who has an enthusiasm for the honor of father and friends—of his countrymen and of mankind. How will you prove worthy to love him? How but by making your country love you and commit herself to you? Be well assured that you can do it. You are of the highest birth, priest of the Erechtheid gods, who campaigned with Iacchus against the barbarians, and now in this festival you have appeared more high priestly than all that have been before you, and most admirable of all the city for the nobility and the vigor of your person. If this seems too serious talk for a drinking company do not think it strange; for I, and our city alike, are always in love with a noble nature which is emulous for true manhood."

Then Autolycus looked at Callias, but Callias looked past

him and said to Socrates, "So you are trying to make a match between me and the city, so that I should go into politics, and make myself well pleasing to her!" "Yes, indeed, if they shall see you, not in seeming but in sincerity, seeking true manhood. For false show is soon exposed in the trial, but true nobleness, if a god harm not, renders the honor even higher in the ' practical issue.' "

Plato also has written a "Banquet," at which he represents Alcibiades, the most brilliant of all Athenians, whose fascination was fatal to his friends, his country and himself, as praising Socrates thus: "I say that he is just like the Silenus images in the sculptor's shops, with pipes and flutes; but open them and there are images of the gods. * * You do not know Socrates. You see him very affectionate and smitten with the beautiful, and then he ignores all, knows nothing, as if all this bearing of his was just a Silenus mask. For this is a mere outer covering like the carved Silenus. But opened within, my boon companions, how full he is of sober mind. He cares nought for beauty or wealth or anything else which men count happy. He counts all our goods and ourselves for nothing, and is always making irony and sport of all human life. But when he is in earnest and his heart is opened, I know not if any man has seen the images that are within. I saw them once, and they seemed to me so divine and golden and all beautiful and marvelous that one must do at once whatsoever Socrates bids." * * * "When I hear him, my heart leaps up more than any Corybant, and my tears pour at his words. And I see many others affected just so. I have heard Pericles and other good orators, and I thought they spoke well, but they did not affect me so. My soul was not troubled nor indignant at my slavish condition. But this Marsyas has often made me feel that I could not live as I am. So as under the spell of the Sirens I close my ears and flee lest I should grow old sitting there by him. But when I am gone my ambition overpowers me, and I flee from him. When I see him I am ashamed. No other man can make me ashamed. Often I wish I might see him no more among men, but, if that could be, I well know that I should be much more grieved. So I know not what to do with the man." Alas for Alcibiades! that he did he knew not what to do! Overpowered by ambition and passion he drank every cup of pleasure, climbed every giddy height, made shipwreck upon every shining promontory, and " died as the fool dieth."

Alcibiades was right in saying that his companions did not know Socrates. He spake to the people in parables. Athens was full of intellectual Scribes and Pharisees, and he spent this public life in unmasking them, acting as he said under the bidding of the Delphic god, who had pronounced Socrates the wisest of men. Socrates says, that, knowing that he had no wisdom, he interpreted the god to mean that no man was wise, and so that he, as the only man who knew that he was not wise, was therein the wisest of men. And so he went on his mission of vindicating the god by proving that all men were fools. Now it is undoubtedly true that, as a rule, he that saith to his brother " thou fool " shall be in danger not only of " the council " and " the judgment," but of " hell fire." It is a perilous, well nigh a fatal, attitude of mind and soul. The sincere kindness, and truth of his own soul could save Socrates from the great condemnation, and could vindicate him in the judgment of posterity, but it could not but be that he should be brought before the council, and it was not strange that the council condemned him. Such a man must make many and bitter enemies of those whom he convicted of folly or of sin. He could not but be liable to misrepresentation and to popular prejudice. The world is too dull and blind to understand those who are in advance of it. It is too sincere to tolerate those who it thinks are leading it astray; therefore whosoever proposes reform, of law or life, does it with the halter about his neck. Socrates knew that and consented. He understood that he who introduces reform must come into collision with the old, with the prospect that the first collision will be fatal to himself. In that conviction he, like Christ, avoided public and official life, because, as he says in his defense, "If I had assayed to engage in politics I should have perished long ago and done no good to you or to myself. For no man can save his life who honestly opposes himself to you or any other people and hinders the doing of many unjust and lawless things in the state, but he who really fights for the right, if he is to live for even a little time, must do it in private and not in public life." So he, like Christ, applied himself in private to his real work. Meanwhile he continued his public ministry, which he likens to the mission of a gadfly, sent to rouse a high bred and great horse, which from his very greatness was rather sluggish and needed to be roused. So he says, "God seems to have set me upon you and I never cease waking and urging and reproaching every one of you, besetting you everywhere and all day long! You will not easily find another one like me. You might easily strike and kill me, and then you might sleep all your life, unless God in his mercy should send you such another." They struck and he died, a death which crowned his life with honor and his race with blessing.

This public work of Socrates was a discipline, but it could hardly be called his teaching, except it be in such a sense as Gideon "took thorns of the wilderness and briars and with them he taught the men of Succoth." (Judges viii. 16.)

I wish it were practicable to give one of the discussions by which he at once confuted his antagonists, disciplining them like those men of Succoth, and educated the eager young men who listened; for example, the encounter, which Plato gives us, with Gorgias, the magnificent rhetorician, to whom Socrates comes asking to know what his art is. Polus, one of the friends of Gorgias, undertakes the answer with many words and no point, and is squeezed like a puff-ball and thrown aside as an object lesson. Gorgias then defines rhetoric as the art of persuasion; vaunts that by it he can make his craft of words worth more than the understanding of his subject. Socrates then leads him to say that the orator's persuasion is with regard to right and wrong. Socrates asks: Must he know the right, and if he does not know it, will Gorgias teach him? The rhetorician, for very shame, says yes, and is helplessly inconsistent with himself. Then up springs the irrepressible Polus and would have Socrates define rhetoric. He makes it an imposture—like confectionery, a craft of disguising the simple truth and evading justice, and so of no use, because the first interest of the man who has done wrong is to get his deserts and to do justice for the wrong. Whereupon Callicles, a representative of the generation which was growing up without conscience and without shame, joins issue with him, and we have, in naked grapple of logic, like Olympic athletes, the two principles which are warring in the world—the bold selfishness of the devil and the clear loyalty of the Son of Man. They come at last to the question, shall the statesman speak smooth things and be popular, or shall he speak the truth if he die for it? The man of the world has felt that he had a soul; as the talk has gone on we have seen the pungent words go home; and he shrinks from the answer. Socrates does not draw back, and he goes on to justify his answer by summoning the powers of the world to come, those dread judges before whom the naked soul must stand, and must receive and meet the due reward of its deeds. Then follows an application searching as from the lips of Whitefield, concluding, ''I therefore follow the truth as it has appeared to us in our study, that the best way is to follow justice and all virtue in life and in death, and not to follow the way to which you would persuade me. For it is worth nothing, oh Callicles." It was the same persuasion which he sealed with his blood.

From such conversations Gorgias and Polus and Callicles might go away defeated and therefore not won, convicted and therefore not convinced, and so ready to crucify him, but those young men that stood around were bright as well as light, and, as they heard, their minds enlarged, their souls were waked, they had caught the thrill of life. Shall we say that they did not know how it was. Neither did Socrates know, but the word that was in the world, coming to his own, though his own received him not, was quick as light to enter where a soul was opened, and "as many as received him to give them power to become sons of God."

Since we went out of Eden the earth has brought forth thorns and thistles for us, and they have done us good, but they are not the word of God by which man is to live.

The teaching of Socrates or of Christ was not for Scribes or Pharisees, for sophists or demagogues, but for sincere souls, that were ready to hear the word and do it.

Xenophon, the pupil of Socrates, says there is no education to any man from one who does not please him; by which he means not only that the pupil should be in sympathy personally with his teacher, but in sympathy also with his thoughts; that he should seek the truth for the truth's sake; that he should cultivate his mind, not so much that he might be a stronger, but a better man. It meant that in the case of a pupil of Socrates.

Socrates in the street, Christ by the wayside, confounded those that claimed to be wise, and interested the throngs that gathered around them, but they were also doing what was nearer to their hearts, as they attracted to themselves, one here and another there, those that were prepared to follow them in the way of truth and life.

These were their pupils, their disciples, and it is especially in the training of these, his pupils, that we are to study Socrates as a teacher. He did not call them pupils, but friends, and the first trait we should notice was the personal affection with which he sought and cultivated his companions. "He often said that he was in love with some one, but it was manifestly not a love for beauty of person but for souls that had capacity for virtue." He says, " I, myself, Antiphon, as any other man delights in a good horse or dog or bird, so and yet more do I delight in good friends, and if I have anything good I teach it, and I introduce them to others by whom I may think they will be helped toward virtue. And the treasures of the wise men of old, which they have left written in scrolls, I unroll and go through with my friends, and if we see anything good we cull it out, and count it great gain if we are becoming friends one to another.'

As this mutual affection was the attraction, the satisfaction, so it was the reward of his teaching. "He thought it strange if any one should take money for teaching virtue and not think he would have the greatest gain in getting a good friend, or should be afraid that the one who had become noble and good would not have the greatest gratitude to the one who had given him the most help."

We have here, then, a second motive of the life-work of Socrates, as it should be of every teacher. It was not only a work of duty, it was a work of love; of love to minds and souls, as well as love to God and truth.

Correspondent to these motives are the rewards, the prize set before him, which governed the life and inspired the work of this teacher. "Do you think," says he, " that from all gains of land or sea there is such satisfaction as from the realizing that one's self is becoming a better man and getting better friends?" Such was his idea of wealth. Wealth is virtue, and it is stored in one's own soul and in the souls of those who have become as one with him.

Both these motives united to fit him for a teacher. He cultivated himself, not merely for himself, but that he might teach others by his example. For their sakes he sanctified himself that they also might be sanctified through the truth. Magical as were his words, his pupils felt even more the impression of his example. "Strange," says Xenophon, " that any should think that Socrates corrupted the young. No man had such continence, such fortitude to bear and to do, and, furthermore, he was so trained to moderate desires that having very little he very easily had enough."

A character of such weight, such appetencies and such attractiveness, thrown into such a nebula of quick and bright spiritual elements as Athenian society was in the age of Pericles, naturally drew to itself congenial elements, and a new star appeared in the firmament, which has remained a fixed star in civilization. It is sometimes called the school of Socrates. The name is not a bad one, if we remember what the word school signified in his day. It is a Greek word, and it means leisure. Socrates says in his Defence, " The young men of the wealthiest families, who have the most leisure, *Schole*, enjoy hearing men examined, and follow me of their own accord " (Ap. 23 c.). From these throngs of men of leisure who followed him, Socrates, as a " Fisher of men," could gather those whom he thought fit for education, to spend their leisure with him in mutual helpfulness, that they might be no more what Horace calls " nebulones," floating atoms in a nebula of vanity, but a constellation, a system, a fellowship of minds seeking truth, of hearts seeking wisdom, like Christ and His disciples, except that Socrates did not assume so to speak "as one having authority." He would not have them call him Master and Lord, for he was not so. And yet to that chastened heart and that cleansed ear there came words which other men did not hear, and which he recognized as out of the depths, the voice of the spirit, τὸ δαιμόνιον.

It was generally a negative voice, saying, "This is not the way, walk ye not in it." As we remember, he affirmed that his highest wisdom was to know that he knew nothing. But even that was a great thing to bring out, to begin to utter, even in the midst of that vanity of vanities, the Athens of Pericles and the Sophists, the voice of the groaning creation which endures that vanity, not willingly, but supported by a hope implanted by its Creator, that it shall be delivered from the bondage of corruption into the glorious liberty of the children of God. In such a hope the school of Socrates formed itself out of the nebula of vanity and wrought on from age to age, and it knew not what to pray for as it ought. But He that knew the mind of the Spirit wrought with it, until He came who "brought life and immortality to light," and certain *Greeks* came to worship at Jerusalem and said, "We would see Jesus," and Jesus answered, "the hour is come."

This school of Socrates was exactly a college: "A society of scholars for purposes of study." He was the "President" and his associates were his "Fellows." We want then to study

SOCRATES AS PRESIDENT OF THE COLLEGE.

His first duty as President was to select and bring in the students who should be in the college. The object of the college was to train men to be able and good men, and to do the state and the world good. Xenophon says (Mom. iv. 1, 2) that he tested good natures by their aptness to learn and to remember, and by their enthusiasm for those studies which would fit them to be good members of the family and state and to deal well with men and the affairs of men. He studied the natures of each, to give each the encouragement or repression, the correction or stimulus, which each might require, and to give all such direction as to studies or pursuits as they needed, teaching them himself or introducing them to other teachers as there might be occasion.

The course of study in the Socrates College might seem to us to fall short of our idea of a University, but Xenophon says that "he was most intent of all men to know what each student already knew, and most zealous to teach what he himself could teach of what a noble and good man should know, and brought them to others to learn what he himself was not master of."

The department which Socrates, like many other college presidents, chose for himself was that of morals, or we should rather say of virtue, of *Arete*, true manhood. For, literally understood, morals, ethics, have to do with *Mores*, *Ethe*, manners, habits, which are the outward show or operations of the man. And Socrates, except that he was a sweeter tempered man, had more loathing than Carlyle himself for any empty raiment. He wanted the heart, out of which are the issues of life. We have, then, to consider

SOCRATES AS A PROFESSOR OF MORALS, OR OF VIRTUE,
OF TRUE MANHOOD.

Probably he might have objected to both terms of his title. He professed, he promised, no such thing. No teacher can make you a man. God helping you, you must do that yourself, and all that any man can do is to do all that he can. He can give incitement and suggestion and example and continual care. All that Socrates did, as scarcely any other man has done, but he did not insure the result. He only "trusted that those of his companions, who accepted his advice, would be for all their life good friends to himself and to one another." (Mem. i. 2, 8.) And that brings us back to the criticism which Socrates might still have made to the title of his department. If he would go beyond the manners to the man, and say virtue, rather than morals, perhaps he would still go beyond the man to the motive. Socrates said that the only subject which he understood was love. (Symp. 177.) So he sought to teach that Love—Love to God and to man—which is the fountain in the heart from which all life flows. As it is written (Luke x. 28): "This do and thou shalt live." "It hath been said by them of old time: 'Thou shalt love thy neighbor and hate thine enemy,'" but Socrates says: "We must not return evil for evil."

Probably, however, it will be better to define the subject of the teaching of Socrates as Virtue: that attitude of soul whose motive is love and whose law is truth, and whose reward is the testimony of a good conscience and the returning love of God and of man. "My friends," says Virtue in his parable of Prodicus, (Mem. ii, 1, 33) "delight in the memory of the past and rejoice in the experience of the present, enjoying through me the friendship of the gods, the love of friends, the honor of their father-land."

For such culture of character, Socrates must limit the number as well as select the members of his college. Christ chose twelve for his disciples. And perhaps something like a similar number might make up at any time the inner circle of the companions of Socrates. A university, which deals with the outside facts of all departments of knowledge, may be numerous as well as manifold. A college, whose office is to make men, should not have so many but that heart can come near to heart as well as mind to mind.

Happy was Socrates in looking back upon a life spent in such opportunities. Happy, in like manner, if not in like measure, may still be a college president who, in like ripening age, may look back upon life spent with such classes, who have been from year to year helping to educate themselves and one another in true manhood or womanhood, and have gone forth to live or to die for country or for mankind, and have left behind them, in the character of the college itself, fruits of their character which are the inheritance of their successors. Whenever there be such a president may his mantle fall, with a double portion of spirit, on his successors —and that of Socrates and a greater than Socrates upon all.

In illustration of the method of Socrates, Xenophon gives an account of his training of a young man, named Euthydemus, whom he found full of weak conceit, but thought him worth educating. He describes the honest art with which he attracts him; then the spiritual surgery by which he casts out all his conceit, by examining him on such questions as

What is right and what is wrong?

What is it to know oneself?

What things are good, and what evil?

What is a democracy?

Each confident answer is riddled by the magic power of Socrates' questioning, until the young man is compelled to confess his emptiness, and to say "I am thinking if it were not best for me to say nothing—for I am in danger of simply knowing nothing." So he goes away disheartened and thinking that he is verily a slave; but he does not give it up, as many do, but attaches himself to Socrates. And Socrates undertakes to teach him.

His first lesson is: Living loyalty to a living God.

His second: Loyalty to right and duty.

His third: Self command as the condition of liberty.

On such strong foundations he builds his education in manhood, enforcing them wonderfully with words, but more mightily by example. He taught piety, and was the most pious of men. So it was as to self command, temperance, honesty and sincerity, modesty, loyalty to God, to truth, to country and to everything which makes a true man. His method of question and answer waked minds. His searching questions probed souls, and his high convictions purified and exalted them.

The conclusion of the whole matter is, that he gave all his life, all his mind, all his soul to making himself and all that were with him the best men they could be made. He died cheerfully, in the consciousness that he had been continually becoming a better man, and saying " I am sure that witness will always be borne me, that I have never wronged any man nor made him worse, but always tried to make my companions better men."

My friends, we may not have capacity or opportunity for such a career as that of Socrates. But may we not so live that witness shall be borne, that we have tried to make every one with whom we had to do a better man?

VII.

MARTYRDOM.

MARTYRDOM.

There are few, very few, words in the speech of man, so
honored and revered, so loved and cherished as the word
martyr. And it is justly honored: for there is no earthly act
of man more striking, more generous, more noble, or more
insane than the act of martyrdom. That a man should,
deliberately and freely, sacrifice his own life for the good of
others, or for what he recognizes as duty or truth, is a deed
which has little in common with ordinary human action; and
yet men, when they see it, praise it and love it and rejoice
in it and exclaim: "That is true manhood!" And it is no
idle praise or selfish love, but an enthusiasm thrilling the
human nature.

What is a martyr? And what power is there in him,
which can so command the hidden keys of our nature and
make them vocal and even exultant in admiration and sympathy for him, and in condemnation of ourselves?

A martyr is, in the original meaning of the word and in
the true essence of the character, a witness. Every true
martyr, in whatsoever cause, is such by virtue of some faith
which was in him, of something which he was persuaded was
the truth, which it was his duty to speak or to do, though it
cost him his life. If there were no more than this, if martyrs were only a severe order of spirits, choosing to die rather
than to swerve, they would command our admiration; but
that love and sympathy and attraction, which attend their
name and wait upon their acts, testify that sternness is noth-

ing more than an accessory and subordinate element of the character which we welcome and embrace. To understand that, we must consider what the witness is which the martyrs bear. We shall find in it an announcement of the greatness and the hopes of humanity.

Let us study the meaning and the importance of martyrdom in a familiar instance, which I take because its familiarity has made it a known and influential witnessing to men: Thermopylæ.

The host of the Persian king, five million souls, the historian tells us, have been kept at bay for six days by a little Greek army under Leonidas, King of Sparta, in the Pass of Thermopylæ. On the left of those Greeks were the precipices of Mount Œta, and on their right, the sea; behind them their homes, and before them the foe; and in that Pass, not wider in some places than a wagon road, they stood, with the mountain and the sea for their allies, an impassable barrier to protect those homes. Now the sixth night is wearing away. The soldiers, weary with fighting all the long midsummer day, are asleep. Megistias, son of the old prophetic race of Melampus, is offering the morning sacrifice. He announces that the omens portend death. In a little time come Greeks who have escaped from the Persian army with the news that a traitor has told the enemy of a secret path by which a force has been sent over the mountain. Then come their sentinels down from the mountain to say that the passage has been made and the choicest corps of the Persians are coming upon them. The Pass is lost, but there is still time for escape. But King Leonidas will not go, for there was an oracle that either Sparta or a Spartan king must fall, and Leonidas will be the offering. Nor will the seer, Megistias, go. He sends his only son away and abides to die with the king. Nor will the three hundred Spartans go, for the Spartan law forbids them to flee from an enemy. As the morning came, they prepared their persons and their armor with studious care, as for a festival, and, when the Persians came, they fought and died in an ecstasy of triumph rather than of despair. One of them was away, sick and blind. He told his slave to lead him to the field. The slave brought him near and fled. The Spartan rushed where he heard the battle din and fell with his comrades.

These men are recognized as martyrs. And what is their testimony? Their epitaph was, "Stranger, go tell the Spartan men that here we lie obedient to their laws."

Ah! There we have something more than a brave frenzy. There was a meaning in their death, and a meaning which could only be expressed in its true emphasis by their death. Those men had a faith which made them strong to die. They recognized themselves, not so much as individuals, with each a single self to save first of all, but as members of a state, and, as such, bound to save the state more than to save themselves.

Such witness comes with authority. The doctrine which has had such power over them must be one which they have read on deep tablets of the soul, whose inscriptions are buried under the corruptions of human nature, but which soul-trying crises lay bare. The doctrine which can so exalt human nature and make it victorious over death itself must be a doctrine worthy of the study of men. See how that faith of theirs was not only a power over them, but a power in them. On that morning they came forth in front of the Pass and fought in the plain, and all the Persian army could not drive them back. And on the field appeared a further illustration of the conditions of greatness in man. As they stood, supported in their stern purpose by the thought of Sparta and her laws, the crowd of their adversaries were driven upon their spears by the lash of slave-drivers. There was the difference between the man who has law in him, and the man who has a master over him. Those poor servile Asiatics, that died at Thermopylæ are also witnesses that a man with a lash over him is not half a man, and so poor unwilling witnesses telling us that man was not made to be a slave. We do not call them martyrs; we reserve that sacred name for those men, whose manhood, exalted by their faith, proved by their triumph over death that man was made to be a citizen, that a man with law in him is ten times a man.

Xerxes felt the power of their martyrdom, and felt that there was a force in Greece, such as he had not considered when he gathered his grand army. Ever since that day, the names Leonidas and Thermopylæ have been reminding and teaching men what greatness there may be in man, and that the condition of that greatness is law, and its life is loyalty.

Similar to this is the testimony of all patriotic martyrdom. There was a day upon which hung the destiny of Rome. Her army was in battle with the Latins on Mount Vesuvius. Publius Decius, consul of the Romans, saw that his men were giving way. He called to him a pontiff and repeated after him a form of words, by which he devoted himself, together with the army of the enemy, to death and the gods below. Then he girded his toga according to the old Gabine cincture, and mounted his horse and dashed among the foe. He fell and Rome prevailed, and her empire grew; grew by that same spirit of devotion to law and the state, till it held the world in its law. So great an issue may hang upon a single martyr, and hang not unworthily. We count men, but men are not counted in history. Men are of force according to the amount of truth and of law—for law is only truth organized and efficient—that is in them. And their most potent expression of that truth and law is by dying for it, and, therefore, they alone who die for the truth are commonly called by mankind martyrs, as being fully accepted as witnesses in the great issue which humanity is trying. For there is a reason why the instinct of mankind loves to regard these men as witnesses. There is a trial going on from age to age in the general mind of mankind, and from hour to hour in the soul of each individual man. In that trial, man—each man for himself and the race of man for mankind—is at once judge and jury, and the destiny of man is suspended upon the verdict to be rendered. The questions at issue in those assizes are these: What is man? And what are the laws and what the issue of his being ?

In our courts, an oath is required as a condition of the reception of testimony. Humanity, too, requires a corresponding pledge of the reliability of its witnesses, and it receives no one as a witness of the first degree—as a martyr—who does not confirm his testimony by the offering of his life, and it rules out all testimony which is not proven by some measure of self-sacrifice. It passes by the evidence of the millions of Asiatics at Thermopylæ, while it records for ever on its heart the witness of the three hundred Spartans. While it calls those who have the martyr spirit its witnesses, it has a corresponding term for those who have no martyr spirit. They are insignificant, that is, there is no meaning in them. slaves, whose motive was the tingling of a scourge, or the clink of money, or any selfish end, are, rightfully or wrongfully, set aside by humanity in its inquiry into the mystery of man, of life, of death, and of duty.

In that very fact, see how great a principle respecting man is decided. The human soul, however it may yield itself to selfishness, refuses to hear the witness who has nothing better than selfishness to present. Man is thoroughly conscious that, whatever may be the true reading of the mystery of his being, he was not made to be a selfish being. He welcomes the martyrs because they present to him a nobler law of life and action. He feels that his nature is degraded, that, under manifold low and base subjections, and especially under the fear of death, he is all his lifetime subject to bondage; and he is looking for some one who can tell him of some better state.

Before this tribunal pass Leonidas and his companions; and of what is man assured by them?

They testify that there is an exaltation above selfishness, possible and native to man; that the heroic life is not a fiction of an imaginary past and of an impossible future; but that the rudiments of such a nature are still in man. Long before Leonidas, Hesiod had sung among the Greeks that the race of heroes was past and gone, and that an age of iron had succeeded it. But the Persian wars were to Greece what great crises of history are to a people who have life in them. Well do we call such events crises, that is, trials, for they try and test the souls of men, and in them come forth manifestations of the nobleness which lies buried in man's nature. Those revelations assure mankind again that life is not mere vanity.

The Persian wars were such a crisis for Greece, and they revived in the nation the thoughts and sympathies of the heroic age. Man has a persuasion that if a man knows the truth the truth will make him free; that the strong man is he in whom the word of God abideth; and he is convinced that that faith which develops itself most in strength and greatness and loyalty is nearest to the truth of God. Accordingly, the moral victory of Leonidas and his men wins the verdict for their faith.

Those times present us an illustration, on a still broader scale, of martyrdom and the greatness which it confers. To states as well as to individuals, the same choice is presented, between noble and ignoble action. There were four leading states of Greece in the generation before those wars—Sparta, Argos, Thebes and Athens. Of these, Argos refused to take any part in the common defence, and was never great again; Thebes submitted and aided the Persians as soon as they had carried the Pass, and for three generations there was nothing great in Thebes; Sparta still led the cause of Greece, and her greatness continued and increased. Athens was called herself to become a martyr. When the Persians swept over the country, the Athenians left their lands to the destroyer and their city to the flames, transferring their state to the Island of Salamis and to their ships. That martyrdom had made their state unquenchable. Xerxes saw their little fleet scatter his thousand ships at Salamis, and he fled to the Hellespont. The Athenian people returned to the spot where their city had been, and from that day the time of Athenian greatness was fully come. And it is remarkable to see how that greatness was pervaded by the free and the heroic spirit. The period of her glory is marked by the impulse of her martyr spirit. That was the time of her great poets, and artists, and statesmen, and philosophers. Socrates, the most living honor of her philosophy, was himself a martyr, and Demosthenes, one hundred and fifty years after the Persian war, when the state was fallen, is assured still of the truth of the martyr principle by the remembrance of the deeds which were done in that year of martyrdom. He exclaims:

"It cannot be, it cannot be, ye men of Athens, that ye were wrong in taking upon you that peril for the freedom and safety of all Greece! No! Not by your fathers that were in the front of danger at Marathon; that stood side by side with their brethren at Platæa; that fought the sea fights at Salamis and at Artemisium; and many more that lie in the public sepulchres, good men, all of whom alike the state has accounted worthy of the same honor,—those that have fallen in defeat with those that have prevailed in victory."

So the greatest and the last orator of free Athens interpreted the record of Athenian martyrdom, and in a few years more his own name was added to the list of martyrs to liberty.　He expresses truly the moral which humanity draws from martyrdom—the revelation of a higher sphere and law of human life; that loyalty even unto death, to state and nation, which is a development of that enlargement of soul by which the single self is to be merged in the fellowship of mankind.

But the best souls, even of the old world, found in the witness of the martyrs something more than that there may be, and should be, and shall be a great unity in the present life of man.　Their victory over death revealed to them the testimony of another life.

We turn from Demosthenes to the orator and martyr of Roman liberty, the most accomplished man of antiquity, and he shall be our guide in interpreting the testimony of martyrs to the immortality of the human soul.　Cicero speaks in the name of the elder Cato respecting the fear of death:

"Concerning which," he says, "it seems to me that there need be no long discussion, when I remember not only Lucius Brutus, who was slain for his country's liberty, or the two Decii, who spurred their horses to their freely chosen death, or Marcus Attilius, who went to Carthage to meet his fate in order to keep his pledge given to the enemy, or the two Scipios, who desired to make even their own bodies a barrier against the Punic foe, or your grandfather, Lucius Paulus, who in that disgrace at Cannæ expiated his colleague's rashness by his own death, or Marcus Marcellus, whose death even Hannibal, the most cruel of foes, honored with a burial; not only these, but even our legions, marching often with a spirit joyful and erect into a position from which they expected never to return.　I see not why I should hesitate to tell you what I think respecting death—a discernment which seems to grow more clear within me as I draw nearer unto death.　I believe that your father, Publius Scipio, and yours,

Caius Lælius, men most illustrious and most dear to me, are living now, and living the life which alone is worthy of the name of life.   *   *   For the mind is a heavenly thing, forced down from a home on high, and, as it were, submerged here in the earth, a place discordant with its divine nature and its immortality."

So great things already have appeared in that forgotten book of the law which the martyrs have found and brought forth from among the rubbish of that ruined house of that Lord—the fallen nature of man. Behold the inscription which tells us that the human mind was not builded for a mere stall for sheep and oxen and the changing of money! "Take these things hence." For man has been taught by the martyrs that the mind has a being as large as the range of thought, as lasting as the truth.

Shall not humanity take to its heart the witnesses who have assured it of such verities?

But we are not yet ready to dismiss the witnesses. They must tell us not only the possibility, but the conditions of such sublimity of human life.

What is the secret principle of the greatness of martyrs? We find it in the principle of faith. They have thought and have realized that self is not the center, and that sight is not the bound of the world in which man lives, but that there is a sphere beyond sight and a being greater than self, to which it is the honor of sight and of self to be subordinate. If they have made their lives illustrious by their surrender of life, it was only because they had first made themselves sublime by the surrender of self; because they had made themselves free by the acceptance of law.

For an example of these principles and for a further opening of the testimony of the martyrs, take our common phrase, "martyrs of liberty." We recognize the term as the title of an actual and most noble order of manhood. But what can such a term mean? What is this liberty for which a man should leave the joys and hopes and affections of this life, should forsake his labors and his duties, and be no more a man upon the earth? Is it any liberty of his own? If it be so, then surely it must be because man has a vision that death is not a going out into darkness and annihilation, but that for true souls there is a better country, where they may escape from the bondage of corruption which rests upon us here.

But if such an anticipation of individual emancipation for the soul by death is present in martyrdom, and in our applause of martyrdom, yet it is not the prominent element of the martyr spirit. It is not in itself the martyr's motive. The martyr of liberty is such mainly because he dies for the liberty of other men.

And is it so, that a man is so bound to his fellow men that it is proper, and even just and honorable, for him to surrender his own innocent blood for their good? The martyrs of liberty affirm that it is; all that praise them affirm that it is; but, if it is, what shall we mean by the liberty or the rights of the individual?

Here is a great fact which all martyrdom for the good of man reveals, and which, when revealed by them, finds its response in all of our minds—the principle that individual men are not separate sovereignties, but that we are all members one of another.

Those Spartans at Thermopylæ died for their country and its laws. What were they dying for? What is this thing which we call our country and say that it is noble to die for it? According to the martyr theory of life, this world is one world, made by the one God, and, therefore, its parts are not disconnected and unharmonious, sprung of chaos and hasting back to chaos; but they continually unite in greater wholes and higher harmonies, in the larger and the sublimer circles of being, until we come to Him who is the All in All.

And mankind has always recognized the civil state as such a greater whole, of which the individual man is a member; and the extent of the recognition of that membership and willing accord to the life and the law of the state has been approved as a measure of the true manhood which was in an individual man. The freest and truest souls have believed that man was made to be a member of the state, and to be fully devoted and subject, not only in outward acts, but, within the province of the state, in thought and emotion, to the state— willing to yield life to it. Socrates, called "wisest of men," steadfastly refused to escape from death when it had been pronounced against him even unjustly by his country. The demand of man for liberty is not a casting off of the authority of the state, rather it asserts and extends and makes the more sacred that authority; only it demands that authority be so constituted and exercised as not to hinder but to foster the best development of the being of man as a child of God.

I have felt constrained to dwell upon this point, because there is a degree of present tendency to forget the true nature and worth of the state. We have a saying that "in old times the individual existed for the state, but that in modern times the state exists for the individual." If this were true, what could it mean except this: that in old times there was a vitality in human society, whereby men wrought together as members of the state and produced the greatness of the republics of old; but that now there is a wide corruption at work reducing human society to the savage state, which is the natural working of the individual or atomistic principle. But the saying does still point, a little blindly, to the truth, which seems to be this: that Christianity has brought in a new understanding of the worth of the individual soul, a new appreciation of man as man. It is needful now that all the structure of human society be reconstructed of living stones, upon deeper foundations, with a broader scope and sublimer elevation. The new ideas have heaved and are heaving the old structures to their foundations, and they are lying or falling in ruins about us. But as we see them fall, shall we exult in the ruin, and say that that dissolution is the glory of modern times? Is it anything for us to boast of that we have leveled the marble temples of Athens to the dust, and that we will go on to burn them to lime, and crumble them to powder, and that such converting of the crystalline marble to the dust of the streets is the inauguration of liberty? Not so! From all these ruins there shall rise a new temple. The recognition of the brotherhood of all men, while it is necessarily breaking in pieces forms of society builded upon a narrower principle, is also working toward the growing together of mankind into a new state, embracing all mankind, and whose law shall fill and pervade every man's nature. As respects mankind alone, that state will be a republic, a commonwealth, its law being the law which shines in all martyrdom for liberty or for humanity, —"Thou shalt love thy neighbor as thyself."

Thus we have endeavored to present the testimony of martyrs, taking for our illustration that which seems at first view most distant from the faith and hope and love, which are the general result of the testimony of martyrdom,—namely, political and martial martyrdom. According to this view, all martyrs for liberty, for loyalty, for humanity, for truth, and for religion, whether false or true, unite in one body of testimony; they constitute one "cloud of witnesses" surrounding us, assuring and re-assuring humanity that man's nature is not deceived in that hope which alone sustains it under this "bondage of corruption," this helpless dissolution in which we seem to lie. Though all without and all within seems like disorganization and vanity—all our race "like water spilt on the ground which cannot be gathered up"—so many isolated and therefore insignificant atoms appearing on the earth and sinking into it again, and each individual man a mere chaos of wandering and warring thoughts, without system or meaning or aim,—yet that there is in man's being a truth and a life, a nobility, a greatness and a strength—that a man has to do not merely with these transient and temporary things which are seen, but with things unseen and eternal, and that his being has fellowship with all mankind, with all intelligence and with God.

With good reason, therefore, do we hail those martyrs of truth, who have assured man that all is not vanity, but that truth will make man free and great; we hail those martyrs of patriotism, of liberty and of loyalty, who have shown how men may be united and exalted together by a common law, whose working is the liberty and strength and greatness of united manhood; we hail those martyrs of humanity, who have taught us that the law of human fellowship which even war declared, is, in its true reading, a law of kindness,—"thou shalt love thy neighbor as thyself." We hail those martyrs of religion, who have given so earnest a voice to our common persuasion, that man and mankind, thus great in their individual and their united being, live and move and have that being in a yet greater being—in God, and that the law of God is the law of man's life.

To such conclusions had the testimony of martyrs brought the best minds and souls of the old world before the Martyr of martyrs came. The consciousness that we are members one of another had organized ruling races into military communities, as in Persia, in Sparta and in Rome, which, in the strength of their own internal fellowship, while they vindicated their own liberty, held mastership over slaves and dominion over nations, until the world was held under the law of Rome and of Parthia, through the strength of that devotion to the state which was illustrated at Thermopylæ. That power of law, grasped by the hand of the Cæsars held the world in order though it had no better banner than: "Thou shalt love thy neighbor and hate thy enemy."

Then the cross was set up as the martyr banner of salvation for all mankind. From that day to this, there have been two powers in the world; they are: first, the military law of exclusive patriotism of country, race or caste, maintaining liberty for itself, and dominion over subject tribes or slaves, whose strength is in the resolute will and the ready sword, and also in that instinct of loyalty through which men grow together. That regime has done a great and needful work in preparing the world for the larger and truer union of all humanity under a royal law of liberty, a union which can only come by the surrender of prerogatives, the sacrifice of self for the greater self, not now of family or state but of all mankind, taking for its banner the cross, not as a picturesque emblem but as actually borne by the Son of Man and by those that receive Him.

The religious victory of the martyr over the sword is the grand pivotal triumph of history; but we have more to do with the political struggle between the rights of man and the prerogative of power, with the great conflict and the grand reconciliation of Law and Liberty.

Man's consciousness of his own rights made the republics and the dominions of Sparta, Rome and Venice, and when they were merged in empires, man's inborn conscience of the rights of other men, of all men, began to gather the nebula of a commonwealth which was to supersede all empire. It has wrought and is working great silent, as well as great convulsive revolutions, and it is to work greater revolutions yet, in Europe and in Asia.

Both regimes, that of liberty and of mastership, had been transplanted to the new continent, and, in the form of assertion of our own rights, had united in the struggle by which our nation declared its own Independence, basing it on the common rights of all men. But in half of the nation slavery existed in bold defiance of those rights, and when the conscience of our people could not forbear the protest, the despot spirit rose in a rage, which could not be pacified even by the utmost forbearance, by which a strong love of the Union had held in check the love of man. That rage demanded the dissolution of our nation. Then came a crisis greater and more sublime than that Greek and Persian war. The cause of the nation and of man were one.

Was there ever such a spectacle as this nation presented four years ago? In a great nation two antagonist principles had grown to mighty power and had not yet come to the deadly grapple. There was the spirit of liberty, pervading and possessing the great body of the nation and making it, in its own good conscience, so peaceful and loyal and loving, that it could think no evil; and there was the spirit of despotism, to which the honest truth of the nation was an offence, and its patient forbearance was a provocation. And so, that spirit brought its action against our mother and demanded her death.

What a sudden crisis was that! We all had slept about our mother's throne during all the menaces that had preceded; for neither she nor we could dream that her sons would seek her life. The assault came, and either she or her true sons must die. And she rose and called for her martyrs, and a scoffing foe and an unbelieving or envious world looked to see if they would come.

It was worth a lifetime to see that day, when the word went forth that America had need of martyrs, and the millions that, till that day, had known their mother only by the ceaseless blessings which her loving care bestowed, answered the call, exulting in the opportunity to speak and do and die for her. It was a scene in history which grows upon us as we come to be more removed from it, and we feel that as yet we are able to take into our field of view only a portion of its vastness. Did you ever observe how the events in history, which we used to wonder at, have grown little since that day?

But even the enthusiasm of that day has been surpassed by the patient steadfastness with which the sons of America have persisted in their testimony. As the call has been for more martyrs, they have come, tide upon tide, "three hundred thousand more" again and again, and still they come, volunteers to take the chances of life and of death for their country. They are from all our community. Our neighborhoods, our congregations, our college classes, our families are thinned, because neighbors, friends, sons, brothers, lovers are gone to their places among the living witnesses, or the martyrs, of our common mother.

Seeing then that we are surrounded by such a cloud of witnesses, let us try to read their testimony. For it means something. Not in a mere idle or blind excitement have those young men gone from friends and scenes they loved to the discomforts and perils of camp and of field. Before me, as I write, lies a letter received a year ago from one of them, a noble Christian scholar and man, who turned aside from studies and from hopes cherished and loved. He says: "We believe we shall not long be soldiers; we are encouraged as we think how much brighter the prospect of preserving our country's life and honor is, than it was a few months ago, when we all felt an imperative call to delay no longer the assistance which our friends and brothers, already wearied and almost discouraged by long and apparently unavailing labors in the field, needed." "Not long be soldiers!" Oh, No! Thou witness brave and true, not long! A few short months more, and that loved name was written among the martyrs whose testimony is sealed. But still there was need of more testimony, and the martyr blood was not exhausted. While I am writing comes another letter from his bosom friend, who has gone to take his place, and he writes: "Though army life is, in itself, the most loathsome and unpleasant condition in which I ever found myself, the cause, liberty, country and humanity, make it a glorious thing to be a soldier, raising the meanest private above all vulgar destiny. I am glad I am here, for the post of duty is the post of safety."

Such men are valid and true witnesses. They testify in behalf of their country and ours, that she is a nation living and worthy to be loved. And no man can reject their testimony. For the nation is but the union of such hearts as theirs. She lives in them and while they live she lives also. And their love of country is a reflection, shining over earth and into heaven, of the loveliness of the land that hath cherished them and for which they freely die.

Solon, wisest of the seven wise men of Greece, came to the court of Crœsus, the richest of kings. The monarch exhibited all his treasures, and then asked his guest who was the happiest man he had found in all his travels. The sage replied: "Tellus, the Athenian." "Why?" said the King. "Because," said Solon, "Tellus saw the prosperity of his country, and children fair and good, and children born to all of them and all surviving; so the course of his life was good, but its end was most splendid, for his country was attacked and he came to her rescue and died in the hour of victory." The King, disappointed, asked: "And who was the next?" Solon replied: "Cleobis and Bito." And who were Cleobis and Bito, that they should be called happier than King Crœsus? They were young men of Argos, victors in the Olympic games, whose mother was high priestess of Hera, the goddess of the city, and on a great festival their mother was to be borne upon a car from the city to the temple, five miles away. The day came and the hour, and the multitude were there to join in the great procession, but the cattle were not yet come from the pasture, and there sat the priestess. A moment's pause and forth came those two sons and took the yoke upon their own strong and true shoulders, and moved on, followed by the wondering multitude, across the five long miles of thirsty plain and then up the steep ascent till they brought the car to the gates of the goddess. "And all the men blessed the strength of the young men, and the woman blessed the mother. What sons she had! And she overjoyed, lifted up her hands to the goddess and prayed that her sons, who had honored her so, might have whatsoever gift was best for man to receive. And so, when the festival was done, they lay down to sleep in the temple, and they woke no more. And therein," says Herodotus, "the Deity showed that it is better for man to die than to live."

Even so we have seen our mother, in the day that was to bear her on to honor as high priestess among the nations or to leave her desolate. We had trusted that she would be borne on, as she had been borne before, by circumstances. We thought that the moral sympathy of the world and the mighty voice of Christianized humanity would give security or victory. But when the hour came "the oxen were not come from the pasture." The nations, upon whose moral support we had counted, stood aloof and seemed willing to profit by the humbling of the high priestess of the hopes of mankind, and so they "passed by on the other side." It was well. For it was our right to vindicate the cause of our own mother. She had sons who had shown themselves Olympic victors in every peaceful emulation of civilized man, and if those sons would not help her, it were shame that she should be borne on by any others.

And the sons were ready. The flag that floated in every sea was not to be lowered and unavenged. The race whose energy was known and felt in every land were not to be motherless by their own fault. The sons have put their own necks to the yoke, and they are bearing the mother on, not only in the fierce shock of battle, but in the patience of long weary marches and dreary anxious night-watches, bearing up amid the violence of foes and the errors of friends; in the suffering of the camp, the hospital and the prison, year after year, through all the manifold martyrdom of war. Many a weary mile is behind them already, marked by the graves of them that have sunk by the way. And as they fall the loving tears of the car-borne mother mingle with their mártyr blood, and make the soil so sacred! It is the soil which was stained by the blood of the slave, and how could it be purified but by the blood of martyrs? But thankfully the mother sees that the car moves on; those sacred graves are not left to be stained again. Where is the son of America that will give them up? We of the West exult to see our Mississippi flow free from its fountain to its end. And yet I know not but that we ought to admire even more the testimony of our Eastern brothers, so steadfast through years of weary labor, wasting disease and cruel defeat.

But still on moves the car. Half the distance is measured, and if the steepest ascent still remains, yet on it is the temple full in sight, and if the sons who remain be worthy of those who are fallen, the day is not far hence, when, by favor of the Most High, our mother shall be at its portals.

And see, as the car moves, how the procession is falling in behind it. The nations that stood aloof, waiting to see the humbling of her that sat as a queen, are "blessing the fortitude of her sons" and preparing to do her honor. And well they may, for though she is our mother, she is, as we have said, a priestess of blessing for them all. When the verdict is rendered, we shall not be able to claim those martyrs as only our own. We are told that the Argives, and not merely their own family, set up the statues of

Cleobis and Bito at Delphi. And so our common humanity, which has long ago claimed our Washington, will set
up the remembrance of these, our thousands of true young
men, in the shrine of its heart of hearts. For, in the language
of that letter which I was reading a little while ago, they
offer themselves, not only for country, but, at the same time,
for liberty and for humanity.

Thus our martyrs have taught us that there are objects
more desirable to man than this bodily life; that there is a
whole greater than our individual self; that there are blessings lying beyond this life. Martyrdom is our assurance
of the greater reality of things invisible; of liberty, country,
humanity, immortality, Deity.

How much more witnessing may be needed before this
present case is decided, we know not. But the martyr blood
already shed, assures us, and may assure the world, that the
future witnesses will not be wanting. Our brothers and our
sons shall not be left to die in vain. If, after they, like
Cleobis and Bito, are "held in that blessed end" of death in
piety for our mother, and so have secured the second blessing
of the Grecian Sage; if, after that, it still remains that the
men of gray hairs, even they who have seen their children's
children, shall rally at their country's call, there will not be
wanting those who will aspire to his first prize, the most
splendid death of Tellus, the Athenian, and will exchange
their gray locks for a crown of glory in the final hour of
victory to the land which has been to them successively
mother and bride and daughter.

Let these, our martyrs, then, teach us the reality and the
beauty of a higher and a better life. Each of them saith
to each of us:

> "Be just and fear not,
> Let all the ends thou aimst at be thy country's,
> Thy God's, and truth's. Then if thou fall'st, Oh Brother,
> Thou fall'st a blessed martyr."

"Blessed," indeed, for that martyrdom shall not be in vain. It is most refreshing and assuring to see how the cause for which martyrs die has been unfolding itself to the soul of man since the ancient days. Leonidas and his Spartans died for liberty and for country. Our martyrs die "for liberty, for country and for humanity." And so at last there is in their testimony a meaning, which will shine even at that great tribunal where shall be gathered all nations. Their longings are sure of their fulfilment at last, in that Jerusalem which is above, which is free, and is the mother of us all, and here in this world, in that "peace on earth, good will toward men," which the angels sung when the blessed Prince of Martyrs was born.

VIII.

OUR MARTYRS.

Our Martyrs.

The closing of the war was a Commencement Day of the nation; the ending of a long term of discipline, and its accession to the new degree of *Magistra Artium*, Queen of Civilization. The ordeal which preceded it was the examination, which tested the results of that Puritan system of education, by which the nation had been trained for more than two hundred years.

The aim of that education was to make men; its organization was the Christian College standing beside the Church, and surrounded by Public Schools. The soul of it was a training in the truths of the word of God, and in the enthusiasms of the most heroic times and peoples, supported by scientific culture becoming continually more manifold as science itself should be enlarged.

As the developments of the war have been reviewed, the question has been pressed upon each of those Institutions which still retained the old idea of the fathers, that the center of a system of education must be the training in the divine and the heroic; the question, What have been the results of your training? Where are the men whom you have prepared for the need of your country and of mankind?

For a general answer, the system can call up the whole nation whom it has educated, the great army of the republic, which sprang up at the country's call all over that region, between the 40th and 48th parallels of latitude, from sea to sea, which King James called New England.

Also in the East, particular colleges have been proud to point to their own sons in the field. In this Northwest, too, whence came the power which decided the war, the question has been put to the young College which had been planted here, Where were thy sons when the land had need of them ?

The answer, modestly given three years ago, was received with such favor, that the guardians of the College appointed that an enduring testimonial should be prepared, in this building, not only of approval of the past but of example for the future. That memorial is now ready; and the question comes again, after three years of thought and further study and reflection, Shall the garland be bestowed, and the young mother, but twenty-one years of age to-day, sit henceforth tower-crowned as foster mother of heroes?

If she is, though by no seeking of her own—for she and her sons alike have only sought to do their duty—if however, she is a candidate for such honors, she must not shrink from standing before you, the parents who have committed their sons to her nurture and the wide community who have called for their service, and answering such questions as these:

1. Did the sons of the College answer the country's call, not in exceptional cases, but in such numbers as to justify the honor to be paid to them as a body?

2. Was their service a local one, or was it so general as to warrant this general testimonial from the wide Northwest, and even from distant parts of the land?

3. Did they show themselves capable men, such as should come from an Institution which professes to train in thoughts as well as in enthusiasms ?

4. Were they brave and true men, faithful unto death, so as to be worthy of an undying honor?

Let her reply to each question.

I. How many and what proportion of the sons of the College answered the call?

When the war came, the College had sent forth but ten classes, and only eight hundred young men had been in it. This number has since been increased to fifteen hundred, of whom, however, more than half were, at the time of the war, too young for service, or had died before, or were otherwise disqualified to serve, or their record is not known. Of the seven hundred and fifty who may remain, we have the names of more than four hundred as in the service; more than half of all who could be there, and more than a fourth of all, older or younger, living or dead, who have ever been in the College; and this proportion may indicate that those who remained at home were not uninterested in the cause, but bore their part in that grand support, which the armies in the field received at home.

II.   Is this a local object and is Beloit College merely a Beloit institution ?

The citizens of Beloit do not fail to recognize the honor done them by the representatives of all this wide region, in not only choosing this, their loved city, for the site of the College of this pivotal section of our land, but in calling it by their name.

They keep in view their pledge to cherish it by their prayers, sympathies and gifts. That their enthusiasms are its enthusiasms, this vicinity has shown by furnishing one hundred of the four hundred soldiers and even a larger proportion of the honored dead. They have come forward also to bear a part in this memorial, and it is in their hearts to do more yet. But these young men, as they fought for all the country, so they represented it all.

Shall we call up the regiments in which they stood, and see what an army they form ? There on the far left is Maine; then Massachusetts, with four regiments, and Connecticut; then New York with seven more; Ohio two; Michigan two; and Indiana one, bring us to the dense center;

fifty-five regiments from Wisconsin; fifty-six from Illinois; ten from Iowa; five from Minnesota; and then the long right wing, Nebraska and Kansas and California. But the muster is not yet complete. In front of the central mass stand Missouri and Kentucky, and Louisiana, and those regiments marked on our rosters by " A. D."—" African Descent" they say it means; Anno Domini is our first thought, and perhaps our last, for, in our night, their dark brows brought light and the acceptable year of the Lord. But this army shall not be unsupported nor uncomforted. There are the mortar boats and the gunboats and the ships of war; the nurses in the hospitals and the Sanitary Commission, the Christian Commission,—all that humane and Christian blessing, by which the elements which are forming the better future glorify the final struggle.

III. But did these many men prove themselves capable men ?

As children of so young a mother, they entered the war, as a rule, as privates. Many had not been long enough in the service to have their merit known when the war closed, or they were disabled, or gave their lives. But of the whole four hundred, two hundred and eighteen, considerably more than half, earned honorable positions as commissioned or non-commissioned officers. One hundred and forty-two bore commissions,—among them, four brigadier-generals, eleven colonels, or lieutenant-colonels, nine majors, four chaplains, fourteen surgeons and lieutenant-surgeons, nine adjutants, quartermasters or commissaries, forty-four captains and forty-three lieutenants. There were also seventy-six non-commissioned officers.

IV. But did they prove themselves true men in action?

When the call to arms came, the present and the former members of the College were, wherever found, among the first to answer it. They appear among the first seventy-five thousand, in the Ohio, Iowa, and California, as well as the

Illinois and Wisconsin lines.   Three of the same name shall represent the spirit of all.

Fort Sumpter fell April 14th, 1861; the proclamation of the President was issued on the 15th, and that of the governor of Illinois for six regiments on the 16th.   Also on the same April 16th, PAUL A. C. GODDARD, returning through Illinois from five years of army service on the frontier, gave his name in the 8th Illinois Infantry without waiting to see his home. He re-enlisted for the three years, and died in the service October 21st, 1863.   FREDERICK W. GODDARD, perhaps on the same day, enlisted in the 1st Wisconsin and afterward in the 3rd Missouri.   The battle of Spring Hill, Tenn., found him waiting for a commission as adjutant in the 22nd Wisconsin and not required to be in the field, except by his own choice.   He chose the battle, and fell there March 5th, 1863. The other, whom we do not name because he lives, was not liable to duty, on account of lameness, but by his entreaties forced his way into service for the short, and again for the long term, and did his duty until disabled by wounds.   During the campaign of 1861, the sons of Beloit were on the Potomac with the 1st Wisconsin at Falling Waters, with the 2nd Wisconsin at Bull Run, and with the 1st California beside Col. Baker when he fell at Ball's Bluff; they were in West Virginia in the body-guard of General McClellan, in those days of his early glory at Philippi, Buckhannon, Rich Mountain and Beverly, and in the 7th Ohio at Cross Lanes, where fell, August 25th, 1861, BURFORD JEAKINS, the scholar and the Christian, whom, though he was here so long ago, we remember as if it were yesterday.

In the West, they were in the force that held Cairo and fought at Belmont.   They were in the 1st Iowa at General Lyon's side when he fell at Wilson's Creek; in the 20th and the 33rd Illinois at Fredericktown; with Col. Mulligan at Lexington; in the body-guard of Gen. Fremont; and, on the 16th of August, GEORGE O. FELT, a soldier full of promise, was killed at Palmyra.

On the 21st of November, LIEUT. J. LYFORD PEAVY left Michigan, leaving enthusiastic professional hopes and a newly wedded wife; on the 30th, before daylight, he died with fever in Baltimore. He had written, "Our brave and precious ones must die." "Should we falter or stop to count the cost? God will guide all."

The search for our men in the campaign of 1862 reveals the breadth of the war. On the 6th of February their regiments were with Burnside at his victory at Roanoke Island, and with Grant at Fort Henry. In ten days more, they were at the fall of Fort Donelson. Meanwhile they were also in Kansas, where they closed the eyes of their loved fellow-soldier, FRANKLIN PRINDLE, at Leavenworth, February 27th. A comrade says: "I never saw one die in such triumph." The 6th of March found them fighting at Pea Ridge in Arkansas, and at the same time sailing out from Hampton Roads with Gen. Butler, bound for Ship Island, where, on the 8th of April, ARTHUR W. MASON died. When Sumpter fell he said: "My father is old and infirm, my brothers have families, I must go to represent our family." He gave up his contract to teach and enlisted by telegraph. On the disbanding of his first company he enlisted again, and kept to his duty until his discharge came and he was laid to rest "in the barren sands of that lonely isle."

The 6th and 7th of April reveal them in many regiments on the field of Shiloh. Thence, true MILTON ROOD of the 12th Iowa is borne away by his foes to die in captivity; and CAPTAIN SILAS W. FIELD, of the 11th Illinois, is borne away by his friends, mortally wounded, to die in hospital at Paducah, May 9th, 1862, leaving a memory full of honor, affection and Christian hope. There at the close of that first terrible Sabbath day, QUINCY E. POLLOCK lay upon the field in the midst of the enemy, and wrote these words on a soiled paper with a feeble pencil: "Dear Father and Mother: While I write I am on the battlefield, wounded, and think I will die, as there is no doctor near. God bless you and me." The victory of the next day restored him to his friends, but could not heal his wound. He died, April 11th, in a hospital at Mound City. He had embraced the Christian hope in the College. He left College to enlist in the army, not expecting to live to the close of the war, but saying "that his life was no better than that of others who had gone." In the camp prayer-meeting he told his comrades "that, if he fell in battle, he knew into whose hands he would fall," and he is now in the bosom of the Father.

Following up the results of Shiloh, many of our men move to Corinth, and Iuka, while others sweep with Mitchell through Tennessee, Northern Alabama, and Georgia; others again go down the Mississippi and occupy Columbus, and Island No. 10, where some remain in command of the garrison, while others still move on to Memphis, and before midsummer are in communication with their old schoolmates who had gone round by way of the Atlantic and the Gulf. On the western border also, they are moving on to Fort Riley, where EUGENE H. TUTTLE dies May 11th, 1862.

By this time the Army of the Potomac is in motion, and our men have their share in all the battles and the sufferings of the Peninsular campaign. In May and June, among those who sank under them was JEROME B. DAVIS, a true soldier, man and Christian, who died May 21st, 1862. In the heat of July we glance westward to see the 2nd Wisconsin cavalry in the fight at Cotton Plant, and the ride of the 1st Wisconsin cavalry through the mazes of Arkansas. We return in August to find the Iron Brigade doing all that men could do to save the army and the country at Gainesville and the second battle of Bull Run. In September again, in the same brigade and in many more, they are at South Mountain and at Antietam, where, in the 57th New York, falls HENRY COOPER, stanch and true there as he was here. At the same time others are engaged with the Dakota uprising in Minnesota, and others again are hastening to join the force which met Bragg at Perryville on the 8th of October. As the year draws to its close we are called away to Missouri, where JOHN GREGG LAMBERT of the Benton Hussars died November 23rd, and then to the extreme northwest of Arkansas, where fell, at Prairie Grove, December 7, 1862, EDMOND DAWES, a true man and "a devoted Christian in the army as well as at home." Then, at the extreme East, comes the battle of Fredericksburg, December 11–15. In this year, too, they are upon the water as well as the land. JEFFERSON D. FLOREY of the mortar boat service died August 9.

The year 1862 closes and the year 1863, the first year of liberty, opens in the East with the Proclamation of Emancipation, firm and clear even in the moment of disasters, and in the West with the successive defeat and victory of the long struggle at Murfreesboro. Among the sacrifices that bought that victory was EVAN W. GRUBB, of the Pennsylvania cavalry, then on Gen. Rosecrans' body-guard. He was, as his comrade testifies, "a soldier who could at all times be depended upon for any duty that required fortitude or endurance." He was instantly killed in the discharge of his duty. There, also, FRANCIS H. CASWELL and DUDLEY H. COWLES sank with wounds, which, aggravated by the sufferings of captivity, brought to each of them the call to pass from a rebel prison to the freedom and rest of the Jerusalem above. Cowles enlisted in the 22nd Illinois, June 25th, 1861. During the eighteen months of his service, "he was in seventeen battles, aside from all his exposures in skirmishes," and the 22nd were generally in the front. In the summer of 1862 they were in Alabama, and during the fall they were in the force which held Middle Tennessee after Buell's retreat.

In December he wrote to his uncle, Rev. S. Cowles, from Nashville: "We have been stationed here for five months. I have heard nothing from the outside world until yesterday. My life has often been in peril, my clothes and cap often cut with bullets, but none has grazed my flesh. Hitherto my Heavenly Father has protected me." "Six days after this date," writes his uncle, "the first day of the battle in Murfreesboro, he was struck by a bullet in his left breast, which came out in his right, inflicting a dangerous wound, but not mortal, if he could have quiet and care. But he was taken prisoner, and forced to march eleven miles, if I am informed correctly, and then trundled in an open car over a miserably rough road to Montgomery, Ala., where he sank down and died on the 20th of January, 1863. The account of his death which a fellow-prisoner gave, was that of a calm, triumphant Christian, sinking away in peace, in the hands of his enemies, far removed from father and mother, brother or sister. Thus his young life closed at the age of twenty-two years."

FRANCIS HEMENWAY CASWELL was born in Siam in Asia. His father lived and died a missionary. He graduated in 1862 and cherished the hope of preaching the gospel in the land of his birth. But very soon after his graduation came a call for 600,000 men, and he felt that his country needed him. He joined the 74th Illinois, which reached Louisville September 30th, and Nashville in December. On the 23rd of December, in view of the expected battle, he wrote to his mother: "Do not allow yourself to be anxious for my welfare or fate; for the purposes of God concerning me have not changed, and if I should lose my life suddenly and soon, it will be no more than carrying out the great purposes of God, and they are all just right, you know." Yes! but they are dark to us! In that same fearful morning, December 31st, 1862, he, too, fell wounded into the hands of the enemy, and was taken to Montgomery, then to Atlanta, then to Richmond, where he died February 4th, 1863. "His comrades testify to his coolness and bravery in time of conflict and to his consistent Christian character." Such was the purpose of God respecting the son of a missionary, who hoped for his father's work. Like his, in spirit, were the aspirations of the other young men whom we are numbering here. If God thought their lives best given for their country's cause, we will remember that "His purposes are all just right, you know."

Such costly sacrifices marked the last day of the year 1862. But they were not for naught, nor in vain. The next day, January 1st, 1863, brought the Proclamation of Liberty, which completed the Declaration of Independence and made a cause in which death itself was a victory. The same New Year's day brought the good omen of a great triumph upon the field of disaster on which they had fallen.

On the Mississippi also, their schoolmates, who had part in the repulse at the Yazoo Bluffs in the last days of December, shared also in the January victory at Arkansas Post, while others were driving back the rebel inroad from Missouri.

During the season of preparation for the great events of the next campaign, died, on the 17th of January, 1863, Henry L. Kingsley of the 105th Illinois, young in years but full of patriotic enthusiasm; and on the 28th, at Memphis, Thomas L. Seacord of the 72nd Illinois. He had looked forward to the ministry of the gospel of peace. The Master had another call for him. On the 5th of March, at Spring Hill, Tennessee, Frederick W. Goddard met the fate which has already been recorded. In the same month, Edward R. Barber of the 24th Wisconsin, was sinking under the disease with which he died at a hospital in New Albany on the 7th of May, sustained by the faith which he embraced while in College. There was no truer man. It was our loss, but true manhood cannot die.

Meanwhile the spring finds those who are in the field full of action. In the last weeks of April they ride with Col. Grierson through the length of the state of Mississippi, and with Hasbrook Davis up to the fortifications of Richmond.

Both were parts of great designs. The plan of Gen. Hooker's great battle of Chancellorsville was commenced by throwing the Iron Brigade over the Rappahannock at Fitts Hugh Crossing, below Fredericksburg, on the 29th of April. A broad river was to be passed in open boats under the fire of the enemy's sharp-shooters. It was bravely and successfully done, but on the hither side, his nobility of form making him a conspicuous mark, fell CAPTAIN ALEXANDER GORDON of the 7th Wisconsin, a soldier without fear and without reproach.

It would be glory to bear an equal part in the work of the Iron Brigade, to which that regiment belonged. Of Captain Gordon we have the testimony of the commanding officer of another regiment of the brigade " that in the field of battle, in the camp and on the march, he always seemed to be the ruling spirit of his regiment." And from another: " I saw him in one battle save his line from giving way at the critical moment, by his presence and daring. I have seen him conspicuous for his good conduct always, and so prominently that upon two occasions I thought him in command, as he seemed to be the soul and spirit of his line, and it was not until the battle was over that I found he was but a subordinate."

While the battle was raging on the Rappahannock, Gen. Grant has thrown his army across the Mississippi, and a rapid succession of victories, at Port Gibson, Grand Gulf, Raymond, Jackson, Champion Hills and Black River, brought them to the rear of Vicksburg on the night of the 18th of May.   Without delay, on the morrow the lines are formed for the assault, but before the charge is ordered a rebel shell cuts down WIILLIAM W. WORKS of the 72nd Illinois.   On the same day, just before the battle, he had written in his diary: "If I fall, I lay down my life, deeming it only a fit sacrifice for the life of my country."   He did not overvalue the life of his country, but how precious it grows as such lives are hidden in it.

But more were yet to be added; while the siege was in progress, PARDON E. CARPENTER, of the 12th Wisconsin Battery, died at Memphis—gentle, faithful and not forgotten.

At Port Hudson, the other key of the Mississippi, the men of the 4th Wisconsin were coöperating with their fellow-students in many regiments at Vicksburg; but we must return to the Iron Brigade and their fellows on the Potomac.

After Chancellorsville the war rolled through Virginia and Maryland into the heart of Pennsylvania, and on the 1st of July, 90,000 rebels were confronted by 60,000 loyal soldiers at Gettysburg.   The Iron Brigade was again in the front, and in the ranks of the same 7th Wisconsin, fell JARED H. KNAPP.   His lieutenant testifies that "he was singularly brave and daring, always at his post, never shrinking from duty."

Like most of the slain of that first day, his body was not recognized, and "rests beneath that sad, solitary, melancholy wo_d 'Unknown' which marks so many hundreds of graves of our dear braves."

So our particular griefs are lost in the common sorrow and thanksgiving, and it is for us to resolve in the words pronounced over those same graves, by him whose martyrdom was destined to crown all of theirs, "highly resolve that the dead shall not have died in vain."

Next came the Fourth of July, 1863, that high day, signalized for all time by the triumphs of Gettysburg and Vicksburg.

But all the war was not at these two points; our men in the 28th Wisconsin joined in a celebration of the same anniversary by repelling double their number at Helena, in Arkansas. On the 11th of the same July one of them was among the white officers who led the historic charge of the 54th Massachusetts on Fort Wagner, at Charleston Harbor.

The Army of the Cumberland also has moved at last, June 24th, from its New Year's battle-field at Murfreesboro, and, in ten days more has driven the enemy from Middle Tennessee. During its next season of rest and preparation for passing the Cumberland mountains, the 24th Wisconsin, from which Barber had died in May, is again called to lose JEREMIAH DOOLEY, who died at Anderson station, on the line between Tennessee and Alabama, on the 5th of August. He was born in Ireland but loyal and true to the land of his adoption. In the operations of the remainder of the year, especially in the great battles of Chickamauga and Chattanooga, our men were everywhere in action, or on guard; and on the last day of October, PAUL A. C. GODDARD of the 8th Illinois Infantry, already named as the first of the sons of the college to enlist in the war, expired at Vicksburg.

The autumn witnessed the strife for the key of the South. September saw the Army of the Cumberland broken at Chickamauga, beleaguered at Chattanooga, but still resolute. October brought them relief and the "Coming Man." November saw three victories at Lookout Mountain, Mission Ridge and Knoxville. In these operations the sons of Beloit bore their full share, though we are not called to record the fall of any one of them.

On the 16th of March, 1864, died J. DWIGHT STEVENS, sergeant in the 20th Wisconsin Infantry. His father was one of the original trustees of the College, and had been for many years before a missionary, first to the Indians and afterwards to the pioneer whites of the Northwest; the son had done his duty as a true Christian soldier, and sank at last under disease contracted during the siege of Vicksburg.

On the 15th of February, 1864, WILLIAM L. KNIGHT, though but a boy, enlisted as a musician in the 59th Massachusetts Infantry. Detailed to care for the sick, his earnest attention brought sickness upon himself, of which he died May 21st of the same year. So young, but he had earned a place in our lasting gratitude.

In ten days more, May 31st, 1864, LIEUTENANT HENRY MEACHAM of the 2nd U. S. C. Troops, died of the yellow fever at Key West, Florida. He enlisted in the 2nd Michigan Regiment, May 25th, 1861; was true to his duty, and died as his officer testifies, "like a Christian," leaving remembrances pleasant though sad, among his comrades and brave friends.

Already in the same month the same 2nd Michigan Regiment had been in the fearful battle of the Wilderness. As they enter the fight on the 10th we see among them a face which many of us saw in its childhood, WILLIAM PEARL LATHROP, eldest son of one of the earliest Professors both of Beloit College and of the University of Wisconsin. The remains of the father repose in our own cemetery. The son, born in Vermont, educated in Wisconsin, serving in the ranks, first of California and then of Michigan, disappeared in the Wilderness of Virginia. No man knoweth his resting-place, but he is not forgotten.

In two days more yet another in the same Michigan line, HORACE TURNER of the 2nd Regiment, fell mortally wounded at Spottsylvania and died May 16th. His captain says: "He was a brave and true soldier, a faithful and consistent Christian, and lives fresh in the memory of his loving comrades."

On the 24th, died WHITNEY TIBBALLS, of the 5th Wisconsin Regiment, from a wound received in the Wilderness on the 10th. Within the last six months he laid hold on the

Christian hope. On the 1st of May he had written six resolutions in his diary, of which the fifth was: "I will be brave in the battle-field," and the sixth, "I will be brave in refusing to do evil." Thus prepared to die and prepared to live, he saw the battle coming. He was detailed to tarry with the baggage, but he went to his captain and begged the privilege of going into the battle. "You are unwise," said a comrade, "we are going to have a fearful fight." He replied: "I know that perfectly well, and choose to take my chance with the rest of the boys." He took his chance. God knew what was best for him. He was borne to the rear and in two weeks more received the prize of him that overcometh.

The record of that month of May is not yet closed. CAPTAIN MARSHALL W. PATTON is known to many here as the boy with the bearing of a man, whose distinguished valor in the Iron Brigade gave him promotion beyond his years, but not beyond his merits. He fell on the 15th as he was leading his company in the 22nd Wisconsin to the charge at Resaca in Georgia and he died on the 18th.

The army moved on; and in front of the 74th Illinois at the terrible assault on Kenesaw, sank LIEUT.-COL. JAMES B. KERR, whom all Winnebago County knows, as a scholar, a hero and a man. He threw his sword toward his friends, his person fell into the hands of his foes, among whom he died at Atlanta, July 3rd, 1864.

Meanwhile had occurred the disaster at Guntown in Mississippi, where fell, in the 95th Illinois, the noble COLONEL, and by brevet after his death, GENERAL, THOMAS W. HUMPHREY, and with him LIEUT. STEPHEN A. ROLLINS, known and esteemed by many here to-day, as well as by his fellow-soldiers. COL. HUMPHREY was grandson of a colonel in the Revolutionary army and was worthy of his parentage.

While these things have passed, the Army of the Potomac has gathered around Richmond. On the 18th of June, cheer-

ing his men to the assault on Petersburg, falls LIEUT. FREE-
MAN B. RIDDLE.   I need not praise him here among the
multitude of those who knew him and loved him and will not
forget him.   He was what all knew that he would be.

Next we are hurried back to Georgia, where falls ALBERT
WALKER of the 22nd Wisconsin, who had just entered College when his country called him and he gave her his life.

Then again we are called to Petersburg, where we find a
regiment of those new-made men with dark skins, ready for
the onset.   It is not our first view of these warriors.   In
thirteen at least of their regiments, sons of Beloit bore commissions; among the rest one whom their suffrages have now
placed in the Congress of the United States, worthily repre-
senting in the capitol of the nation the capital of the state
which he had educated.   Also we claim one of the captains
who led the 24th Massachusetts in the historic charge upon
Fort Wagner.   He happily still lives; not so his fellow in
renown, so were he equaled with him in his fate, who led
the 29th United States Colored Infantry to the breach at
Petersburg, where CAPTAIN HECTOR H. AIKEN fell July 30th,
and died August 1.

In the same service, on the 25th of the same July, but far
away in Arkansas, died CAPTAIN AZEL D. HAYWARD of the
70th United States Colored Infantry.

During this summer many of you, who were students of
the College, served as "Hundred-day men," stationed at Memphis, and your loved and revered PROFESSOR BLAISDELL was
your chaplain, and here on the 14th of August you stood
round the dying bed of WILLIAM H. SHUMAKER, and on the
21st around the remains of FRANK E. WOODRUFF, killed at
his sentry post by Forrest's raiders, and you wished that you
might be no less true to the love of God and of man than they.

Yet again on the 3rd of November of the same year, the
battle of Franklin, Tenn., is marked by the fall at the head

of his regiment of the gallant COL. PORTER C. OLSON of the 36th Illinois.

There yet remains one more martyr's name, ALMERON N. GRAVES of the 3rd Wisconsin, who fell at Averysboro, N. C., March 15th, 1865, the last, and faithful to the last.

Thus twenty-seven of the forty-six died by wounds, and the rest, good and true men all, proved how brave men can suffer bravely and die bravely without the excitement of the field. Their lives and their deaths were not, and they shall not be, in vain.

SERMONS.

I.

THE PREACHER TO THE POOR.

THE PREACHER TO THE POOR.

Matthew xi: 4, 5.

Go and show John again those things which ye do hear and see, the blind receive their sight, and the lame walk, the lepers are cleansed, and the deaf hear, the dead are raised up, and the poor have the gospel preached to them.

This was Christ's own argument in proof of His Messiahship. John the Baptist, having accomplished his illustrious mission of proclaiming the coming of the Lord, was now in prison, reaping the reward which the rulers of this earth are accustomed to give to fidelity when it reproves them. Here he heard much of the progress of Jesus of Nazareth, and, as we elsewhere learn, rejoiced in His increase. We cannot suppose that after the witness which he had borne, both to the character and the person of the Christ, John was himself in doubt as to whether this Jesus was indeed He of whom Moses and the prophets did write. But his disciples, those especially who had been attracted by the striking features of John's appearance and career, may very probably have found some difficulty in recognizing in the plain carpenter's son, who came eating and drinking, even with publicans and sinners, the glorious Messiah, whom their imaginations had pictured as about to come upon the earth with a splendor worthy of the expectation of so many ages. With their doubts and questionings they came to John in his prison-house, and it must have been to satisfy their incredulity that John sent two of them to Jesus with the question: "Art thou He that should come or look we for another?"

Christ's reply was exactly addressed to their state of mind. It is in the form of a climax. "Go and tell John

what things ye have seen and heard; how that the blind see,
the lame walk, the lepers are cleansed, the deaf hear." Ye
have seen my power over all maladies and infirmities of the
body, and ye have seen yet a greater work, "the dead are
raised."

This was evidence which they could not gainsay. But it
left the cause of their doubt untouched. They were still
unable to reconcile His mighty works with this meek and un-
assuming deportment. His miracles they had seen; and now
they wished for a solution of the contradiction between His
powers and His course. Nor were they disappointed,—though
we may judge of their surprise at hearing Him state the very
ground of their doubts, the preaching of the gospel to the
poor, as the crowning evidence of His Messiahship.

If we examine this answer we shall find that it comprises
the evidence which the every-day life of Jesus gave of His
character, and that all the parts of it are necessary to the
completeness of that testimony.

And, standing as it does, it furnishes full proof of the
truth of his claim; and that in three several ways.

First: It presents the fulfilment of prophecy.

Secondly: It states the present visible evidence of His
superhuman character and mission.

Thirdly: It sets before us the life and spirit of Christianity in such a way that it commends itself to the belief of the
thinking man.

First: This reply records the fulfilment of the prophecies
respecting the Messiah.

The question had a particular reference to these. "Art
thou He that should come?" And the answer is so framed
as to remind the inquirers that Isaiah had not only said:
"The eyes of the blind shall be opened, and the ears of the
deaf shall be unstopped, then shall the lame man leap as an
hart and the tongue of the dumb shall sing," but that he

had also declared that the Christ, Messiah, the " Anointed," was "anointed to preach good tidings to the meek,"— was " sent to bind up the broken-hearted, to proclaim liberty to the captives and the opening of the prison to them that are bound."

All this was necessary to the completeness of the evidence from prophecy. It must be shown, not only that He had powers like those of the promised Deliverer, but that His character and career agreed with that of " Him who was to come."

Second: We have here the testimony which the life of Jesus presented of His exalted character and office.

" It is written in your law," says the Savior, " that the testimony of two men is true. I am one that bear witness of myself, and the Father that sent me beareth witness of me." " The works which the Father hath given me to finish, the same works which I do, bear witness of me, that the Father hath sent me." And when the Jews came to Him in Solomon's Porch, and said: " How long dost thou make us to doubt? If thou be the Christ, tell us plainly," His answer was : " I told you and ye believed not; the works that I do in my Father's name, they bear witness of me."

The passage which we are now considering presents the evidence from miracles in the form in which it most inevitably precludes the possibility of any explanation which denies the truth of the claims of Jesus. First we have the miracles themselves,—healing all manner of diseases, and raising the dead. They were done in the presence of the people, the spectators were there, those who asked the question themselves had seen them. Were they not the very seal of God set to the truth of His claim? God would not give the special sanction of miraculous interposition, in order to give authority to a falsehood. If these works were from God, then they proved beyond question that he who did them was what he professed to be. And was any other supposition possible? Could it be that these works were not from God? Was it skilful magic? Could it be collusion with the evil one? First, neither of these would account for such works. For who ever knew magician or devil that could raise the dead? Still there might be a doubt remaining in some minds. For they had seen such wonders done by magic and knew so little of the powers of Beelzebub, that they were not prepared to affirm that anything was beyond such power.

Christ was not accustomed to answer doubts as to the evidence of miracles by denying that such works could be attributed to other than divine agency. He knew that the minds in which such doubts arose required an answer of a different kind. They said: "Thou castest out devils, through Beelzebub, prince of devils." Does Christ deny that Satan could cast out Satan? Not at all. But he presses the consideration that it is impossible to suppose that he would do so. So, here in the text. These disciples of John might have said: "Certainly we see all these works. But it is easier to believe that it is all sleight of hand or Beelzebub, than to believe that this preacher to the rabble is the Christ, upon the distant anticipation of whose coming pious hearts have been looking with rapture ever since the fall of man." To minds in such a frame as this, the argument in the text addresses itself with inevitable directness and power. It explains away nothing. It offers no apology. That calm voice of one having authority simply states the fact, "I heal the sick, I raise the dead. I preach the gospel to the poor." And there He leaves it. It was for them to take the facts and meet them fairly and draw their own conclusions. Was it the work of the devil? If so, then the arch-fiend has sent upon earth an agent endowed with powers such as he never gave to man before, and all for the purpose of preaching the gospel of righteousness and peace to the poor, whom his previous machinations had loaded with sorrows. Satan never sent such a missionary. Though, blessed be God, we believe that all his malice will be made to contribute to the glory of God, yet he never was known to task his utmost powers to contrive and to carry out a plan whose direct and immediate object, as well as result, was to destroy his own kingdom.

And the idea that all these works were done by some secret skill, or by some newly discovered principle in physiology is equally incompetent to account for the facts of the case. For, supposing that legerdemain were omnipotent, can we believe that one who was endowed with the free power of working such wonders at his will, would be content to spend his life as Jesus of Nazareth did? The man who could lead after him such multitudes; who could feed five thousand upon five loaves; who could heal the sick and raise the dead, and walk upon the waters and command the tempests, and pass alone and unarmed through crowds that were frantic for his destruction; such a man might choose his place at the court of any monarch upon the earth, or, in defiance of earthly monarchs, He might have established himself upon the throne of universal dominion. And yet He spent His life in preaching to the poor. This was the problem which these doubting disciples of John were to solve. And it stands as an everlasting problem for those who maintain that Jesus of Nazareth was an impostor. Let them solve it if they can. If they can account for such powers united with such a course of life, in a man whose whole life was an imposture, then they can comprehend a greater mystery than "God manifest in the flesh."

We must come, then, to the conclusion that this fact of Jesus preaching to the poor, so far from being proof that He was not from God, is not only strong evidence of His sincerity, but it is utterly irreconcilable with the idea that He acted under the influence of any evil or ambitious motives;

and, moreover, is so very singular as to make it difficult to believe that this prophet was a mere man, and swayed by the motives which ordinarily govern human action.

But, so far, our reasoning has been of a negative character. We have found ourselves unable to account for the life of Jesus upon the ordinary principles of human action. And now we are ready for the positive inquiry. Is such a life as this consistent with the claim that this Jesus was the Son of God? If it shall appear that it is so consistent, then our first surprise at such a course will become proof of the truly divine origin of the dispensation. For it is the prerogative of God to see, and in His own time to reveal, that fitness which is so hidden in the nature of things—those harmonies which are so deep and perfect as to escape the casual notice or the undirected search of the human mind, but which, when pointed out by the finger of God, become luminous and eloquent testimonies to the unsearchable wisdom of the Architect of the universe.

Suppose that a blind man could be made to comprehend the physical structure of an eye, and then should attempt to divine the purpose for which it was intended. It would be an utter mystery to him still. But let the light in upon his own vision, and you reveal to him at once the design of that exquisite organization. The novelty and the completeness of the explanation concur to produce upon his mind the impression that the contriver of such adaptation was in truth the master of the secrets of the universe. So with the great doctrine of the Atonement. It is its perfect adaptation to the condition of a race that had sinned against a God of inflexible justice—together with the fact that it is such a scheme as man's intellect could never have invented—which proves it to be from God. If it had been left to us, the most sagacious human mind must have despaired of being able to devise a way of return. But, when the plan is unfolded, the sincere soul feels the grace of God bringing salvation. This is the evident mark of the wisdom of the Deity, and such proof of divinity we shall find in the life of Jesus, if it shall appear that a course of life so utterly the reverse of what we should previously have expected, commends itself to our judgment, as having been, after all, the course most exactly fitted to illustrate the character and perform the mission of the Christ, the Son of the living God. We come then to the question: Is this preaching the gospel to the poor an employment fit to be the favorite occupation of the Messiah? Was such a course consistent with the dignity of a divine person? Did it comport with the greatness of the errand upon which He had come? Does it show that understanding of man's being and character and condition which indicates the mind of one who has the Creator's acquaintance with the works of His hand?

Was such an appearance, then, consistent with the dignity of the character of the Christ? Can we believe that He who was the Ruler of the world would come in such a garb?

If that love, which is illimitable in its condescension as well as in its grandeur, could stoop to take the form of man, how was it fit that He should come?

God in the beginning made man a living soul, with thoughts that wandered through eternity and immensity, and deathless capacities for suffering or enjoyment, and He placed him here for a brief space to choose for himself what he would be for eternity.

Man, thus left, had surrounded himself with various trappings, and was spending that brief moment of life in striving, for that moment, to outshine his fellow man. Now, when it became necessary for the Son of God to appear on earth, how did it become him to treat this pomp? Would you have him come decked with the emblems which denote earthly royalty, or in that simple dignity of man as God made him?

These outward badges are all very well in their place, but, wherever they occur, they are a confession of the weakness of human nature. The colors of the various precious stones are beautiful, but the perfect gem is the diamond, whose surface no substance can mar, but light shines freely through it and glistens in it. It was well for Herod and Augustus Cæsar to surround themselves with the visible emblems of majesty. It was well for John the Baptist to come with raiment of camel's hair and a leathern girdle about his loins. But wherewith will ye array the Son of Man? No outward adorning that man could look upon and live was worthy of His character. If, then, the Christ could come upon earth and dwell among men at all, the garb of a man seeking no aid from the badges of this world's greatness, and preaching His gospel to rich and poor alike, was a fit garb; was it not the only garb in which it was worthy of His exalted character to appear?

Again, was the manner in which Jesus came suited to the purpose of Christ's advent? It was a serious errand upon which He had come. He was to bear the sins of a world and to restore fallen man to communion with his Maker. His business was not with kings as kings, but with men as men, standing all alike in the eye of God. It was no visit of form and ceremony. He would not leave the throne of His glory to deck Himself in the finery of oriental courts, nor to gain a temporal throne among the feeble atoms which He had created in this corner of His dominion. No! The Son of God had a far other errand here. He lived among men to give to men an example of holy life, and to teach them the truth which is able to make them wise unto salvation. And to do this He lived in that plain, familiar, common life, in which man's actions and character are known to all. He addressed Himself to that class to which belonged the great multitude of the souls whom He had come to save, and, by so doing, He practically proclaimed the great truth, which He was continually inculcating in His preaching, that the soul, the soul is the man. Such a being, voluntarily divesting Himself of all outward splendor, disregarding and contemning everything except the one end of doing good and working out the salvation of a fallen race, was a constant answer to the question: "What shall it profit a man if he gain the whole world and lose his own soul?" He came to men whose thoughts were so engrossed with the things that are seen and temporal, that they had forgotten alike the soul that was within themselves, and the world of spirits that lay boundless and endless just beyond the feeble, perishing fabric of temporal things, which had shut out from them the light of heaven. And He came to show them how worthless were the things upon which they had fixed their attention, and to lead them to look inward and forward and upward. They had indeed a most imposing form of worship. But their eyes were dazzled by the gold of the temple or covered with broad phylacteries. He wished to teach them to look at the things of the spiritual world in their impressive simplicity. Stern and fearless as He was in defending the temple from the profanation of traffic, He had come to bring in the day when neither on Gerizim nor yet at Jerusalem should men worship the Father, but when the true worshipers should worship Him in spirit and in truth. Accordingly we find Him teaching indifferently in the temple, the synagogue, the mountain, the desert, the wayside, the house of the publican.

He spoke the truth to high and low, to the proud and to the despised, without other distinction than such as was required by the state of heart of the person addressed.

He did not manifest that reverence for dignities which makes them of more value than the qualities of the soul, nor, on the other hand, was there any of that hostility to eminence as such, which is the tribute which cringing envy pays to

merit, which the lost spirits render to the glorious arch-
angels. His was the spirit, which, without fear or favor,
spoke the truth in love.

Such was the harmony between the grandeur of Christ's
office as a teacher and the humility of His demeanor. It
proved Him to be the Son of God, by manifesting that sovereign love which is the character of Deity, fixing itself upon
that soul, which God's eye always sees as the one thing of
value in this world.

There is another point of view in which this course
displays the wisdom of God. It shows that Jesus understood
the human mind. With the powers which He continually
manifested, He might certainly have created, in His time, a
far greater excitement. While He was walking about among
the villages of Galilee, not having where to lay His head,
He might have been borne in triumph through the world. It
would have been an easy thing for Him to overthrow
all the systems of idolatry and false philosophy in the world,
and make Himself to be worshipped by the whole race of
man. But He understood the nature of man too well to
enter upon any such career. He knew that such worship of
Himself would be mere idol-worship still. He knew how
prone man is to forget the soul in looking at the form. The
religion which He wished to reveal to man was one of the
heart, and He knew that it was of more value that it should
be planted within one soul than borne upon the lips of millions. He knew that the principle of true piety, if once
planted in the earth, must, by the aid of the Spirit, prevail
over all; but He also saw that its great adversary would ever
be that tendency to put the worship of some outward form,
or some outward form of worship, in the place of that holiness of heart, without which no man can see the Lord. He
therefore appeared as a humble man, and called humble men
for His Apostles, and sent them to preach the gospel of love to

every being that had a soul. He forbade them to be called Rabbi. He pronounced His blessing upon the poor in spirit, upon them that mourn, upon the meek, upon the persecuted for righteousness' sake; while His own life of constant, patient, quiet devotion to the good of man, united with such powers as He displayed, was to His own age, and it is to ours, a living illustration of the system which He taught, as well as a reflection upon earth, of that infinite mercy of the Heavenly Father, Who every day "causes His sun to rise on the evil and on the good, and sendeth rain on the just and on the unjust."

If we look into the mind of Jesus, we shall find proof that that mind was something more than human, in the way in which the great doctrine of the equality of mankind lay in it. The idea that no man has a right to lord it over his fellow man, is one of fearful energy. This was the soul of the steadfast movement that made our nation free. This, abiding and growing for centuries in the English mind, has made that nation what it is. And this, gaining possession of the French people, where the equally mighty conservative influence of an enlightened fear of God was wanting, showed suddenly to the world that terrible but sublime Revolution. But in the precepts and the life of Jesus of Nazareth this doctrine shines with a clear, fair, healthful, constant light and glow. He saw it and felt it fully. It was an essential part of that great system of things which He had come to reveal. Yet that truth, whose partial apprehension has made the wisest men of the wisest times madmen, dwelt here in all its breadth and strength and fulness, in the mind of a Jew,—one of a nation who were in bondage to a distant and a hated people,— a nation famed from of old for their impatience of a foreign yoke; a nation whose ancestral recollections were as glorious as their present bondage was degrading. And, moreover, these glorious memories were connected with the very family of Jesus. Himself was the Individual to whom the nation would look to deliver it from slavery; and, as we have seen, in His own hand were powers which might easily have bidden defiance to the Cæsars. Would any man in such circumstances have led the life that Jesus did? Can the facts in the case ever be accounted for upon the supposition that Jesus was a man? But suppose Him to be what He claimed to be, and the difficulty disappears. The ability to hold fully a truth at once so great and so novel, and yet preserve the balance of the mind, bespeaks a mind more than human. And we should infer the same from the aspect which the doctrine assumed in His mind. It has that calmness, and clearness, and scope, and universal adaptation which mark Divine things. There is none of that spasmodic action which attends the movements of a human mind under the influence of a great idea. He saw, of course, the obvious bearing of the principle upon the political condition of His country, and upon the subject of political government in general. But He saw, too, that this was only one of the incidental results of the fundamental principles which He had come to destroy or to establish, and He spent His life in impressing, in its simple purity, that foundation principle of the immediate responsibility of each individual soul to God, which, when once fairly mastered, would, in the process of ages, apply itself to all the relations of life in future generations, as it did every day in His own life. And He showed the far vision as well as the wide scope of the Divine eye, in thus, without agitation or bewilderment, striking at the root from which grew the evils which existed in society, and in thus quietly preparing the ground and planting the seed of the tree of life, whose leaves should be for the healing of nations, instead of thrusting into the hard ground detached branches laden with some one of the twelve manner of fruit which the tree should bear. Now that time has revealed it, we can see the perfect wisdom of such a course, but it was a Divine Mind that could lay the plan!

So the disciples of John go back to their Master, and what should they say of Christ?

They saw Him in fashion as a man, and yet they saw Him do the works of God. He spake so gently, and yet He spake as "never man spake." He did not assume the majesty even of Scribe or Centurion, but what command was in Him! And, with all His power, He lived to preach the gospel to the poor. What should they say of that? Surely this is not human, and yet, how humane it is! Certainly, we say, this is not humanity, and then the very echo of our words corrects the thought of our minds and of our hearts. Verily this, and only this, is humanity,—humanity purified from selfishness. A human spirit in full sympathy and vital union with all mankind,—the "Son of Man." And yet His works and His word, and the whole manifestation of Him, proclaim Him Son of God. So He is the God-Man, come from the "Bosom of the Father" into the heart of humanity, that he may enable them that will "believe into him" to become Sons of God, and may take them home again with Him to the blessedness from which He came. So let us, "poor in spirit," receive His gospel. "Blessed ye poor, for yours is the kingdom of God."

How precious a legacy to the church and to the world is the history of Christ's life.

It is amazing to see what an inconsistency exists between the professed principles and the life of almost every man. This Jesus was the one Man whose life was in perfect harmony with His own precepts. In Him every act is in natural accord with every doctrine. To this His followers look, in every age, for an example of a true life and for the principles which are to guide them in every situation. The beauty of that life, shining there in the view of all coming generations, while it has awakened the rapture of infidel as well as Christian, has ever pointed steadfastly up the way that leadeth unto life, and it is a light that can never be hid.

II.

THE GREAT MERCY OF GOD.

The Great Mercy of God.

Psalm ciii: 11.

For as the heaven is high above the earth, so great is His mercy toward them that fear Him.

The Psalms, like all the poetry of the Old Testament, are full of the impression of the awful greatness of the created universe in which this world is set. It is an impression common to all great and thoughtful minds, and the greatest minds stagger most under it, because they are able to feel more its unspeakable immensity; but yet, human as they are, they can no more grasp and sustain such a thought than the feeblest of intellects. In such an overwhelming contemplation mere man can be only passive, great to suffer but never to bear up under the burden. So we discern the approach to the presence of purely divine power. The mightiest human intellects show more and more tokens of might as we see them in contrast with other human intellects and their works. But as those same chief human minds come into the presence of divine power, they become a spectacle no more of strength but of feebleness, and all their development of intellect only adds emphasis to that expression of impuissance. They express feebleness as smaller minds cannot, by virtue of their very greatness and through the dread relief in which they stand in consequence of their separation from the ordinary ranks of mind.

Thus Daniel Webster, as death drew near to him, wrote these words for his epitaph:

"Lord, I believe, help Thou mine unbelief! Philosophical argument, especially that drawn from the vastness of the universe, in comparison with the insignificance of this globe, has sometimes shaken my reason for the faith which is in me; but my heart has always assured and re-assured me, that the Gospel of Jesus Christ must be a divine reality. The Sermon on the Mount cannot be a mere human production. This belief enters into the very depth of my conscience. The whole history of man proves it."

That is the natural working of a great intellect under the various teachings of God. "When I consider thy heavens, the work of thy fingers, the moon and the stars which thou hast ordained; what is man that thou art mindful of him?"

Human minds, that can only come to great things by leaving small things, find it a hard labor to receive the idea of an Intelligence which can fill and contain all this immensity, and yet whose full and sympathizing presence is with even such atoms as we are. And it is most natural that this difficulty should be greatest with the greatest minds, because they have most experience of the littleness of common things as seen in the perspective of greatness. And so it is most philosophical that praise should be perfected out of the mouth of babes, that those minds which have not been overwhelmed by the effort to comprehend a greatness more than they could bear, should most freely give glory to the God whose blessing and whose presence it requires only a pure heart and a single eye to see and to feel; just as it is not the eye that is dazzled by the noonday sun but that which is gladdened by its morning beam, that rejoices most truly and intelligently, as well as most freely, in its shining. But the heart of man is not liable, like his mind, to lose its elasticity as it grows great, and so the great statesman's heart answered as simply as a child to the voice of the Son of God speaking upon the Mount. For the heart is ever young, it does not grow stiff and weary and unwieldy like the body or the mind. Its emotion, if it move at all, is always free and unlabored like a child's, and its perceptions are just so spontaneous, if the mind will heed them.

From a Webster, with his sometimes wavering mind made steadfast by the assurance and re-assurance of his heart, we turn to this "Psalm of David." And here we see a noble sight and hear a noble voice; the full and concordant "Amen" of a great mind to the teaching of a great heart enlarged by God. That overpowering vastness of the universe becomes to him the dwelling—the not too spacious habitation—for the great love of God which is speaking to his heart.

He says: "As the heaven is high above the earth, so great is His mercy toward them that fear Him."

It is the awe of a soul standing upon this earth and beneath the infinite heaven that is lifted over it, and looking up into its immensity; and as it looks, it fears, and is hushed in awe; and, as it stands thus still and fearful, it feels the Divine presence filling that space, and it feels the Divine breath upon the heart, and it is a warm breath of kindness, and the assurance springs up, that God's love fills all that expanse, yea, that this sky, and that deep heaven and heaven of heavens are a pavilion of God's mercy spread over us, His own infinite love over-arching them that fear Him; and that it is all not too great for the dwelling of the love of God; and so the fearful awe of the mind becomes not confusion or prostration, but a most peaceful and cheerful, though most solemn, psalm of praise.

For these grand objects of contemplation were not unfamiliar to David. His childhood was that of a shepherd-boy at Bethlehem of Judea, and, as he kept his flocks by night, the stars were his companions. As he looked up among them night by night we may well believe that he came to love them even more than he wondered at them, and that he wondered with the rapture of a Hebrew poet, shut up as he was to solitary thought, and to conversation only with the most in-

spiring natural objects, and with the sheep of his pasture and
his harp. So to him the heavens declared the glory of
God, with no speech nor language, with a voice not heard, and
yet as with words going forth to the end of the world, and
mingling themselves with all his soul.

The vastness of the universe in comparison with the insignificance of this globe did not shake his faith; but the
"multitude of the heavenly host" sang to him, as to those
other night-watching shepherds of Bethlehem, one thousand
years after Him, not only, "Glory to God in the highest,"
but "on earth peace, good will toward men."

So the boundless heaven was to David full of the love of
God, and he needed, as we need, some such association as its
vastness and its loftiness, in order to express the idea of the
height and breadth and depth and length of that love which
he felt as passing knowledge.

So David, as he looked up to the heavens, did not feel their
vastness oppressing his soul with skepticism, but to him
"the heavens declared the glory of God." There was no speech
nor language, their voice was not heard, yet his soul felt a
music in that heavenly host; "their line," as it were a harp
string, a chord, a strain of music, going forth through all the
earth, and all his soul trembled with the vibrations of that
harp, and felt that it was in communion with God.

And not David alone. After David's harp was joined
to that harmony on high, Isaiah stood and looked up to the
heavens, and did the sight crush Isaiah's faith? He says:
(Isa. xl: 26, 27,) "Lift up your eyes on high, and behold
who hath created these things, that bringeth out their host by
number; He calleth them all by names by the greatness of His
might, for that He is strong in power; not one faileth." So
he is impressed by the vastness of the view. Does it make
him doubt the care of God for man? He goes on to say,
"Why sayest thou, O Jacob, and speakest, O Israel, My way

is hid from the Lord, and my judgment is passed over from my God?" The grandeur of the firmament is to him an assurance of his faith.

But perhaps those old Hebrew poets were carried away by the enthusiasm of a poetic soul not instructed by the light of modern science. Perhaps they thought that this earth was the center of the universe, and that all the sky was made for its embellishment, and if they had known what the telescope reveals to us, that this earth is but a poor, insignificant, opaque planet, while those stars are mighty orbs, blazing suns of light, they would have been perhaps sadder but wiser men, convinced that the great God that made those heavens could have no time or thought for such poor creatures as we are.

If that be so, if this be the fruit of all our science, if the telescope has removed heaven further off from earth than when the world was young, we must accept the result, and eat the bitter fruit of our tree of knowledge, though it be a tree of death; we must say, "Peace! fond heart, there is no yea and amen for thy hopes, no communion with God, no immortality for thee." Why not? Why not? sighs through the soul. "Because this earth on which thou dwellest is so little and the universe is so great." Oh! cries the soul as it sinks, Oh! that there were a God, that could see even me!

Is it so? Has science brought any such fatal present to man? No! Not so! When she brought the telescope to show the vastness of the heaven, which is God's throne, she brought also the microscope, to tell us that God is not more manifest in the vastness of the heavens than in the perfectness of each atom which goes to make up the whole. Indeed, we may imagine that we see some grossness in the great aggregations of matter, but our closest analysis leads to the conviction that its ultimate forms, too minute for our discernment, are perfectly finished. We may truly say that the telescope has not added so much of oppression to our view of the vastness of the universe as the microscope has added of assurance to that expostulation of the Saviour, "If God so clothe the grass of the field, which today is, and to-morrow is cast into the oven, shall He not much more clothe you, O ye of little faith?"

Practically, it is not so much a mistake after all, that first impression of every man, that the spot on which he stands is the summit of the earth and the center of the sky. It is so for him. Physically, every particle of matter is a center, from which and to which influences go and return in straight lines, connecting it with all other matter. Spiritually, every living soul is a center of spiritual influences radiating and returning, a center of the working of God, who worketh all and in all. Each one serves all and is served of all.

If we can purify our idea of God, we shall no more be staggered at the thought that the Son of God should die for such a little world as this; but we shall feel that if there were in the universe but one fallen soul that could be saved, and if that soul were the feeblest tenant of the smallest as-teroid that God had made, yet it would be worthy of God to give His Son to die for that soul, and the Son would hold a new claim to the adoration of the angels by reason of that sacrifice.

So that very infinity of God, which fills all the universe, assures us that our way is not hid from the Lord who hath created these things.

The thought presented for our contemplation then is,

THE SUBLIMITY AND GRANDEUR OF GOD'S LOVE.

"As the heaven is high above the earth, so great is His mercy toward them that fear Him."

We stand here upon the earth and look up into space. It is a sight imposing and magnificent at the first, but as we look it grows upon us. There are planets so many times larger than this earth, which are but points of light in the sky; and beyond them other planets which are hardly less, which our eyes cannot discern; and they are close upon us compared with those fixed stars, and other stars beyond them; and so it goes on. It passes all our thought, we cannot measure it; yet the imagination, made to seek God's throne, though weary and bewildered cannot rest, but goes on, star beyond star, star beyond star, until it comes to the limits of the creation, to the infinite outer desert of blank space, and all that domain, set with suns, and all that void space, if such void there be, is the heaven which rises above the earth. And as high as that heaven, "So great is His mercy toward them that fear Him."

We, the dwellers upon this footstool of God, look up into the heavens, and an awe comes over us, and if it be a holy fear, then straightway, all that expanse, even to its utmost height, is full of the love of God, centering upon each one that stands, fearing God, beneath that awful arch.

I. The love of God is sublime in its magnitude. It fills all this wide universe. It fills it with worlds, and so far as we are able to know, it fills those worlds with life, and fills those lives with blessing. "His tender mercies are over all His works."

See how great and wide is any one of His gifts. His sun, which He caused to rise this morning, how great a blessing it was to you as an individual! It brought you light to rejoice your heart, to guide your way, to reveal to you all His wonderful works, and to show you the face of man. It brought to you warmth, dispelling the cold, and with that light and warmth it brings newly every morning and every springtime the assurance of seedtime and harvest, unfailing through God's covenant. These blessings are manifold life and joy to you, but not more to you than to hundreds of millions more of men upon this earth, and to the beasts of the field, and to the birds of the air; and even all inanimate nature seems to rejoice in the sun. And then, there is all the rest of the solar system, rejoicing in the same periodical return of day. And our day is but a little fraction of that great blessing of light, which, pouring forth from suns countlessly more than all the stars which we see, is, as we believe, bathing all the universe and every soul in it that fears God, with blessing as full as that which morning brings to you. And yet this sunlight is only one of a multitude of mercies which make up our being here.

Night is a wide blessing to a weary world, and as the grateful shade comes over us, it is grateful, too, to think that we may suppose that all those stars, which it shows to us, are representatives of systems, the half of whose inhabitants are enjoying the "sleep" which "He giveth to His beloved." And then there is all that bounty wherewith "He openeth His hand and satisfieth the desire of every living thing." There is this free and liberal air which we breathe, and which sends such life through every fiber of the being of every one of us, and of all the living creatures which the Lórd God created and made; and there are those bountiful and sparkling waters, at which the wild asses quench their thirst, as well as man. There is all the bounty of fruits, and the beauty of flowers, and wealth of crops; and all these sentient beings, which the Creator has made to rejoice in all this bounty.

But what shall we say of that love that gave us these minds that grasp the truth and love it, and placed before them all this world of truth, in which they might revel, which they may take to themselves and convert to their own substance, and in the strength of it go on to new and yet more victorious conquest upon the field of truth? And He gave these minds their tastes, by which they recognize and enjoy beauty and harmonies, and then He has surrounded us with various and unspeakable loveliness and music. So it is now. How was it when He planted that garden Eastward in Eden?

What a thing is sin! that hath marred such beauty, that hath broken such music, that hath changed those senses of unfallen humanity to "this body of death!" Yet even now God giveth us capacity and subjects for rapture. But the passive blessing of acquaintance with truth or loveliness is not the limit of the greatness of God's love, as shown in our mental constitution. He hath shown His love to us, in that He hath given us the power of thought. And who can measure the greatness of such a gift? The power of thought! That a man, so feeble and so young, can look abroad in this world and off into God's universe, and can make all the creation not only to instruct him in knowledge, but also to afford him the material and suggestions for reasonings, by which his own mind may repeat processes like those of the great God Himself, that we may not merely see the grandeur and loveliness of natural things, but may interpret their plan and trace out the inner harmonies of them, and that, taught by them in first principles of order, harmony and law, of kindness and truth, we may go on even to reasonings on unseen things, and talk of spirits and their faculties.

So our minds may go on climbing the heavens—star beyond star—until we may, in imagination, come to the topmost pinnacle, to the star which stands out beyond all the rest and sends its twinkling on both sides into void space. But even there we do not think that the mind has done its greatest work; for it can reason of God, and of abstract right, and deem that that right is the law of God's own being; and of free generosity and nobleness and love, which is the motive of God Himself. And not only that, but man may make all these high thoughts operative again upon his own being;

and he may regulate his own acts by that law of right, and
his emotions by that benevolence, which inspire God's own
action.   And so, doing the works of God, and thinking the
thoughts of God, we may be formed in the image of God—
I was about to say—may become almost as God, as "it is
written, I said ye are gods."

Do our minds recoil from the thought, as if it might be
blasphemous?   We remember that God, the Son, "is not
ashamed to call us brethren," and that we may be "sons and
daughters of the Lord Almighty," and that is the same
thought in its greatness, though not in its dreadfulness.   Oh!
how fearful it would be to stand out independent, unsupported,
at such a fearful height of being.   If so it please the Infinite
One, that we are to stand beside His throne, let it not be except as sons, that we may lean upon that throne, and feel the
love of a Father, blessing all that strange greatness of our
being.

Verily, sublime in its greatness is that love which fills all
this great universe with crowded blessings.   But how "high
toward them that fear Him" is the love of that God who
bends from His own heaven of heavens, and touches such a
creature as man, and indues him with a power of thought
which can go forth exulting to the bounds of His own universe, and has given him a soul, eternal as the Deity Himself,
and destined to rise and stand beside His very throne, and to
be His own companion forever.   Is not that love high above
the earth as the heavens to which those thoughts ascend, yea,
high as the very heaven of heavens to which the soul itself
is to rise?

II.   The love of God is sublime in its magnanimity.

Here is a higher style of greatness.   We honor greatness of
power and affluence of bounty.   But we recognize a great
and noble heart most by its superiority to caprices, and irritations, and prejudices, and narrow ends; by the power of

maintaining an independent generosity of heart under provocations and irritations. It is noble to be first in bounty to those who may not have done kindness to us; it is magnanimous to forgive. "He that ruleth his spirit is greater than he that taketh a city." All the world would say that as the Bible says it.

God, then, displays the magnanimity of His mercy in that He is "good even to the evil and the unthankful," in that He "sendeth rain on the just and on the unjust." It is not so with men. If we do any man a favor and he does not thank us, our impulse is to do no more for him. Indeed, it were well if we were always ready to return even the favors which we do receive. Oh, what a stain to a nature is this ingratitude! Here appears the great disparity of being. Man stands, as it were, upon a little projecting shelf, beneath a measureless height, above a bottomless gulf. The height is the generosity of God. The depth is the ingratitude of fiends; and we here waver to the one and to the other, and with the one or with the other shall be our portion forever more. Our Father bends to draw us to Himself, and our passions continually strive to thrust us down. Where and what should we be if, as we turned away and insulted God, He were also to leave us? But He "is God and not man," and so He bears with us, and so His goodness follows us, morning and evening and on every side, with its gentle persuasion, if we will yet return and love Him. The Father surrounds us with His mercy; the Son came and died for us; the Spirit comes to dwell with us; and we spend the Father's bounty upon our lusts; we trample upon the blood of the Son; we close the door upon the Spirit; and yet God bears with us and fills our cup with blessings; the Son appeals to us still by His blood, and the Spirit knocks at the door. Is not that sublime magnanimity?

III. But this same love of God is also sublime in

the freeness of its bounty. We have our estimates and measures of finite things, as we exchange with one another the gifts which God has given us; and we go on adding to the price, according to the increasing value of our commodities. But soon we come to our limit; we come to goods which transcend all our valuation; we come into the presence of Him from whom, as children, we receive all our possessions, and all that with which we buy them, to our Father; and there we are, destitute before Him; and He possesses all things. We have nothing to pay, and He gives without price the priceless gift. There is the mark of the sublime bounty of God Him-self; as Omnipotence is still in its action, as Omniscience is calm in its thinking, so Infinite bounty is free in its be-stowing.

IV. Moreover, God's mercy is sublime in its ten-derness.

"Like as a father pitieth his children, so the Lord pitieth them that fear Him; for He knoweth our frame; He remem-bereth that we are dust." It is a sympathy filling the universe; not standing aloof by itself, like a finite thing, and sending blessings to us, but like an all-pervading Pres-ence, as it is, filling all our being, and pouring through it all a sense of a tender love, which, when we have felt it in ourselves, we may read in all about us, and so rejoice as we view the tenderness of that mercy which "is over all His works." In this very fact of tenderness, that love which be-fore appeared so great in extent, becomes great in character; for tenderness is the perfectness of all kindness and even of all politeness.

V. But there is another view of this great mercy of God. It is a fact full of great awe, and of critical fear.

Every approach of God to man is full of awe. And here, in His mercy, He comes nearest to us. In the intercourse of men with men, nothing stirs a deeper or a juster indignation than benefits scorned; and Jehovah our God is a jealous God. The just God, giving the law on Sinai, is terrible, but there is a solemnity also in the still voice of the Gospel. For what saith the Scripture ? "Therefore," it saith, "because ye are not come unto the mount that burned with fire, but unto Jesus the Mediator of the new covenant, and to a blood speaking better things than Abel, see that ye refuse not Him that speaketh, for if they escaped not who refused Him that spake on earth, much more shall not we escape if we turn away from Him that speaketh from heaven. Wherefore, let us have grace whereby we may serve God acceptably, with reverence and godly fear, for our God is a consuming fire."

So we should stand in awe, most of all, beneath this mercy of God, which stands high as heaven over us. And so the Psalmist says, in another place: "With Thee is forgiveness that Thou mayest be feared." And, as we look, so it is in our text: "As the heaven is high above the earth, so great is His mercy toward them that fear Him." To them that fear Him not under this sublimity of His goodness, all this heaven is no longer full of pure mercy. The wrath of God is gathering in it, as a storm gathers in a summer's day, and it will come with clouds, covering but not filling that deep heaven of love; but though the hand of wrath should rest over the wondering despisers, yet all the time the vast universe beyond those clouds will be basking serenely in the light of God's love; and only they who dwell under and look up into the infinite openness of that heaven of love, can really see the awful greatness of the Infinite God, and not they who shrink in terror under these clouds of wrath which rest so close upon the earth. Therefore it is for them, to whom this awful greatness of God is revealed, to know His terrors, and knowing them, to persuade men. For "according to Thy fear," according to the awe which His greatness inspires, "so is Thy wrath." So we must measure the greatness of God's

Being by the greatness of His love, and then imagine all that great Being revealing Himself in wrath to the uttermost. What shall that mean? We should "perish from the way, when His wrath is kindled but a little." Do we shudder at this perdition? We choose it if we reject God's love; God cannot save us in our sins. He sends His son to save us from our sins.

There is the great example of God's love, in the light of which all the rest are lost like stars at sunrise.

"God commendeth His love toward us, in that while we were yet sinners, Christ died for us." Here is "the breadth and length and depth and height, the love which passeth knowledge." Its depth, it reaches to our low estate of sin; its height, it lifts us to the throne of God; its breadth, "far as the east is from the west," from one to the other border of space, "so far hath He removed our transgressions from us." It fills the breadth of our being, the breadth of His dominion; and then, its length—"His mercy is from everlasting to everlasting toward them that fear Him;" it goes on with them through eternity.

Such is the mercy of our God; behind and before, above and beneath, it surrounds and overwhelms us. He invites— it is a blessed invitation, the invitation of God. He entreats— it is a fearful entreaty, the entreaty of God. Standing beneath this great love of God, what answer shall we return to it? Here, Lord, are our little hearts—oh, take them and fill them with Thy love.

III.

THE PERFECT MAN.

The Perfect Man.

Ephesians iv: 13.

Till we all come in the unity of the faith, and of the knowledge of the Son of God, unto a perfect man, unto the measure of the stature of the fulness of Christ.

Man's most ambitious study is himself. He delights in the maxim that "The noblest study of mankind is man," as if he did not know that the noblest and the truest study of mankind is God. Ever since the Tempter said, "Ye shall be as gods," man has made himself the competitor of God for the central throne in all his thoughts; and so he sends his thoughts roaming over the earth and among the stars, and they come back and report that they have found nothing so noble as the living soul from which they sprung, and so they chant together, "O, man, man, how excellent is thy name in all the earth!" But the wisdom that is from above, seeing man's feebleness thus exalted, cries out, "O Lord, our Lord, how excellent is Thy name in all the earth! Out of the mouth of babes and sucklings hast Thou ordained strength."

Proud man, retiring thus into the study of his own royalty, has rejoiced in fashioning unto himself ideas of manhood, searching, like Diogenes, through all his own dark and crooked thoughts, as well as through all outward life, that he may find a man; and in general, the more he has sought, the more those lineaments of justice, and truth, and generosity, which he had looked for, have faded away and left a falsehood and a mockery. But still, after the various heroes which man has set up have proved to be mere "kings of shreds and patches," the mind clings to its persuasion that the idea of the hero soul is not a fiction—that it is possible for a man, out of the independent nobleness of his own soul, to live a life truly just and generous, truly great and good. It is a mistake. There is no such hero, in fact or in possibility; man cannot have an independent greatness, and the hero is a mere fiction, if we consider him as one out of whose own greatness of soul great results spring forth. There lurks at the core of all our human conceptions of manhood that worm, self, which by seizing to itself the vitality which God had given, blights the fruit bearing of the soul. It is at the heart of our hero, as well as of the miser; and so the searching examination for real wealth of soul finds in the treasury of the one, as of the other, nothing but withered leaves; and so we find that in this world nothing is great of or for itself, but all is part of a whole, and is great chiefly in some greatness of ministry as part of the whole. So it is with the smallest thing that is; for the grain of sand is a distinct and perfect creature of God, doing His will in its own office, and thus it is the peer of the planet. So it is with the greatest of creatures; for Gabriel rejoices to be a messenger of God to the humblest heir of salvation.

We cannot find the real, living nobleness of man by any introversion, or by dissection of his nature. You may dissect an eye, and you will wonder at the curious and fanciful mechanism of it, and you may fill a volume with plates and letter-press describing the phenomenon, and when your work has set forth the whole, even to the utmost minuteness of chemical analysis, have you told what the eye is? Has all your science defined that little word? You have described a most curious and fantastical arrangement, and left, after all, the impression of some Chinese toy, without any meaning, and remarkable, at first, only for the idle painstaking of him who made it, and now remarkable, again, for the idle industry with which you have retraced his work. After all your description, what is an eye? What does it mean? The eye is made to see light, and all the rest has a meaning only as it stands in relation to that purpose.

So, when we ask, "What is a man?" we must know first what is the end and purpose, that is, the meaning of his being. The answer to this inquiry, an answer which arose in the thought even of ancient philosophers, must be that man, in the true intent of his being, is a lover of God—that as the eye was placed in the body that it might receive the light, so in this lower world was placed man, in order that the love of the Father might be discerned by an intelligent soul which could return love for love. Man is the organ in this world for recognizing the love of God, and he is the psalmist, to express in articulate thought and word the praise of God, and he is the living soul to learn the love of God, and to receive it as the light and the law of his own life.

A true view of man, then, must consider him in his adaptation to the end of his being—as a lover of God. We are to study him, not as standing apart, an independent being, but as a being on every side defined by God. In God he lives and moves and has his being, and therefore his being is defined when we have told his relations to God, and his being is noble and true, or false and ignoble, accordingly as he is or is not in true union with God.

Our subject, then, is "The complete man," the law, the nurture, the exercise, and the end of his being.

The law we have from the lips of Him who made man:

"Thou shalt love the Lord thy God, with all thy heart, and with all thy soul, and with all thy mind, and with all thy strength, and thy neighbor as thyself."

The complete man is a thoroughly pious man. He loves God with all his heart.

The sources of the character are in those deep emotions and affections of the soul which human laws do not even try to reach; in those secret springs of action which are, like the fountain head of a river, hidden in inaccessible recesses of mountains; or shall we rather say, like those "waters above the firmament," those vapors dissolved in air, which float in God's light, mingling undistinguishably with that serenity, until God's law shall bid them gather into clouds to make the morning and evening glorious, or to descend in raindrops, millions upon millions of witnesses to every man that God is good. Even thus it is with the pious heart. Its emotion, before it is formed into volition or begets thought or action, is a love to God, rising silent and unseen, and mingling and losing itself in God's love to it, which called it forth, as the vapor of noonday fills all the air and sky in particles lost in the warm brightness of the sunlight; and again, when occasion calls, in this peaceful sea of love gather emotions of love, which answer the particular expression of God's love, as the moisture of the sky gathers itself into clouds, that they may shine in the benignity of the sunset; and still again, when the time calls for good deeds, they, too, come forth from the treasures of the heart's love, like the rain and dew from heaven, and they make the love of God to shine among men, as the raindrops form the sunbeams into the bow of promise.

Here, then, in this undivided love of the heart for God, is the spring of the character of the man of God, and from it flows a character diverse in all its principles from that of the hero of this world. For his self-sufficiency it has poverty of spirit, because it has nothing and is in the presence of God who possesseth all things; for his complacency, it has mourning for sin; for his vaunting, it has meekness; for his self-satisfaction it has hungering and thirsting after righteousness; for his arrogance it has mercy, remembering that it needs mercy; in its purity of heart it sees God; and, loving peace, it is called the child of God.

All the heart! Not in some ranges of affection and emotion but in all, the perfect man loves God. He does not repress any pure and true emotion of his nature; for if he did, he would not be loving with all the heart; but the emotional nature is cultivated and developed in a genial and kind sympathy with the joys and the sorrows, the enthusiasms and the repentings of humanity. He is to be a whole-hearted man among men; a man that knows how to be heartily glad, though his laughter is never "the laughter of the fool;" a man who can come and sit by you in your affliction and you shall feel that his sympathy is no set form of words, and yet sorrowing not as they that have no hope, for his sorrow is "after a godly sort," and he "rejoiceth in the Lord always." He shuns not those domestic affections which bless the life of this world, for he feels the love of God in them all. For they all work together to train the soul to the love of God: it was even a Divine voice which said, "Whosoever shall do the will of my father which is in heaven, the same is my brother and sister and mother."

So that the man of God may be perfect in heart, let him be full of love—loving not only the abstract idea of God whom he hath not seen, but all the children and the works of God. Let his whole heart be in free and healthful exercise and play. Thus let him become even as a little child, with all his emotions springing to praise the Father. So shall he show forth the character of the Lord's free man.

The heart which has communed with the heart of Christ turns to other human hearts with a love which it has learned of Him who died for us. The disciple whom Jesus loved saith, "He that loveth not his brother whom he hath seen, how can he love God whom he hath not seen ?"

No! The man of God is not narrowed in the range or in the greatness of his pure human sympathy. For as all the love which flows into his heart from all earthly friends is but a flowing, in many streams, of that great love of God which is ever pressing to find an entrance into his soul, so all his love, if it be the pure love of a true heart, toward whatsoever object it may immediately go forth, is still a part of his own love which goes back, seeking God again through these same channels by which the love of God flows first unto us. "I will run," saith the Psalmist, "I will run in the way of thy commandments, when thou shalt enlarge my heart." So let the man of God learn largeness of heart by all those teachings of which God has made up the intercourse of life, that the experience of every hour may bring his heart more into the likeness of God, who doeth good to all, whose tender mercies are over all His works. Such an heart was that of Moses, "the man of God." But such beyond all human comparison was the Prophet of our brethren like unto Moses, that Divine heart, whose great and pure love so sought out and embraced humanity that He is called "the Son of Man." So great-hearted and so true-hearted should be he that loves God with all his heart, "that the man of God may be perfect."

Again, the perfect man must love God "with all his soul."

He must be an earnest man. His love is not merely to be a general state of complacence, floating in emotions or settling in reveries, but it must form itself into acts of soul, into purposes and principles and strivings. The heart, in its own secret piety sits with God, "to hear what God the Lord will speak," and "He will speak peace unto his people," and that sitting before God with all the soul rapt in His blessed words of peace is the attitude of the heart in the exercise of pious emotion. But out of that heart flow all issues of life. The heart that loves God perfectly, is kept in perfect peace, it hath entered into God's rest, but that rest is not a motionless quiescence, for God is not quiescent and he that loveth is born of God, and the Father worketh hitherto, and so must the soul, whose life is hid in God, be ever working the works of God. Its peace and rest is nothing other than a perpetual spontaneous flow and gush of most blessed activity. God saith, "Seek ye My face" and the heart saith unto him "Thy face, O Lord, will I seek." "Lo I come! in the volume of the book it is written of Me, I delight to do Thy will, O My God"—"yea, Thy law is within my heart." There is the secret spring of the activity of "the man of God." God's law is within the heart and so that same law which governs the great and manifold activity of God, is perpetually developing various and earnest activites of soul. Therefore, this loving God with all the soul implies, not merely that the man of God be free from purposes opposed to the will of God, but that all his soul be alive with purposes, volitions, and acts, all joyfully and harmoniously working out the will of God. Like some great manufactory, in which are a thousand men each intent upon his several department, but all working together to produce the perfect fabric in which no part shall be lacking, so all the manifold emotions of the heart are working out manifold desires and purposes and acts of good will, each in its own particular direction and with its own immediate object, but all working together to make up that perfect sum of good willings, which is, for that soul, its perfect loving of God, and which answers in its lower sphere to that perfect love of God for the soul which so directs all things that they work together for good to them that love God.

So at once by the purity and by the fulness and earnestness of the vitality of the soul, let him that nameth the name of Christ learn to love God with all the soul, that in the acts of the soul the man of God may be perfect.

Moreover, the complete man must love God with all his mind. God has given him an intellect, and it is his duty to be a sound and Christian scholar and thinker.

Some men, perverting the meaning of those words, "I

determined to know nothing among you save Jesus Christ and Him crucified," have despised the exercise of the intellect. Not so does the Word of God, for Paul in that same passage says, "Howbeit we speak wisdom among them that are perfect." And the Hebrews are exhorted to leave the principles of the doctrine of Christ, and to go on unto perfection, searching into the "deep things of God," as the only exercise by which a Christian mind can preserve its health, and so prominent among the "things that accompany salvation." Not such is the testimony of the works of God. For God has made all this world full of hidden wisdom, crowding all the objects of all His universe with testimonies of His power, of His wisdom and of His love, and then putting us among them with these minds, which recognize His challenge and spring to the search into these hidden mines of truth, and from this search the mind grows keen and strong and ardent, and able to discern good and evil, and all these works of God, rightly studied, lead the mind to God; yes, and may we say, into God. In all its searching the mind walks in the midst of God's wisdom, power and love. The mind feels, in its best activity, that it is working, not with and in dumb materials, but in the midst of eternal thoughts; that itself is continually in the midst of an infinite mind, whose thought is everlastingly active all round about it and throughout it—which is the atmosphere in which the mind lives and thinks. So it is ever joyfully thinking with God the thoughts of God. Shall the life which is hid with Christ in God lie passive and listless in the bosom of that infinite and ever active Intelligence? Shall it not rather apply itself to all the wisdom by which God summons it to action, and thus love God with all the mind, and thus be "renewed in knowledge after the image of the Creator." For God smiles upon man's search for wisdom, giving to all liberally and upbraiding not, giving even His own spirit to lead our minds "into all truth." Let the man of God, then, diligently apply the faculties of a mind, purified and enlightened by the spirit of God, to the study of the truth of God, and to thinking the thoughts of God, that his constantly expanding mind may be continually coming more and more to know God and Jesus Christ whom He hath sent, whom to know is life everlasting. So shall he love God with all the mind, that in mind also the man of God may be perfect.

Still, again, the man of God should "love God with all his strength." It is his duty to the extent of his ability to be a strong man, strong not with the vain strength of man that would be a hero, but "strong in the Lord and in the power of His might."

This is a strength which flows directly, like the right will and the clear, sound mind, out of the pure fountain of a pious heart. For the true heart has as its ally the everlasting strength of the Lord Jehovah. And the very natural effect of sincere piety is to bring strength out of weakness—the strength of an honest man, the strength of an earnest man, the strength of a man who believes that there is a God and that God "is with the truth." With all that strength is the man clothed who has learned to put off all the craft of human sophistry and vain wisdom, and simply as a child to seek the pure truth of God, and honestly and artlessly to tell it and to do it. So out of the mouth of babes doth God ordain strength. The philosopher and the scribe are amazed at the strong truthfulness of the child, the monarch quails before the martyr, the Roman centurion goes from the crucifixion exclaiming, "certainly this was a Son of God."

So strong is every simply true man. And if round about this strength of inner truth he has put on the whole "armor of light" is he not strong? It is the duty of the man of God to be strong in the faithful development and exercise of every faculty of body, mind and soul, strong in every connection which man may form with the strength of God; so by his strength shall he glorify God, "Who ordaineth strength in babes because of his enemies, that He may still the enemy and the avenger." Let the love of God shine forth, then, in the strength of the man of God, that the man of God may be perfect.

In our text we have the means by which man is to attain this perfectness, "till we all come in the unity of the faith and of the knowledge of the Son of God unto a perfect man," the one faith and knowledge of God. We are to come fully and trustingly to God in Christ as the way, the truth and the life, and so, committing our whole souls unto Him, continually to learn of Him, mingling our souls with the Son of God, and in proportion as we see Him we shall be like Him—learn to be Sons of God. And those emotions and desires which filled the heart of Christ shall fill our hearts, and out of that love shall spring, even as the life blood leaps from the heart to carry health through the system, such works of God as He came from heaven to do. So directly out of that first and great commandment shall flow the second, which is like unto it, "Thou shalt love thy neighbor as thyself." For into that same heart of Christ flow all the hearts that love Him, and then in that heart they are united in one, all their individual desires and ambitions and affections coming into membership of that great love of Christ, which desires the true good of all that love Him and of all whom He loves. Thus in that one heart, in proportion as we know Him and love Him, we are all united in one, and we love Him, who is the whole, with all our love, and we love each other as ourselves. And behold now, and not till now, do we come to the true meaning of that "perfect man." It is not the maturity of any individual man, but rather that perfect whole of humanity, which is to make up the body of Christ, of which we all are members. No one human soul will in any period of eternity be that perfect man, but all together, in the unity of the faith and of the knowledge of the love of God, are to come unto that perfect man, unto the measure of the stature of the fulness of Christ. That glorious whole—that "new man"—is the proper object of these aspirations of our nature. When He shall appear may we be "found in Him."

IV.

JOHN, THE LOVED DISCIPLE.

JOHN, THE LOVED DISCIPLE.

John xiii: 23.

Now there was leaning on Jesus' bosom one of His disciples, whom Jesus loved.

"The disciple whom Jesus loved." This is an expression upon which the religious emotion of the church has dwelt so long and so delightfully that it seems almost like sacrilege to suggest a doubt as to the correctness of the import which pious hearts have been accustomed to assign to the words. Still, I do not know but that justice to the Evangelist may require a re-examination of his meaning; and perhaps, if the result of such a consideration should be a modification of our common impression, we may find his real meaning not only more just to himself, but not less delightful to Christian contemplation.

We have been won to understand John as customarily designating himself as the favorite of his Master. We can well believe that one whose heart was so full of love as his, would occupy even such a place as that in the heart of the Lamb of God. But can we quite suppose that such a heart, in the maturity of its grace, would indulge any desire to give public prominence to such a distinction over his brother apostles, who had already, when this gospel was written, one after another, laid down their lives for the cause of their common Lord? Is such an understanding in accordance with the evident modesty of intention, with which this form of speech seems to have been chosen? Would not the better view be something like this? The living fountain of

John's piety was always the thought of a Divine love which had "first sought" him. "Herein," he says, "is love, not that we loved God, but that He loved us." During the few years when he was with Jesus, his life was in his Master's love, and during his long subsequent life, the remembrance of these privileges became more and more precious to him. At length, in his age, he sat down to write the story of his Master's life. With true modesty he does not often introduce himself as an actor. Not once does he tell his own name; but when the course of the history brings before him that young man, that he was sixty years before, enjoying day by day the unmerited love of the Son of God, he could not avoid designating that young disciple by the circumstance which was more present to his own mind when he thought of him, than was the name men called him by, namely, the fact that "Jesus loved" him, not more than He loved any other, but that His love should have rested, at all, upon such an one.

The whole Christian character of the Apostle John is formed about this idea that Christ had "first loved" him, so that this history is the example given us in the word of God, to illustrate the influence of the sense of Christ's love in forming the Christian.

This Apostle shared with his brother James, who was to be the first martyr from their band, and Simon Peter, who illustrates an entirely different style of personal and Christian character, the most intimate association with their Lord.

John was, by nature, a man whose emotions, impulses and associations were personal and social, rather than general, political or abstract. In this he differed widely from Peter and Paul. He was not naturally a mild man, nor an ill-natured man, but all his personal feelings, of whatever character, were very strong. This view, I think, we shall find sustained by his history, and be able to trace, in some degree, the progress and character of the sanctification of such a heart.

We find him first, with his brother James, upon the shore of the Sea of Galilee, in a small fishing vessel, with Zebedee, their father, and hired servants, mending nets. Jesus passed along the shore, with Simon and Andrew, whom He had just called. He invited them to follow Him, and immediately they left father and business, and followed Him. He gave to them the name of Boanerges, "Sons of Thunder," in allusion, probably, to that natural violence of character which we shall find occasionally manifested in their history.

After their calling, they were the constant companions of Jesus, often admitted to scenes at which other apostles were not present; but the principal representations of character occur after the commencement of the last journey from Cæsarea Philippi to Jerusalem. On their way, they saw the scene of the Transfiguration; then they came to Capernaum. Here occurred an incident, which illustrates the electric nature of the "son of thunder," both by his aptness for personal attachment, and his proneness to personal collisions, as well as the Savior's manner of instructing him. He came and said to his Master, "We found one casting out devils in Thy name, and we forbade him, because he followed not with us." And Jesus said unto him, "Forbid him not; he that is not against us is for us." By and by "the time drew near that He should be received up, and He steadfastly set His face to go to Jerusalem." On this account He was refused entertainment at a Samaritan village. This incivility to their Master exasperated the Sons of Thunder, and they said, "Lord, wilt thou that we command fire to come down from heaven and consume them, even as Elias did?" But "He turned and rebuked them and said, ye know not what manner of spirit ye are of, for the Son of Man is not come to destroy men's lives, but to save them; and they went on to another village.''

These incidents seem so inconsistent with our common idea of the loved disciple, that we do not readily recognize him in this violent young man. Yet it is he, and in his action are displayed the same traits of character which were afterward ripened into that heavenly spirit. For the foundation of his ardor was not a violent or malignant disposition, but an enthusiastic attachment to his Master. It was love, already his engrossing emotion, but as yet unenlightened in its views and narrow in its scope. And see how Jesus answered him. He is speaking to one who had been led, by his attachment to one being, into animosity toward another. And so He opened His own heart, and behold there, instead of such a passion, is a love which could embrace even the object of that animosity. Thus He summoned His disciple to a magnanimity of love, which was the next lesson which he was to learn.

During the last journey of Jesus through the country east of Jordan, occurred an incident which seems to reveal another failing in the apostle. The sons of Zebedee and their mother, Salome, present a request that they might enjoy the seats at His right and left hand in His kingdom. Are we to infer from this a selfish ambition as forming a part of John's nature? Probably not. The movement would seem to have originated with Salome, and so is to be regarded as indicating the affection of the mother rather than the selfishness of the son. Such personal ambition is not like John. His temper was always to be the true and ready supporter rather than the leader, whether we find him associated with Jesus or with Simon Peter. It is easier to suppose that his own kind nature yielded to the entreaties of his parent than that he for himself coveted the dignity. On the other hand, such a desire on the part of Salome is in perfect accordance with that affectionate nature which she always displayed. She was one of the women who, when Jesus was in Galilee, followed Him and ministered unto Him, and who came with Him unto Jerusalem. When He was upon the cross, she, with Mary Magdalene and Mary the mother of James the Less, stood looking in sorrow upon the scene, and when the Sabbath was past, the same three "had bought sweet spices that they might come and anoint him, and very early in the morning they came to the sepulchre." Thus we see that this apostle's kindness of heart was not altogether original with him, but that he was one of those favored men who have been permitted to inherit the disposition and to enjoy the influence of a pious mother.

From such notices as these we derive our knowledge of the natural character of John and observe Christ's method in his education. He was now approaching what were the most important hours in his own life, as well as in the history of the world. Peter and John had from the first been among the disciples objects of Christ's most particular care. In many of the most important scenes of Christ's life, either alone or with James, they had attended Jesus, as at the Transfiguration, and at the reviving of the daughter of Jairus, and afterward at Gethsemane. They were to be examples of two different phases of the Christian character, the one of pious emotion, the other of devoted action. Thus far they had been, like the other apostles, but partially enlightened, and were very immature in spiritual Christianity. A new scene of discipline was yet to be passed by each of them, adapted to his peculiar cast of mind. The ardent, independent, self-confident spirit was to pass through a storm of temptation which should sweep away all his false reliance, everything merely human in his strength; after vaunting his own fortitude he was to tell a lie and to deny his Master at the interrogatory of a maid servant; he was to repeat that treacherous lie and to accompany it by an oath; and then to meet that "look" of the Lord. From that time Simon Peter was an humble Christian.

The scene through which John passed was of a very different character. He had that personal dependence upon the Lord which prepared him to receive at once the impress of His mind and heart. His character needed ripening rather than purging. Accordingly what does the Lord Jesus? When that last supper came, John is called to the place next his Master, to recline upon His bosom. That hour in the bosom of his Lord, was the era in the life of that young man. It was an hour of wonderful interest to all the company; for in it they listened to truths which that night were new upon the earth. But how the soul of that youngest apostle was drinking in the love of Jesus! The minute circumstances of the night were impressed forever on his mind, so that when, sixty years afterward, he sat down to write his Gospel, the whole scene—every look, word and gesture returned to his view. There he was again, reclining—a young man loved of Jesus. Jesus rises and washes their feet and says, "Ye are clean, but not all." He resumes His robe and His place beside the disciple, explaining the lesson of the washing, and the disciple felt the heaving of the bosom upon which he leaned as He uttered the words, "One of you shall betray me." Then came the doubting glances of the disciples and the gesture of Peter, by which he himself, lying upon Jesus' breast, was encouraged to whisper the secret question, "Lord, who is it?" and the private answer by giving the sop to Iscariot. Then the departure of the traitor leaves the way open, especially the mind of that disciple prepared for the conversation which follows;—Christ's anticipation of His glory; His injunction to the disciples to love one another—"as I have loved you." How that injunction sank in the heart which was next His own! Then came Peter's vain profession of fidelity, and the revelation of the heavenly mansions, and the questioning of Thomas and of Philip, bringing out the words, " He that hath seen Me hath seen the Father;" then that blessed promise of the Comforter and the leaving of peace with them. Here they rose from the table, but the heart of the disciple had already been bound to his Master by new tendrils, and we cannot suppose that he was far from His side as He proceeded to tell of the " true vine," which is Himself and His Father the husbandman, and "they the branches." Perhaps that illustration conveyed an indistinct idea to Peter; but the disciple, who had that evening felt the pulsations of the heart of Christ, understood what it was to abide in Him, and with a still rapture of first love, he was beginning to feel how blessed it was. Himself abiding in Christ, Christ's words abode in him. The very thoughts and words next uttered were those with which he long after began His own Epistle. Says Christ, " As the Father hath loved Me, so have I loved you; continue ye in My love; these things have I spoken unto you that My joy might remain in you and that your joy might be full." John writes, "Our fellowship is with the Father and with His Son Jesus Christ. And these things write we unto you that your joy may be full." How full was the joy of that disciple in that moment at the thought that Jesus and the Father loved even him, and in Their love he might " abide as a branch in the vine."

Jesus goes on to speak of His love to them and theirs to one another, and as He speaks all uncharitableness melts from the heart of the listener, and his soul comes out into the free and perfect light of Christian love, so that in his epistle he follows the words just quoted with these: " If we walk in the light, as He is in the light, we have fellowship one with another."

The Master, henceforth calling them friends, went on to tell them that He must go, but that He would send them the Comforter. At this stage of the conversation, the remembrance of the apostle recalls vividly the perplexity and awe of the disciples as they whispered to one another, "What is this that He saith—a little while?" a question which He half answers and half defers.

Then, after bidding them henceforward to pray in His name, and assuring them of His victory over the world, He "lifted up his eyes to heaven," and closed the interview, which was becoming too solemn for human conversation, with that prayer for them, which closed His ministry for that life to them as a body.

They went over the Kedron to the garden. He took Peter and James and John and went on with them; then He left them and went on alone, and passed the agony unsupported, except by that favored angel from heaven. In the meantime, the three disciples, overcome by such joys and such sorrows as no man on earth had ever experienced, slept. When they woke, Jesus was by them and the band of the traitor was just at hand. After a brief tumult they "all forsook Him and fled." Probably most of them did not see Him again, except by stealth, looking through the gloom of the night to where the glare of the torches fell upon the meek countenance, or peeping from some hiding place along the Via Dolorosa, or in view of Calvary, until His resurrection. Peter, however, followed afar off, and John went in with Jesus into the palace of the High Priest. Here we have a beautiful instance of that unconscious courage which love creates. John had probably no martial boldness in his nature which would nerve him for dangers, before which even ordinary men would quail. But he loved Jesus; his heart had grown to the heart of Jesus, and he felt irresistibly drawn to His side. His soul was so full of love that there was no room for the thought of danger. He tells the story without any apparent consciousness that any special nerving of spirit was required for it. In his case it would seem that there was no such summoning of courage. Such cases are not at all unknown, in which an impulse of affection has led spirits of a delicate and even timid cast through scenes which manly courage dared not meet. It is beautiful, as showing how God made love to be the commanding principle of the human heart, and how the gentlest things in the world are the strongest.

Here, then, was John, the only one of that crowd who was Christ's open friend, and there, too, the mingling of his heart with his Lord's was going on. It was good for him to be even there. The same spirit which brought him to that midnight council of the murderers of the Prince of Life, must have kept him near the Savior during all the successive hours of that important morning; and we may suppose that, even among those scenes, an occasional look of gratitude or kindness from the Savior swelled his heart to a new capacity of ecstatic love.

We come to the cross, and there, too, stands the "disciple whom He loved" with those women, whose position is another evidence of the superior strength of simple quiet affection over even ardent attachment, which has been accustomed to rely upon natural fortitude. Here, with almost the last words of the Lord, was finished the lesson of Christian love which the disciple was that day to learn. "He saith unto His mother, behold thy son. Then saith He to the disciple, behold thy mother." After that He said, "I thirst." They gave Him vinegar, He received it and said, "It is finished!" and He bowed His head and gave up the ghost.

The "disciple whom Jesus loved," went away leading the mother of Jesus, a different man from the John who went with Peter, twenty-four hours before, to prepare the guest chamber for the Passover. John was now the first mature Christian on this earth, the first fruit in that kingdom of heaven in which the least is greater than John the Baptist.

We have now considered the natural character of this apostle, and the manner of the operation of grace in his case. It remains to see, in part, the soul that was thus formed.

The Sabbath passed, and with the dawn of the following day came Mary Magdalene to the sepulchre. It was empty! She "ran and came to Simon Peter and to the other disciple whom Jesus loved." What interviews those two brethren had had since the crucifixion! Simon Peter needed such a helper then,—one who had learned Christ's love so that he would not break the bruised reed.

They "ran to the sepulchre." John reached it first, but as affection is rather swift to run than prompt to decide, he went not in, until his more independent companion set the example,—then he went in, "and he saw and believed, for as yet they knew not the scripture, that He must rise again from the dead." He had not known clearly what Christ's glory was, but this he knew, that he loved Him.

We cannot dwell here upon the remaining incidents in John's life recorded in the Gospels and in the Acts. Until they disappear from the inspired narrative, Peter and John remain much together; a noble union of diverse Christian graces, a training of each for the work they had to do.

After these scenes, this disciple lived until he saw two generations more of men gathered to their fathers. There was a suitableness in such an ordering of events; for his was the style of piety adapted to be ripened in this world. If you would see what his piety became, read his artless Epistles and study the spirit of his Gospel. You will find there the traces of this last conversation of the Lord, not only in the love which filled his heart, but even in the thoughts which fill his mind. That night and day determined the course of his emotion and of his thinking for all his long life. He always thought of himself as a "disciple whom Jesus loved, which also leaned upon His breast at supper." That hour, that hour in the bosom of his Lord, it was the recollection of his past life; and well it might be. For was not that the most blessed position which has been occupied by mortal man since the world began? It was good that God should leave him, who had known such an experience, in His church on earth for the longest life of man.

Through that life, he looked back to that night and forward to the day without a night when he should meet his Lord again. "Beloved," saith he, "now are we the sons of God, and it doth not yet appear what we shall be, but we know that when He shall appear we shall be like Him, for we shall see Him as He is." And now he is with Him, in those mansions of His Father's house. They drink the fruit of the vine, "new in the kingdom of His Father" and the disciple whom Jesus loved is forever leaning upon Jesus' bosom.

V.

PETER, THE SMITTEN ROCK.

PETER, THE SMITTEN ROCK.

And the Lord turned and looked upon Peter.

On that look turned the history of a soul, and, in no small degree, the history of a world. A veil seems to be drawn back and light from two other worlds is let in, so that we see not merely a poor Galilean cringing by the fire in the court of the High Priest, but we see a Prince of Darkness and a Prince of Light, in contest for the possession of a human soul.

That same night, the Lord had said to Peter, "Simon, Simon, Satan hath desired to have you that he may sift you (the disciples) as wheat, but I have prayed for thee, that thy faith fail not, and when thou art converted strengthen thy brethren." It seems to be part of the record of a scene which passed behind the curtain that shuts in this visible world, like the opening of the book of Job. More literally translated it reads thus: "Simon, Simon, Satan asked (and gained) you (the disciples) to sift you like wheat; but I prayed respecting thee that thy faith may not fail." That is the ordeal which is now going on. The adversary is sifting the souls of them that are with the Son of Man in His temptations. Judas is lost, the rest have "forsaken Him and fled," except the disciple whom Jesus loved and whom He had cherished in His bosom at the Supper, perhaps that He might have one friend constant in the fearful trial, and this Peter, whom the tempter has marked for his victim. For he knows men or thinks that he knows them.

Peter was a hero, as the world goes. He could fight in the garden against any odds—against the Jewish hierarchy and the Roman Empire. But here he was in the strange court of the High Priest's palace, weak from much excitement and little rest, chilled with cold and with fear, helpless, hopeless, with nothing to lean upon, and nothing to brace against, a man, mighty to do, but who had never learned to suffer. Spiritual capacities, which were made to shake the world, are disordered for the time, and show their power only by the agitation, with which they shake the soul which they tenant. It is the adversary, "sifting wheat" for the Lord's garner. Peter comes in at the door, and the maid that kept it said "he was one of them." He sits by the fire, and as its glare falls upon his face, those that sit by recognize him as having been "in the garden." He tries to hide in the shadow of the porch, but the challenge pursues him. For more than an hour it drives him hither and thither, breaking down his pride, crushing his heart, until what was there left of the strong disciple, who last night "was ready to go with Jesus to prison and to death?" What of the "rock," upon which the church was to be built? Nothing but this bruised reed. At last, as the poor crazed soul is denying, in an agony of cursing and swearing, "the cock crew, and the Lord turned and looked upon Peter."

If we could see that look! What was in it?

There was majesty in it. Through the rest of this story Christ is called Jesus, but here it is said, "the Lord turned and looked upon Peter." As he met that look, captain and chief priest and High Priest sank, and there was but one "Lord" there.

There was Omniscience in that eye. Peter thought how the Lord said, "before the cock crow thou shalt deny Me," and so he learned to say, "Lord, thou knowest all things."

There was power in that look. As he met it, the jarring elements of his soul felt the potency of that word which spoke the world out of chaos. They came together, not as they had been before, but as the new heavens and the new earth shall rise, for the dwelling of righteousness.

There was tenderness in that look, the double tenderness of grief and of pity; grief, at the sight of which Peter is as a bruised reed, ready to be crushed at the first token of reproach; but he does not see that reproach, but the tenderness of a God-like pity, that would not "break the bruised reed nor quench the smoking flax, till he send forth judgment unto victory." In the very tenderness of that compassion lay, that morning, and always lies, the victory of the "Son of Man."

There was forgiveness, and courage, and hope in it. For Peter can remember that saying of the Lord, "I have prayed for thee, that thy faith fail not," and his faith receives strength to lay hold of the promise; he feels the everlasting arms taking up his helpless soul, and he feels himself henceforth, as he says in his epistle, "kept by the power of God, through faith, unto salvation."

Of the effect of this look, we have first, CONTRITION: He "went out and wept bitterly."

The Rock was smitten and the waters gushed forth. It was more than a transient emotion, a nervous excitement passing like an April shower. It was the opening of a deep fountain of tender life within the Man of Rock. Peter was, before, like Arabia Petræa, like "Mount Sinai in Arabia," severe, craggy, desolate. Now he is like the Temple Mount at Jerusalem, no less established for ever, but the soft-going waters of Siloah flow from it perpetually, making glad the city of God. Such, all down the history of salvation, is the manner of God's working to make the desert blossom as the rose. The hearts of stone are smitten, and the gushing tear is the token of the opening of a stream of salvation.

Out of this contrition comes, second, REPENTANCE. From that moment Simon Peter is a changed man. John was changed by the melting influence of the Savior's love, as he lay in His bosom at the supper. We do not know whether John ever felt any bitter conviction of sin. Peter was the stout heart, which needed to be broken. As he stood there without, bitterly weeping, what was there left of him or for him? Nothing now of that rocky armor in which he had trusted. But yet he felt in his soul a deeper and a firmer strength. He rests now on that prayer of the Lord. "I have prayed for thee, that thy faith fail not." And there was something in that look of the Lord, which told him that Christ's prayer still clasped him, and so he is ready to throw himself with simple faith into those everlasting arms.

And then we have the third result, THE SURRENDER OF SELF IN SIMPLE FAITH. There came a deep feeling of love for the Master, possessing all his heart, and a clear and henceforth undaunted strength, of which we shall see more and more as we follow the after-course of his life.

The narrative leaves him, outside the palace of the High Priest, "weeping bitterly." It presents him again with John on the Lord's day morning, running to the sepulchre. What a Sabbath those two brethren had passed! They were the two maturest fruits, thus far, of the kingdom of heaven among men, the melted heart of John and the broken heart of Peter.

We may suppose that they did not fail to come together from time to time during that day of terror, but it was not strange that Peter should shrink from the position at the foot of the cross, to which John was drawn. But the Sabbath must have been a day with them of the blending of new and strange communions, a day of faith, resting upon new and deep experiences of their souls, and prevailing even in the midst of the power of darkness which seemed to shroud everything around them. One of those "days known to the Lord, not day nor night, but at eventime there shall be light," (Zech. xiv: 7). But on the early morrow morning came a wonderful word; the women said that the tomb was empty. It found them together, Peter and the " other disciple." Peter does not draw back now, but seems to have been first to start and first to enter the sepulchre. During the day, the Lord appeared to him again, as it would seem by himself, and we have no record of what passed in that interview, perhaps the first time the disciple had met the eye of the Lord, since that look in the palace of the High Priest.

Next we see him on the Sea of Galilee in the gray of the morning. In a stranger on the beach, the quick sense of the loved disciple discovers the Lord, and at the word, Peter throws himself into the sea. After their breakfast Jesus searches his heart with the question, " Lovest thou me?" Three times the question, and three times the unshaken answer, rising on the third to that high confession and that bold profession, "Thou knowest all things. Thou knowest that I love thee." The heart that had been searched by that look of the Lord, had learned a lesson respecting vain confidence and of the deceitfulness of the heart. But the heart, which had been sought out by the tender compassion of the Lord even in such a fall, and had been sustained by His prayer in its fearful danger and its bitterness of remorse, did know that it loved Him, and standing even in the light of His searching eye, and with its own apostasy for the dark background, it could not say less than " Thou knowest that I love thee." But there is here none of the old self-confidence, but rather the fulfilment of the prayer that his faith fail not, and the preparation for the strengthening of the brethren. He is the Rock, but not that isolated Rock of the Desert which Christ found him. He has now become a hewn stone for the Temple of the Lord, as he himself describes it in his Epistle. He says, " As new-born babes desire the sincere milk of the word, that ye may grow thereby, if so be that ye have tasted that the Lord is gracious, to whom coming as unto a living stone, disallowed indeed of men but chosen of God and precious, ye also as lively stones are built up a spiritual house." So Christ who built the worlds, was building His church, so that the gates of hell should not prevail against it. Himself is the chief corner-stone, and the twelve foundations were to be the twelve apostles of the Lamb. All His life has been spent in preparing them, and especially in His last agony He has fitted, and now by His blood has cemented to Himself, those two, that were to be built next Himself, one on the side of fervent zeal, and the other on that of deep communion.

Thus have the scenes of that trial changed the style of the rocky texture of the disciple's character. It has been disintegrated and dissolved by that fierce temptation, and crystallized anew, under the influence of that look, after the model of the Rock of Ages.

The most marked effect of that scene, through the whole life of Peter, was the merging of himself in his Master. With such an one as John, the forming of himself into the image of Christ was a gradual process. He beheld in the "Word made flesh" the glory full of grace and truth, and "of his fulness he received and grace for grace," and Paul "beholding as in a glass the glory of the Lord, was changed into the same image from glory to glory." But not so with Peter. Up to the moment when he put his sword back in its sheath in Gethsemane, he was Simon Peter, a staunch adherent of the Lord, because he was a staunch man. His countenance stands before us fixed and rigid and self-willed. But from the time it was bathed in those tears we see that expression no more. It is not in the eager face of him that ran to the sepulchre. It is not in the earnest gaze of him who said, "Thou knowest that I love thee." It is not the tender aspect of him that looked upon the lame man at the Beautiful Gate. By what magic have those strong features caught the aspect of that Lamb of God, who "turned and looked upon Peter?" And his words are changed too. "Ye men of Israel, why look ye so earnestly upon us, as though by our own power or holiness we had made this man to walk?" Or read those addresses of Peter at Pentecost, or at the healing of the lame man, and see if the blended power of truth upon the mind, of faithful reproof upon the conscience, and of loving kindness upon the heart, is anything else than a translation into words of that look, which the Lord, when He turned, imprinted upon Peter's soul?

The subject is full of illustration and suggestion. It shows us the secret history and the relations of the temptations which befall men.

Here was a soul fearfully entangled in the snare of the adversary. But it was only by the permission of the Father, and the temptation itself was the means of bringing about the purification, though so as by fire, of a soul which needed an ordeal. It was a great part of the struggle and of the triumph of the Son of Man over the prince of this world. The same strife with the rulers of the darkness of this world, with spiritual wickedness in high places, goes on to-day. Satan sifts the chosen ones of Christ, and the Savior prays for them, not for his apostles only, but for them that should believe on Him through their word. Simon Peter is our example. "And when thou art converted," Jesus said to him, "strengthen the brethren." So in his Epistle he calls upon them that are under temptations to rejoice, "that the trial of your faith, being much more precious than of gold that perisheth, though tried by fire, might be found unto praise and honor and glory at the appearing of Jesus Christ." A great temptation is an opportunity for a great purifying of the soul and a great glorifying of God. But sometimes we do not consider what the great temptations are. Peter had braced himself against them. If the High Priest had called him into the presence of the council, perhaps he would have stood firm and gone with Jesus to prison and to death. But when he was talking with those girls and servants by the fire and the door, he was off his guard. How many a man, who would go to the stake, denies the Lord that bought him, by his little follies. Look up! The eye of Jesus is upon you!

See again Christ's method of dealing with a soul—so faithfully, so tenderly. If he sees that Satan has a snare for the soul, He says so. He has none of that civility which will stand out of the way and let a soul go down to death. But how does He save it? First, He prays for it, and then he warns it, and then he watches it, and in the critical moment he meets it with truth, with reproof, with love, slaying the old, creating the new, and in place of the vain and fatal pride and passion and ambition of man's heart, forming there a soul "kept by the power of God through faith."

Thus we get some idea of what is meant by the new man, and by the forming of Christ within us. John, the sweet spirit, after that blessed hour in the bosom of the Lord, loved to translate his name—"Johanan," "Jehovah's Grace"—into the dear form "Jesus loved." It was still the same combination of thought, but full of the sweetness of the old commandment made new in Christ. So Peter, the strong spirit, after that night at the High Priest's palace, was still the rock, but not left to stand in the midst of the new world, like Petra, the old Rock City of the desert, wonderful but desolate. He is a precious living stone in the New Jerusalem. He is no more a rough crag of old Sinai, but, like Mount Athos hewn to the likeness of a king, he stands as part of the mountain of the Lord's house, presenting, even in his rocky brow, the loving aspect of the Savior of men.

What Jesus did for Peter and for John, He is ready to do, and, so far as His work is concerned, is hourly doing for you and for every soul that will receive Him. He calls us to His bosom, or He casts us into manifold temptations, according as, by one or by the other, He may form us to His image and fit us for His work and for His blessedness.

So let us, as we close this study, lay to heart those words with which Peter closes his last Epistle: "Ye therefore, beloved, seeing ye know these things before, beware lest ye also, being led away with the error of the wicked, fall from your own steadfastness. But grow in grace and in the knowledge of our Lord and Savior Jesus Christ. To Him be glory both now and forever. Amen."

VI.

BARNABAS, THE SON OF CONSOLATION.

BARNABAS, THE SON OF CONSOLATION.

Acts iv: 36.

Joses, who by the apostles was surnamed Barnabas (which is, being interpreted, the Son of Consolation).

Let me introduce to you an old acquaintance, whom I hope that you will love to know hereafter as a friend and helper.

Among the men chosen of God to preach His new Gospel, was one of such marked qualities that the apostles gave him a new name, which fitted him so well that it entirely took the place of his former name. The Hebrew name, Barnabas, would signify Son of the Inspired Word, using the same term which in the book of Chronicles described the word of Azariah, the son of Oded, to King Asa, " The Lord is with you while ye be with Him; be strong, therefore, and let not your hands be weak; for your work shall be rewarded;" and which is used again for the exhortation by which Haggai, the Prophet, and Zechariah, the son of Berechiah, inspirited the builders of the second temple. The Greek term signifies, "Son of exhortation," or " of cheering on." We may say that the Hebrew means the son of the inspired word, and the Greek means the son of the inspiriting word, and that both were in the idea of the character of him whom the apostles called the Son of Inspiration. The Hebrew expresses the word as it wells up, like a gushing fountain, from a heart which is full of the Spirit of God. The Greek expresses the same word as it comes to another human heart, full of the fruit of the Spirit.

239

What it meant, as applied to Joses, the Levite from Cyprus, may appear the better, as we see more of the man.

We see him first in the first practical crisis of the Church. A multitude of poor Jews and strangers from all parts of the world had received the Gospel. They could not bear to go away and leave the word of life behind them, and they could get little employment from the rich men of Jerusalem. The Church is disheartened. It needs the word of cheer, and in such a case the word of cheer is the deed of help, and the "Son of the Cheering Word" comes forward; "and Joses, who by the apostles was surnamed Barnabas, a Levite and of the country of Cyprus, having land, sold it, and brought the money, and laid it at the apostles' feet." The problem was solved, and the narrative warrants us to suppose that Barnabas was, if not the first, at least the most prominent example of that liberality with which those first disciples "had all things common, and sold their possessions and goods, and parted to all, as any had need, and continuing daily in the Temple, and breaking bread from house to house, did eat their meat with gladness and singleness of heart."

We do not meet him again, by name, for some years. No doubt he had his part in those discussions in the synagogue of the Libertines, Cyrenians, Alexandrians, Cilicians and Asiatics, from which the vehement Stephen and the furious Saul came out, the one as martyr and the other as "consenting unto his death." We will not doubt that he was among the "devout men," who "carried Stephen to his burial, and made great lamentation over him," while, "as for Saul, he made havoc of the Church," and his persecuting rage hurries him off to Damascus. We may easily credit the tradition that Saul and Joses were old friends, pupils together under Gamaliel. Years pass. Communication is cut off by the agitations of the country, in which Damascus has passed for the time into the hands of Aretas, King of

Arabia, and yet, no doubt, the prayer of Barnabas has gone after his old college friend, whom his generous heart will not give up, even though he has seen him keeping the garments of the murderers of Stephen.

Suddenly Saul appears again, and approaches the disciples, "but they were all afraid of him, and believed not that he was a disciple. But Barnabas took him and brought him to the apostles, and declared unto them how he had seen the Lord in the way, and that He had spoken to him, and how he had preached boldly at Damascus, in the name of Jesus." Perhaps there were none in the company of the living disciples who had suffered so much abuse from Saul of Tarsus as his old acquaintance, Joses, and Saul's heart was touched at finding his hand and heart so open to receive him. Paul needed Barnabas, as Simon Peter needed John, to teach him elements of Christian character, which were not easy for him to learn. Tongues of men, or even of angels, prophecy, mysteries, and all knowledge, and even faith that could remove mountains, did not astonish the mighty soul of Saul so much. The lavish bounty which could give all its goods to the poor, or even the devotion which could give its body to the flames, did not overcome him, but the charity, which "suffereth long and is kind, which is not easily provoked, and thinketh no evil, beareth all things, believeth all things, endureth all things," stood before his mind as the greatest of all. He had seen Stephen's miracles, and they did not move him, but Stephen's dying prayer he never could forget. Barnabas, giving his goods to the poor, did not convert him, but when Barnabas took him so kindly by the hand, red as his hand was with those blood-stains which would not out, he led him like a lamb. Most precious to himself and to the Church was the education, which, beginning that day, and reaching on through many years, the vehement apostle received through his generous friend.

Years pass again. Saul has gone to Tarsus, and Barnabas has remained at Jerusalem, in usefulness constant but unrecorded, for history tells what is done by storms, but not often what is done by the shining of the sun. New tidings come to the ears of the church at Jerusalem. Some men of Cyprus and Cyrene have gone to Antioch, and there have preached to Grecians that Jesus is the Lord, and a great number of them have believed and turned to the Lord. Here is an irregularity. Can such things be allowed? "They sent forth Barnabas that he should go as far as Antioch." Barnabas was a Levite, full of learning, full of dignity, versed in the law and in the gospel, and, moreover, being himself of the country of Cyprus, he will be better able than any other man to correct these extravagancies. Here then we have the Son of Inspiration as an inquisitor. How does he perform his office? "When he came and had seen the grace of God, he was glad, and exhorted them all," (those Greeks who were fearing the sentence of exclusion) "that with purpose of heart they would cleave unto the Lord, for he was a good man, full of the Holy Ghost and of faith." The effect of his inspired and inspiriting word was soon manifest, "for much people was added unto the Lord." How precious a grace it is to be able to throw ourselves with heart and hand and word of cheer into a good work of the Lord! There was the smoking flax; the hand of Barnabas might have quenched it. His breath encouraged it, and up flamed a light to the Gentiles.

That story tells us what the apostles meant by the name Barnabas, "the son of the word of God which wells up in the prophet's heart," and how Luke came to interpret it by the Greek, "the Son of Cheering on." When he saw the grace of God, he did not ask the scribes if this was according to the tradition of the elders, but he spoke out the voice of the Spirit which was in his heart, and said, Go on! or rather,

Come on! "Come with us and we will do you good," as Moses, the Levite of old, had done and would have done again. For you remember how "there ran a young man and told Moses and said, Eldad and Medad do prophesy in the camp. And Joshua the son of Nun, the servant of Moses, one of his young men, answered and said, my Lord Moses, forbid them; and Moses said unto him, enviest thou for my sake? Would God that all the Lord's people were prophets and that the Lord would put his Spirit upon them! And Moses gat him into the camp, he and the elders of Israel." Moses, who was so ready to go into the camp-meeting when he saw that the Lord was there, would have rejoiced to throw himself into that first revival which was sweeping in Gentiles as well as Jews, and to say to those Greeks, as he said to his Arab friend, "Come with us and we will do you good."

In the great revival which sprang up around them they needed help at Antioch, and "Barnabas departed to Tarsus for to seek Saul; and when he had found him he brought him unto Antioch. And it came to pass that a whole year they assembled themselves with the church, and taught much people."

In those days came the prophetic warning of the famine which came to pass in the days of Claudius Cæsar, and the church of Antioch sent relief to the brethren in Judea. The Son of Inspiration, who had animated the liberality of the infant church after Pentecost, was probably not the last suggestor nor the least subscriber in this movement, and so he, who had come down to Antioch a year before with his heart full of the word of cheer, goes back now with his hands full of the act of gratitude and help. Barnabas probably, and Saul with him, comes to the house of his kinswoman, Mary the mother of John Mark. They come at the Passover, but they find sorrow and fear among the disciples.

Herod Agrippa, grandson of him who slew the babes at Bethlehem, has received the government of Judea from the Emperor Claudius, and has killed James the brother of John with the sword, and Peter now lies in prison and is to be brought forth to the people after the feast, and prayer without ceasing is going up from the church to God for him. The very night has come which was to be his last. Peter was sleeping, but not the church. As the evening gathered they came quietly into this house of Mary, and joined their prayers. That was a prayer meeting worth recording. There, perhaps, was John, full of love and sorrow for the brother he had lost; there was Saul, full of zeal, and there was Barnabas, full of faith; there were the women, full of prayer; there was Christ, unseen but full of grace and of secret bounty. There is a knock at the door. They are startled, and look at one another, remembering how in the former persecution such a knock as that would be their first intimation that Saul of Tarsus had found out their resort. But this time it was no second Saul, but a visitor more startling still to feeble human faith, the very Peter for whom they have prayed.

From a visit signalized by such a scene, Barnabas and Saul returned from Jerusalem, when they had done their errand, and took with them that same John Mark, at whose mother's house that strange prayer meeting had been held.

The Lord had brought his first missionaries to Jerusalem just before they were to enter upon their great work, and had called them there to pass through scenes which were invaluable as preparation for their life-work. But it is to be observed that their commission as missionaries is not dated at Jerusalem. Not there, or on Gerizim, or at any spot on earth, was to be the center of His worship. The center of Christianity among men is wherever is most of the Spirit and of the truth. He brings them back to Antioch, and there, " as they ministered to the Lord and fasted, the Holy Ghost said, separate me Barnabas and Saul, for the work whereunto I have called them." And when did He call them? See how patiently God educates His chosen ministers. Twelve years have already passed since Saul was called at Damascus "to bear Christ's name before the Gentiles," and Barnabas has been in the church for a still longer time. Both were mature and leading men before, and highly educated in both Jewish and Gentile accomplishment. Barnabas was a wealthy Levite from the country of Cyprus, an island not more surrounded by the waters of the Mediterranean than it was bathed by all the currents of ancient culture. And Saul was a Jew of Tarsus, the chief seat then of Gentile learning, and himself brought up in Jerusalem at the feet of Gamaliel. He had the miraculous teaching of the works and the Spirit of God, and yet he must have years in Arabia, and years more in Tarsus and in Antioch, before he is ready to go forth with the Gospel for the nations.

But now they go forth, two men in middle life, Barnabas, the Levite, and Saul, the Benjamite, with the young John Mark for their helper. First they sail to Cyprus, the old home of Barnabas, where, perhaps, his own personal standing gained them an undisturbed audience in the synagogues, as well as access to the Roman Proconsul, Sergius Paulus. Thence they cross to the south coast of Asia Minor, and labor among the lawless tribes who lived about the Taurus Mountains; tribes who from century to century refused to be tamed by the empires of Nineveh, of Persia and of Rome, as now they are not tamed by the Turkish Empire. The heart of their young associate failed him, and he drew back before they entered the mountains; but the matured men went on, and in city after city they found the same barbarian entertainment—first welcomed and then driven out by the mob. Lystra is an example of all, and illustrates the character of the mission as well as of the people. Here a cripple lay at the gate. His ready faith prepares him, when Paul gave the word, to leap up and walk, and his countrymen are ready to recognize their gods in the men who had done the miracle; and with them a thought was a word and a deed, and the thought and the deed, as well as the speech, were in the idiom of Lycaonia.

On that same plain, the legend ran that in old time Jupiter and Mercury came down and walked among men, seeking hospitality, but no one received them, except a poor and aged couple—Philemon, whose name was borne by Paul's friend, and Baucis. The deities change the inhospitable town into a lake, except the poor cottage of their hosts, which becomes a splendid temple with themselves for its priests, until, in a good old age and in the same hour, they are changed, he to an oak and she to a linden tree, on which they that passed by used to hang garlands, and to say " Cura pii, dîs sunt et qui coluere coluntur." "The pious are God's care, and them that honor Him He will honor!" There, too, Apollonius of Tyana, who studied at Tarsus, and may have been classmate there with Barnabas and Paul, was worshiped as a god. These people, then, cried out in the speech of Lycaonia, "the gods are come down to us in the likeness of men." And they called Paul, Mercurius, because he was the chief speaker, but Barnabas they called Jupiter. This title may give us an idea of the noble presence which accompanied that generous heart, from which used to come those inspiring words in one crisis after another of the church, and which made such an impression that not only did those rude men, in the speech of Lycaonia exclaim, "The gods are come down to us in the likeness of men," but the apostles themselves, in their own Hebrew tongue, called him Barnabas—"the Son of Inspiration." These pagans recognize in Barnabas a power not of many words, but of that sway which goes out from a great, true man in his silence as well as in his speech, a still might, from which the very vehemence of Paul drew a chief element of its power. But when the priest of Jupiter brought oxen and garlands and would have done sacrifice, out of the abundance of the heart the mouth spoke. For we can hardly be mistaken in ascribing to Barnabas, to whom the sacrifice was to be offered, those great simple words, "Sirs, why do ye these things? We also are men like you, and bring you glad tidings, that ye should turn from these vain things to the God that lives, that made heaven and earth and sea and all things that are in them, who in past generations permitted all nations to walk in their own ways; and still left Himself not without witness, doing good, giving us rains from heaven and fruitful seasons, filling our hearts with food and gladness."

When we remember that Palm Sunday and Good Friday are in the same week, we need not wonder that we next hear of Paul stoned and dragged out of the gate of this same Lystra and left for dead.

We have not time or need to dwell upon the rest of their mission, their return to Antioch, their visit to Jerusalem and their subsequent labors in Antioch.

Upon the proposition of a new missionary journey, the old friends and co-laborers are separated. We see their parting with a degree of pain, and yet probably it was for the best. Paul had been long enough with Barnabas to learn much which it was good for him to learn as of that large Christian generosity and breadth of soul, which he needed as the complement to his own directness and vehemence. Saul was a Benjamite. Perhaps his quick left hand could sling a stone at a hair and not miss. If he needed anything in order to be a complete Christian, it was a large open right hand, and it was good economy to keep even the largest heart in the Christian church behind him, with reference to his own education, as well as for the present effect of their ministry; that the dignity of the one might give power to the force of the other, as the weight of the deep phalanx urges the point of the foremost spear.   Paul's Epistles are full of the evidence of the value of the influence of his friend, who was so great in charity, and if that element of the apostolic character is as important as Paul makes it, we Gentiles must ever be thankful for the influence by which it was made to grow upon a stock, which had naturally so much of the wild olive as had the apostle of the Gentiles.

But it was time for each of them to take his own work; and their separation was characteristic.   The fervent Paul could not think of taking with them that John Mark, "who left them in Pamphylia and went not with them to the work." The generous Barnabas could not think of rejecting his young cousin and friend, who was disposed again to be a missionary.   Both were right.   It was not best that Mark should go with Paul.   Where Paul went storms gathered; Paul had nerve enough to fight through them; Barnabas had character enough to be unshaken by them.   Perhaps Mark had neither in such eminence as such a case required.   But still he was a choice spirit, and we, that have Mark's gospel, may be grateful that the noble Christian, through whom the Lord had done so much for Paul, did not cast him off.   And Paul himself is our witness, that his generosity was not lost.   Paul's witness is a noble evidence of the work of grace in both himself and Mark.   In ten years more, Paul was in prison at Rome, and Mark was with him, and is commended by him to the church at Colosse as a fellow-worker who had been a comfort to him.   In six years after that Paul was a prisoner again, and the time of his departure was at hand.   We have the last gushings of his heart, as he poured them forth in his last letter to Timothy, and among them is this, "Take Mark and bring him with thee; for he is profitable to me for the ministry." No doubt the mellowed heart of the great apostle brought forth rich thankfulness for the grace poured forth upon Barnabas, that he did not break, when it was bruised, the reed on which Paul, the aged and the dying, now longs to lean.

Such was Barnabas, "the Son of Inspiration." A chief light in the early church; a light, not as of lightning, but as of the sun; a chief power, not to destroy but to build. Perhaps it may have been a fault in him not to be able to say, "No." But when we see again and again how much salvation there was in the full and round "Yes," that rose from the bottom of his heart, when every other man would have said no, we may learn to rejoice, as Paul did, in that preaching of the gospel of Jesus Christ which "is not yea and nay, but in Him is yea."

If there is too much in the world of the yes, which expresses only the weakness or the hypocrisy of the natural heart, there is also too much of the no, which expresses man's sourness and alienation from his brother, and there is all too little of that yes, welling up like the word of the old prophets, from the honest depths of a heart in which the love of God is perfected, and which answers on earth to the voice from on high, of "the Amen, the faithful and true witness, the beginning of the creation of God," of that Son of God, in whom "all the promises of God are yea and in Him amen unto the glory of God by us."

Such a "Son of Inspiration" is precious in what he is, even more than in what he does. What Barnabas gave to the poor was large, but the charity which his word and example called out was, and is, boundless. The generosity of his own heart was noble. That which he kindled in others ennobled all the church in his day. It should enlarge your soul and mine to-day, and will enlarge hearts till the time when all are gathered in the great heart of the Savior. Like his is every

day the influence of a large heart in any community. Out
of it are issues of life, of that full true life, which, rejoicing
in the Lord always, runs in the way of God's commandments, mounts up with wings as eagles, runs and is not
weary, walks and faints not, until it enters into the joy of
the Lord.

VII.

PAUL BEFORE NERO.

PAUL BEFORE NERO.

II Timothy i: 12.

I am not ashamed; for I know in whom I have believed, and am persuaded that He is able to keep that which I have committed unto Him against that day.

This Second Epistle to Timothy is the last written of Paul's Epistles, and the only record which Scripture gives us of a most striking event in the history of Christianity—the appearance of Paul, the Apostle, before the Emperor Nero. The point of view in which the scene is brought before us is that which presents to us the inner heart of the martyr, at the moment when he unbends himself from the bracing for a fearful trial, to hold refreshing communion with the human spirit upon which he most relied.

Written from "Paul the aged," to his young pupil, Timothy, it is full of that peculiar, mellow grace which marks the attitude of one who is spending the last days of a good life, if he has been so happy as to find a young man in whom he may recognize, as it were, the spirit of his own life beginning a new course, and with whose young fervor and strength he may blend his own mature wisdom and grace. In such a light, this Epistle to Timothy seems like Paul's mantle falling from the midst of his chariot of fire upon his Elisha. There is with it also a grand pathos in the refreshment and new strength which seems to come to the old hero in his need at the thought of such young and true devotion.

It would seem, from the Epistle itself, that the time when it was written was after Paul's first appearance before Nero, during his second imprisonment at Rome. Nero is a name

which is going down, like that of Judas Iscariot, to the ab-
horrence of the successive generations. There have been many
traitors, and many bloody tyrants among men since the world
began, but among them all, it has been the peculiar distinction of Iscariot and of Cæsar Nero to have become the proverb
of the civilized world; the one for falseness, and the other,
though he died at the age of thirty-two, for demoniacal
tyranny.

In order to understand Paul's situation, we should understand Nero and his persecutions. Nero was the union of the
two kinds of tyrants—the exalted brute and the fallen angel.
He was educated in Asiatic lust, in Greek philosophy and
art, and in Occidental barbarity. He loved music, as he loved
blood; he took pleasure in beholding the movements of gracefulness, and the writhings of pain. Cruelty and slaughter
were not so much an employment with him, as a racy flavor
to give zest to the brutal entertainments which he used to
enjoy with his populace.

We have it upon heathen authority that he was wont to
take delight in uniting the gratification of his taste with that
of his cruelty, in the persecution of Christians. For Nero
was a man of taste; he had his love for the beautiful. He
was a delicate, beardless youth, until his gross indulg-
ences disfigured his comeliness, passionately fond of music,
enjoying the Grecian games, rejoicing in magnificence of
scenery, exulting in the grandeur of the scene when Rome
was in flames, and expressing his transport in bursts of music.
He was not without an eye for more quiet and picturesque
beauty. His palace was surrounded with gardens, in which
he delighted; and the view of them which pleased him best
was when the living body of a martyr had been smeared
with pitch and placed in some choice position, so that, as the
flames rose from it, the light shone up among the boughs of
the over-arching trees, and spread itself over the lawns and

among the rose beds and the playing fountains. He loved, too, in the amphitheater, to behold his victims, clad in the skins of beasts and beset by hunting dogs.

It was, as has been supposed, before this "smooth-faced demon" that Paul was called to appear. It was a fearful ordeal to pass, because he had to fear not only injustice but that vulgar passion for cruel insult, by which Nero always studied how he might make brutal sport for himself and the populace of the sufferings of the innocent.

And now there was a rare opportunity for the indulgence of so fiendish a taste. Paul, the chief preacher of the Christians, was in Rome, an old man. Every one knew him who knew anything about Christianity. There could not be a more merry spectacle for that brutalized emperor and rabble than to bring him forth into the amphitheatre to glut their thirst for sport and blood.

This peculiar feature of Nero's persecution, the vulgar delight of the emperor in turning his cruelties to the brutal amusement of the rabble of which, in spirit, himself was one, explains the emphasis laid throughout this Epistle upon the temptation to be ashamed of Christianity.

The occasion of Paul's first appearance seems to have brought together in the Imperial Basilica a great multitude of people; for Paul speaks of "all the Gentiles" hearing his plea. This multitude was probably composed of those who most enjoyed such entertainments as Nero was accustomed to furnish; a populace who had beheld mortal combats of gladiators "butchered to make a Roman holiday," until that had become a tame amusement. It was not strange that such a judge, surrounded by and sympathizing with such a multitude, made an assemblage into which a Christian would not be forward to enter.

If any one should, in sympathy for the prisoner, try the experiment, it would not be unlikely that the mob would

assault him, to relieve the tedium of awaiting the progress of
the cumbrous forms of judicature in the case of the chief
prisoner, as the Greeks in Corinth beat Sosthenes before
Gallio's judgment seat, or as the Roman soldiers mocked
Jesus in the Pretorium at Jerusalem. Yet it was just the
scene in which the accused most feels the need of some sympathizing friends upon whom his eye can rest. But Paul as he
looked around the multitude found not one. Now that he was
past the trial and pouring forth his heart to his young friend,
the shock which that forsaking gave to his feelings recurs
again and again. He writes: "Greatly desiring to see him."
He says, "Be not thou ashamed of the testimony of our
Lord nor of me his prisoner," and a little further on, "I
suffer these things: nevertheless I am not ashamed; for I
know in whom I have believed," and again, "This thou
knowest, that all they which are in Asia be turned away from
me." Again, after he has refreshed his mind with counsels to
his pupil and recurrence to the scenes through which they
had both passed, his mind reverts to the same scene, "At my
first answer no man stood with me, but all men forsook me;
I pray God that it be not laid to their charge."

There stood Paul, the aged servant of God, unbefriended
in such an audience. It was a contrast of weakness and
might, a double contrast; on one side was the strength of the
iron empire which ruled the world; on the other was Paul.
There was a contrast, too, of moral force. With Paul was a
"spirit, not of fear but of power and of love and of a sound
mind;" and on the other side was moral timorousness and
weakness and hate and insanity. The one man stood not
alone, but "the Lord stood with him and strengthened him;
that by him the preaching might be fully known, and that all
the Gentiles might hear." It was a fair meeting of physical
with moral strength; of audacity with courage; of frenzied
passion with the collectedness of a right mind and heart.

Imagine the scene as he enters. The Jew that sets himself forth for a prophet and decries the gods of Rome, stands alone between the pomp of the court and the wild populace. No man appears as his advocate. The accusation is read and opportunity is given for any to speak for the defense, and the prisoner rises.

The curiosity to hear what the Jew will say produces a stillness in the assembly. They thought to make new sport of his apology or supplication. They beheld his weak bodily presence, and now they waited for his contemptible speech. But they had mistaken the man. He was the same who had in his earlier years been arraigned before their governor, Felix, and he had then reasoned of righteousness and temperance and a judgment yet to come, so that the judge trembled before the prisoner. And now the Lord was helping him, as he stood before a judge and in the midst of a people, illy prepared to resist the command of moral power, the dignity of a benevolent heart and the phalanx of a sound mind. It had been worth something to hear that plea. We know its subject, "By him the preaching was fully known, and all the Gentiles heard," and we know its effect. "He was delivered out of the mouth of the lion." But we can only imagine how its winning words and forceful sentences made their way alike through court and crowd, enchaining attention and commanding respect.

Shall we venture to imagine the tone of that plea?

"I count myself happy, most august Cæsar, and ye Romans, the ruling people of the world, that I am permitted to stand before you, and make my plea here, in the citadel of the nations; that I may vindicate myself, as a Roman citizen, who has always been loyal to Rome, ever rendering to Cæsar the honor which is his due; and also that I may proclaim the words of salvation for all the ends of the earth, even the Gospel of our Lord Jesus Christ, who hath abolished

death, and brought life and immortality to light, through the
gospel, whereunto I also am appointed a preacher and an
Apostle and a teacher of the Gentiles; for which cause I also
suffer these things; nevertheless, I am not ashamed. They
threaten me with crucifixion; I preach a crucified Savior;
from long ago I am crucified to the world and the world to
me.   If I suffer with my Lord I shall also reign with Him!
This is a high tribunal, and I stand before it a stranger,
without a single advocate to support my cause; nevertheless,
I am not abashed; for this tribunal, the most august of this
world, reminds me of another, more august than this, where
all of us, the small and the great, shall stand before God,
and shall be judged, every man according to his works.
Then, more than now, shall I stand in need of an advocate,
and I know in whom I have believed; and am persuaded
that He is able to keep that which I have committed to Him
against that day.   God grant that thou, O Cæsar, come not
before that judgment seat, as I come now before thee, a stranger, without an advocate."

With such and more winning and cogent words, does
Paul, in his spirit, not of fear but of power, gain the command of his audience.   Now was the critical opportunity for
the orator, who has so suddenly become not a culprit but a
preacher.   Now the spirit of courage and power which has
quelled their passion becomes a spirit of love, which wins
their hearts; and then, the spirit of a sound mind, which
instructs their strangely wakened intelligence in the truths
of God's salvation. So as the Lord stood with him and
strengthened him, the preaching was fully known, and
he was " delivered out of the mouth of the lion."   And
this was the victory by which he overcame the world,
even his faith.   And now that we have seen how great a
triumph was wrought, we are ready to inquire, what was the
faith which was so victorious?

Paul expresses it in our text: "I know in whom I have believed, and am persuaded that He is able to keep that which I have committed unto Him against that day."

He was not afraid of any crisis, because he had entrusted all that he cared to keep to One who he knew would keep it for him against the day of reckoning.

What was it that Paul had entrusted? Some men entrust their property, their persons, their fame, but neither of these was Paul's trust. Paul, with all his power, was a simple hearted, pious man, and he had entrusted the keeping of his own soul to a faithful Creator, and in this honest simplicity lies much of the sublimity of his character. He, himself, had believed the word that he spoke. Thirty years before, his own eyes had seen the Just One in His glory, at midday, by Damascus; and then he had said, "Lord, what wilt Thou have me to do?" Thus did he consecrate himself to the Lord that appeared to him in the way, and thenceforth "he was not his own, but bought with a price." He had given his soul to Jesus, and that phrase meant something with him.

As Stephen said, "Lord Jesus, receive my spirit," and died; so Paul, from the hour when he gave his spirit into the keeping of Christ, accounted himself as dead, and his life as hid with Christ in God. Other men, "through fear of death, are all their lifetime subject to bondage." For they dread to leave these scenes, where all their treasures and their hearts are, to enter a state for which they have made no provision. But Paul had already died to this world. He had begun the life of another world, and so all the bitterness of death was passed; and who should harm him now?

We have sometimes followed with our sympathies a victim of brutal tyranny, or of the Inquisition, or of slavery, suffering all that the malice or caprice of man could inflict, " the bitter in soul which long for death, but it cometh not;

and dig for it more than for hid treasures." But at last, in some extremity of agony, that great deliverance suddenly sets them free, and in a moment the soul is fled forever from the tormentors. Then it is a relief to look upon the lifeless form; the members that just now were writhing in agony are pliant and soft; the countenance, perhaps, in the sudden joy of the escaping soul, has changed its anguish to a peaceful expression and the first smile that has lighted it since infancy. There he is, escaped at last, to "where the wicked cease from troubling and the weary are at rest; where the prisoners rest together; they hear not the voice of the oppressor."

So serene and beyond human assault, though full of intensest life, was the aspect of Paul before Nero. Such was the victory by which his faith then overcame the central power of the world. He was dead, his life was on high, and the utmost that Nero and his Pretorians could do, could only sever the little cord which still bound him an unwilling captive to this world, and let him "fly away and be at rest." As when a violent man seeks out his foe to wreak his wrath upon him and is appalled to find that he has taken refuge from him in the peaceful grave, so when Nero, the vicegerent of "the prince of this world," "came" to Paul, the minister of Christ, he found "nothing in him." They beset him thinking to overwhelm him with their violence, but when they found that none of those things moved him, they were thrown back by the recoil of their own assault. Behold a greater than Nero was there; a greater than Rome. The prisoner was remanded to his confinement and the assembly was broken up.

Remember now what was the secret of this victory of Paul.

He knew in whom he had believed. His belief had consisted in the entrusting of his own soul to his Savior. He knew that he had so entrusted it. He was persuaded that He is able to keep that trust in that day. His life now was hid with Christ in God. But it was waiting for him, and whensoever Nero, or any persecutor, should set him free from this prison of the body, then he would go to receive that spiritual body; that brow crowned with the garland of justification.

And now the question comes to each one of us—Dost thou know in whom thou hast believed?

How many answers will such a question meet in such an assembly as this! How many more would it meet if the heart, deceitful above all things, were not continually deceiving itself! One man believes in money, and his soul shall be required of him, and then whose shall those things be? Another believes in reputation, loving the praise of men, and verily he has his reward. Another believes in himself, and so withdraws himself from that sympathy which is essential to life. Another believes in his religious observances, or in his rectitude of life; another in the judgment of his friends who seem to think that he is a Christian. Some do not know in whom they have believed. They think it is a dark subject. They are not certain in whom they ought to believe, and so they let the matter run on, thinking that they may come upon more light. But in the meantime the truth stands inflexible, and by it they shall be judged in that day, and no man knows how near that day may be.

There are those here who will say, "I hope that I have believed in Christ." Would that you might know in whom you have believed. Assurance like that of Paul is indeed a high attainment. It seems that none of the Christians of Rome had faith enough to stand by him at his first appearing. Yet he shows us that there is such an attainment, and he shows us how much it is worth.

We all need a faith which can stand through such an ordeal. Do you think to say that in these quiet, Christian times we may dispense with that tension of clinging to eternal realities which the days of the martyrs required? Is it not true on the other hand that there are dangers to our faith growing out of this very quietness? In the fiery trials of the early church the pure gold was refined. Men had severe tests by which to determine in whom they had believed.

It is our duty, as it was Paul's, to be witnesses for God. His were fiery trials, and he needed that God should stand by him, that he might witness a good confession, and he needed that Christ should pray for him that his faith might not fail. He stood, not because he was strong but because Christ was able to make him stand.

If we have had any experience in the Christian way, we know, and if we are just entering that way, we need to be well assured, that we want the upholding hand of Him who is able to make us stand as much as Paul did. If you will study the letter which even in that crisis, Paul, the hero Apostle, wrote to his "son Timothy," you will see and perhaps wonder that he dwells upon the simple principles and the daily duties by which the Christian man is formed, rather than upon his arming for such extraordinary battles. He charges him to "hold fast the form of sound words;" the Holy Scriptures which his parents had taught him, and the Gospel which Paul had brought; to depart from iniquity, to shun lusts and vain speculations. He seems to dread the guile of the serpent more than the rage of the lion.

The fierce adversary is not the most fearful. Remember how he came to Eden; not in his own proper character, as the spirit of hatred, but with soft words, words of love, as if kinder and milder than God himself. "Yea," hath God said, "ye shall not eat of every tree of the garden?" "Ye shall not surely die;" and he showed them "that the tree was good for food and that it was pleasant to the eyes and a tree to be desired to make one wise;" and so they took the fruit and here are we.

Just so he will come to thee, who art trying to follow Christ, suggesting that it is a severe and hard service; that the views of those about you are rather strict and puritanical; that it is unnatural to keep the Sabbath so stiffly; or to be so reverent as Paul and Timothy were of their "holy Scriptures," and of the faith of forefathers and grandmother and mother; that a newer theology is "to be desired to make one wise ; " and that the fashion and gaiety of the world is "pleasant to the eyes ; " that a man in this world needs to be a little selfish, as well as his neighbors, it is "good for food." And so, little by little, you will be drawn away from Christ. You are not in so much danger from the profanity and drunkenness which you shudder at; though let him who thinketh he standeth take heed lest he fall even into such depths as these! But those beginnings of evil, by which the spiritual life leaks out, drop by drop, you are in danger from them; and in order to resist them, we need to commit our way to Him who is able to keep that which we commit unto Him.

We need a clear faith and a pure light. For it is a wily, lurking tempter that besets us. We need to know in whom we have believed, and to have our hopes resting upon that sure foundation of God, which hath this seal, " The Lord knoweth them that are His," and this, " Let every one that nameth the name of Christ depart from iniquity."

It is the great attainment in Christian knowledge to know Him in whom we have believed. To the young believer it is a new mine of knowledge, and to many an older one he says, in loving reproach, "Have I been so long time with you, and yet hast thou not known Me, Philip?"

Did you ever mark the value that Paul puts upon this knowledge? "I count," saith he, "all things but loss for the excellency of the knowledge of Christ Jesus my Lord, that I may know Him, and the power of His resurrection,

and the fellowship of His sufferings, being made conforma-
ble unto His death." So did he desire to know his Lord,
that he even desired to die as He had died, that he might
even thus get some sense of the suffering love of Christ.
Thus, pressing toward the mark, Paul arrived at that knowledge of Him in whom he had believed which strengthened
him so at his appearance before Nero.

And what is it to know Christ? It is to know a friend,
who loves us as no friend on earth can love, even beyond
death. It is to know a sympathizing brother, to whom we
may go with every grief—kind to pity, wise to counsel, mighty
to save. It is to know a sinless exemplar, a model in our
own nature of every beauty of character and of mind, and
to dwell with Him. It is to know a Priest who hath offered
Himself as our sin offering, acceptable to God. It is to
know an Advocate—the only one admitted to plead before the
bar of our Judge, and one to whom we may commit our cause,
and be assured that he will bear us safely through the trial of
"that day."

It is to know, in all the trials and temptations of this
world, One "who is able to keep you from falling, and to
present you faultless before the presence of His glory with
exceeding joy, even to know the only wise God, our Savior,
to whom be glory and majesty, dominion and power, both
now and ever, amen."

This is He in whom we have believed, if we have believed
in Christ. Dost thou know in whom thou hast believed? If
it be in Christ, He invites you to that intimacy of fellowship
in which lies all blessing possible to man. "Behold, I stand
at the door and knock; if any man hear my voice and open
the door, I will come in to him, and sup with him, and he
with me." Yet though this be blessedness almost beyond the
lot of man, there is a higher blessedness of knowledge in
store: "Now we see in a mirror" the mere shadows of the

true, "but then face to face; now we know in part, but then shall we know even as also we are known." "When He shall appear we shall be like Him, for we shall see Him as He is."

And oh, in that day may the Lord know us with "them that are His!"

VIII.

THE PURE IN HEART.

The Pure in Heart.

Of this passage, Henry, in his commentary, says with beautiful truth, "This is the most comprehensive of all the beatitudes; holiness and happiness fully described and put together. Here is the most comprehensive character of the blessed; they are the pure in heart. Here is the most comprehensive comfort of the blessed; they shall see God."

In the delightsome contemplation of such a character and such a comfort we shall naturally inquire:—Who are the pure in heart? what is it to see God? how do the pure in heart see God?

I. Who are the Pure in Heart?

Purity of heart, in its more comprehensive Biblical sense, denotes not merely freedom from those filthy imaginations and unclean desires which we commonly understand by impurity, but in general, freedom from any form of evil in the heart—a "heart washed from wickedness," to use the expression of Jeremiah (iv. 14)—a clean heart, cleansed of earthly ambition, of pride, of the greed of filthy lucre, of the rust of selfishness, of the gangrene of lust, of malice and envy, of all defilement and debasement of flesh or of spirit— a heart fitly clad in that "fine linen, clean and white, which is the righteousness of saints;" the virgin purity of heart of "them in whose mouth was found no guile, because they are without fault before the throne of God," whom he that saw the Apocalypse beheld standing "before the throne and before the Lamb, clothed with white robes "—the " Israelites indeed, in whom is no guile." "Out of the heart," said He who knew what is in man, "proceed evil thoughts, murders, adulteries, fornications, thefts, false witness, blasphemies; in these are the things which defile a man." And so he that hath a pure heart must be free from all those springs of evil, from which flow such streams or droppings of evil.

And the Son of God hath said that he that is thus pure in heart is blessed, "for he shall see God."

Such a statement from the Son is full of import, for "no man knoweth the Father, save the Son and he to whom the Son will reveal Him." This only begotten Son hath thus declared him.

II.   What is it to see God?

God is a spirit.   Eye of flesh is not capable of discerning His form or distinguishing His presence.   Yet may we draw near to Him in spirit, we may " worship Him in spirit," we may hold communion with His Holy Spirit.   To see God is with the spiritual sense—with the heart, to recognize His being and His presence, to discern His spiritual attributes, if we may so speak, His spiritual form and aspect.   The one intellect of man is associated with a double system of senses and perceptive faculties.   There are the bodily senses, by which we are apprised of the facts of the external world; we see, and hear, and smell, and taste, and feel.   Through these, too, we in general converse with one another.   These are the senses of man, the mortal.   But there is another system of senses of man, the living soul, senses by which we spiritually discern the world above, by which we commune with God, and feel the attraction of heavenly things.   Thus man is made to live on this earth two lives at once—a life of conversation with earth, and a life whose conversation is in heaven.   And so, too, there are two deaths possible to man.   For death is the ceasing of those processes and sensations, by which any living thing keeps its vital connection with the system of things in which it lives. And so, while the mind lives inextinguishable, except by the word of the Creator, it may pass one death by the dissolution of that organism by which it associates with the material earth; it may suffer another death by the fatal derangement of those sensibilities and perceptions given it to maintain its communion on high. This is the second death, the outer darkness of the blinded soul, the deathless worm of the incurable spiritual essence.

It is, then, with the eye of the spirit that we are to see God; and mark the expression, "the pure in heart shall see God." Not that they may feel after Him and find Him, not that they shall hear Him, not that some joyful taste or savor shall indicate His presence, but they shall see Him. He shall be present to the most ready, spontaneous and happy sense of which man has any knowledge—that sense which presents to us at one glance the full form in all its grace or majesty of proportion and attitude, its beauty of complexion and comeliness of attire, and all so easily and so fully, that the figure carries the idea of the most immediate and perfect revelation of Deity to the soul; not by any laborious process of search and inference, but as a vivid reality plainly present before it, a clear perception coming in the repose of the soul, coming as the sunlight comes into the clear eye; it will present its picture, unless the eye be closed against it. Surely thus to see God must be a blessing indeed. And this blessing Christ says the pure in heart shall enjoy. And His word is true—true for this world and true for the world to come.

The pure in heart shall see God.

III. How do the Pure in Heart see God?

Purity of heart is a clearness and cleanness of all the spiritual senses and faculties, so that the soul can truly discern the various suggestions that are continually presented to it. This purity produces the two essentials to the soul's vision of God, viz.: The disposition and the ability to see God.

Impurity of character does not incline him that cherishes it to desire the sight of the true God, for He is of purer eyes than to behold evil. So it has been ever since the first human soul that was conscious of corruption, hid among the trees of the garden from the face of Jehovah "because he was naked." "He that doeth evil hateth the light; neither cometh to the light lest his deeds should be reproved." But the pure heart seeks the light and longs to come to its fountain. "He that hath clean hands and a pure heart, who hath not lifted up his soul unto vanity, nor sworn deceitfully, this is the generation of them that seek him, that seek thy face, O God of Jacob." This world is full of the manifestation of God. He displays His power, He illustrates His wisdom, He pours forth His bounty. Yet as a general thing the witness of God, universal as it is, is unobtrusive. "He maketh His sun to rise on the evil and on the good, and sendeth rain on the just and on the unjust;" as the stream of blessing flows, He that pours it forth remains unseen, ready to manifest Himself to them that seek him, yet not interrupting the even dignity of His bounty because some of His creatures do not have Him in all their thoughts, for He is God and not man. And most godlike is the still beauty of that gentle persuasion, unceasingly wooing man, whether he will hear or whether he will forbear, to come to his God, to trust His wisdom and His strength, and to repose upon His love. "He left not himself without witness, in that He did good, and gave us rain from heaven, and fruitful seasons, filling our hearts with food and gladness." The pouring forth such bounty is a joy to His benevolence, even as He pours it forth, but when the grateful heart is lifted up to God in recognizing thankfulness, then it sees God, and as it looks and listens, behold all is full of beauty, and that beauty is the smile of God; all is full of music, which is the gentle voice of God; and all is full of strength and majesty and consummate skill, which are features of God; and all this presence of God is made manifest to His sons, simply by lifting that eyelid of self-will, which obstructs the vision of the carnal man, and, so discerning and responding, they enter into the joy of their Lord.

But this is not all the truth. The impure heart lacks not only the will but the faculty of seeing God. His pure and perfect loveliness is shielded from the impure gaze of men by a veil, a mist, a film, which overspreads the evil eye, or an inner palsy of the nerve, so that God may walk among His people but His enemies shall not see Him. The pillar which gave light by night to Israel was cloud and darkness to the Egyptians.

And how, again, is this? How is it that the pure in heart can see God more clearly and truly than other men? Purity of heart is not mental acumen or penetration, and cannot more scientific and philosophic men, better than the merely pure in heart, analyse the manifestations of God and deduce from them the character of the Creator? Oh, no! "Out of the mouth of babes and sucklings God hath ordained praise." "He hath chosen the foolish things of the world to confound the wise." "The natural man cannot know the things of the spirit of God, because they are spiritually discerned." All this is no marvel. It is simply according to all the analogy of nature. We wish to see God. If we are to see Him it must be with a spiritual eye. Now, intellect is not eye, either of body or of spirit. John Milton was a wonder of learning not less than of genius, but he, at the period of his most consummate flowering of mind, could not see man, whom the youngest boy in this congregation can see without an effort. So Voltaire was a wonder of talent and study, but he could not see God; he was blind in soul, and so many a little girl, that knows almost nothing else, knows what Voltaire, with his philosophy, could not know. And what is the philosophy of this?

One part of it is that the pure heart is able to understand and recognize God.

No man can understand a feeling such as he never had, or a motive which he never felt. The impure heart is continually perverting the gifts of God. This scheme of nature, so pure and holy in loveliness, in all its multiplicity of elements and of operations, is to the impure heart all filled with impure associations. "Unto them that are defiled and unbelieving is nothing pure," but on the other hand "to the pure all things are pure." And so to the pure heart all things manifest the pure God. There are those to whom the very Word of God is full of carnal suggestion, but to the pure heart "the words of the Lord are pure words." God's "word is very pure, therefore he loves it," and so with the visible manifestations of God. There is a suggestion of divine purity rising above human guile through all the objects of this world, and on high are the pure stars, and they, too, suggest a yet higher purity—the purity of Him in whose sight the stars are not pure—and so in the contemplation of such purity the heart continually purifies itself "even as He is pure," and as it grows purer, the pure light flows in more purely still, cleansing the heart that it may see Him more and more, until at length it shall "behold His face in righteousness," and "be satisfied, awaking in His likeness." [Ps. xvii. 15]

We see spiritual things here as in a glass—in a mirror—and we know how entirely the impression of an object so viewed depends upon the quality of the glass. A discolored glass cannot present a pure white image, and a distorted glass can give none but a distorted image, and therefore they that trust to such media can never see God. The mirror, the imagination, which is defiled with unclean defacings, cannot present any reflection of Him at all, and that which is scratched and twisted by the self-willed philosophy of men can only render an unseemly caricature of the perfection of beauty, which the clean and simple heart sees.

So man has proved it by experiment, for he has a nature which looks for God, and which in its corruption has supplied its own longings by making to itself gods, that is, by trying to embody in some distinct form its conceptions of Deity. It makes its gods as Aaron made gods for the children of Israel. It takes the precious gifts of God, with all the rich and blessed meaning and suggestion which there is in them, and throws them into the fire of its own passion, and pours them upon the soil of its own debasement, and fashions them with the graver of its own crooked thoughts, and there comes forth " this calf." All the gods of all paganism are presentations of the idea of Deity as rendered by the various minds which have attempted to catch and represent it. There was the Phœnician religion of the Canaanites—the deification of lust and brutality; the Egyptian worship of the brutes themselves, a more humane religion than the Phœnician, by as much as a real brute is more human than a brutal and beastly man. And then there were the Grecian gods, a mythology as cold and superficial in its gracefulness as that of Sidon was hot and sanguinary in its hideousness; and the Roman gods—fierce, imperious, proud and stern—each made in the image of its worshipers. The soul of the Roman religion is will; of the Greek, fancy; of the Canaanite, passion; but neither presents the true image of God, the perfect in love and grace and justice, because in neither was that pure and unbiased state of soul which was prepared to present them all.

We have been speaking of God as presented by His works of nature and bounties of Providence to the observation and gratitude and worship of men. But all these, as we see, are but the drapery of our idea of God. The image itself of God is the human soul. "In the image of God made He man." And as all this outward world, in its Sabbath loveliness, is like a still lake reflecting heaven, so the image of God Himself is seen in the depths of the human soul, but only when that soul is unruffled and clear. A gust of passion sweeping over the surface destroys the image, a discoloring of the element perverts it, but the pure human soul, in its free and symmetrical and healthful development, is the presentation of the character of God. The image is finite in proportion, as are our minds which are to grasp it, but still it points to the infinity of God, partly by its own power of endless expansion, directing our imaginations in the line along which they may run toward the Infinite to the utmost stretch of imagination, and partly by the fact that the attitude of such a pure soul is that of continually looking up to an Infinite One, in whom are realized the fulness of all those perfections of being which the soul longs for, and in whom are all those riches of bounty upon which the soul must depend, and who is all that the soul worships.

Here in the depth of the pure soul, then, it is that men are to see God. Sir William Herschel wrought for his great telescope a speculum of pure and burnished metal, which, when duly adjusted, gathered the rays that came from heaven, and presented for his study the stars and planets with a distinctness and lustre unknown to the naked eye. He descried a new planet far off beyond the circuit of Saturn. So God, not visible to our mortal eye, may be discerned in the wondrous speculum of the pure heart. If the astronomer pointed his neighbor to a dark and apparently vacant spot in the sky, and told him that in that spot was a great planet, and his neighbor should refuse to believe it because he did not see it there, he would be like some men who will not believe in Deity except on higher external evidence. But suppose the astronomer to say further, I see the planet in a plate of metal which I have, and the other to go and see if he could see it in the plate of his plowshare or his silver table service, and seeing it not, should disbelieve it, he would be like some other men who do not accept God because they do not find His image in their own minds. The fact is that the reflection of God is not in the rusty iron of selfish toil, nor in the gold which bears the image and superscription of Cæsar, but in the heart which God hath refined as silver is refined, and tried as gold is tried. The astronomer might permit another to see the wonders of the sky in his telescope, but not so with the spiritual mirror. Each man must keep his own heart pure if he would see God. He cannot see the vision of Him which is in the soul of another. Yet the man of pure heart is in some degree a reflection of God for all the community about him. His character as it shines is a likeness of God, and men, seeing his good works, glorify his Father which is in heaven; or seeing his faith, as the disciples looked into the eye of the Only Begotten Son and saw the image of the Father there, they may also catch His likeness.

So in still communion with his own heart the Christian sees God. When he hath gone into his closet and shut the door, then his mind, resting from the annoyances of toil and care and earthly trouble, presents to him the likeness of God as clearly and distinctly as the mind itself is at peace and is clear of the clouding of sin; and not only does he see God there, but if he can preserve that same heavenly composure when he goes abroad, the light itself of day may make the image vivid, and the works, which God has made very good, may become a fitting frame for it, and the voices and the motions of all nature, inanimate, animate and even human, may all

give expression and life to that view of God which is so full
of grace and majesty and benignity in the silence of private
contemplation.

But to see God as the pure heart sees Him is something
higher than all this. He is permitted not merely to contem-
plate God, but to commune with Him. God loves the pure
heart more than the pure heart loves God, and so God, of His
special favor, manifests Himself to such an heart. It is not
merely to look down to unapproachable spiritual depths
beneath, if we may so say, the placid surface of the soul,
and there to see a ravishing reflection of the features of
Deity, a vision for its beauty blessed beyond all human
thought, but still the image of a God, removed as far above
us as that image is deep below the surface, even as far above
the stars as it is purer than they; but God Himself comes
and dwells in such a soul, and His name is called "Immanuel"—"God with us."

"Jesus said, If a man love Me, he will keep my words; and
my Father will love him, and we will come unto him
and make our abode with him" (John xiv. 23). And so
the soul, in the stillness of its secret contemplation, not only
sees the likeness of God, but it has direct communion with
God. It has come to the Father of Spirits, to the source of
all spiritual life, and now it seems at last to live. There
have been many who, having tasted the joys of such solitary
communion with God, have deemed a solitary and ascetic life
the best life for men in this world. And so they have sought
deserts or monastic cloisters for a purely religious life; and
doubtless many and ecstatic have been the enjoyments that
they have known. Yet that is not the life which God
intended for men upon this earth. Men may and must commune much with God in secret, in order that His image and
His presence may be continually with them, as every true
earthly friendship must be cherished by private acquaintance.

But the God of the pure heart does not stay in the closet and wait for the visit of the soul there, leaving it to go unsustained through the ways of the impure world. "Enoch walked with God." God, if the soul asks his company, will go with it through the labors and the business of the day. If, however, the soul would have God go with it, it must walk in a pure way, "for the ways of the Lord are right and the just shall walk in them" (Hos. xiv. 9).

The need of a pure heart in order to see God was illustrated in the coming of the Word to the world. "He was in the world, and the world was made by Him, and the world knew Him not; He came unto His own and His own received Him not. But as many as received Him, to them gave He power to become the sons of God." "The light shone in darkness, but the darkness comprehended it not." Why? "Because they would not come to the light lest their deeds should be reproved;" because "the natural man receiveth not the things of the spirit of God; for they are foolishness unto him, neither can he know them, because they are spiritually discerned." Satan "worketh with all deceivableness of unrighteousness in them that perish because they received not the love of the truth that they might be saved." Therefore those things which "prophets and righteous men desired to see," the men among whom they were done did not see, because their eyes were covered and their ears were stopped by the pollution of this world. But the "just and devout" Simeon, who was waiting for the consolation of Israel, tarrying upon the earth until he should see the Lord's Christ, when the infant Jesus was brought into the temple, "took Him up in his arms and blessed God, and said, 'Lord, now lettest Thou Thy servant depart in peace, according to Thy word, for mine eyes have seen Thy salvation.'" And when He commenced His public mission "the Israelite indeed, in whom was no guile," exclaimed, "Rabbi, Thou art the

Son of God, Thou art the King of Israel." To the people in general, He was without form or comeliness, and when they "saw Him there was no beauty that they should desire Him." But to those whose eyes were open, like the pure-hearted John, He was revealed, "the Word dwelling among them," "and they beheld His glory—the glory as of the only begotten of the Father, full of grace and truth;" for the pure heart is able to discern heavenly beauty and truth because itself is lovely and true ; and in proportion to the purity of their own hearts were they able to discern His true character, while He was with them ; and after He had gone, and sent the Spirit to sanctify them and to lead them into all truth, " the Spirit took of the things of Christ and showed them unto them."

How did He make that manifestation ? It was only necessary to purify the heart, so that they might recall and spiritually discern the meaning of the words which Christ had left in their memories, as within our own day a likeness of an old Italian artist has been brought to light simply by removing a coating which had been plastered over it. To take perhaps a more accurate comparison, we have an art, in which a clean and burnished silvered plate, after a peculiar preparation, is placed in the camera and receives the image of a human countenance. Thus only the hearts which God had cleansed and prepared were able to receive the Divine lineaments of the Savior's character. Again, the silvered plate, after receiving the impression, must be exposed to the vapor of mercury in order to make the image visible; so must the Spirit breathe upon the soul that has seen God, in order that the Divine likeness may become manifest. Thus He takes the things of Christ and shows them to man ; and still further, now that we are upon this illustration, the plate must be exposed to yet another chemical washing in order to cleanse away all the film, which is not covered by the image, and to render it permanent. So must the followers of Christ be baptised with the baptism which He was baptised with—the baptism of fire, as well as of the Holy Ghost—which shall thoroughly purge away all the dross and take away all the tin, so that Christ may be revealed in them, and the image made enduring even in all the mingling of the soul in the unholy world.

By such a continual and varied process of purification must the image of God be brought out and fixed in the soul. Thus, too, it was altogether natural that the apostles, as they were sanctified by the Spirit, should turn back with a fresh, wondering love to that vision of God manifest in the flesh, which had gone about with them in the years of their young manhood, when their eyes were so holden that they could not see Him; and as they remembered, after He had vanished out of their sight, how unaccountably their hearts did burn within them as He walked with them by the way and opened to them the Scriptures: how their ripened hearts must have longed for a renewal of such heavenly intercourse now that their hearts were better prepared to "know Him."

Their longing was to see Christ again. Nor was it a vain longing in them, nor is it in us. It was a sure hope, and this shall be the last and most blessed topic in our present consideration.

The pure in heart shall see God hereafter. "We know," saith John, "that when He shall appear we shall be like Him, for we shall see Him as He is."

Such a blessedness and crown of rejoicing did the apostles of our Lord anticipate as laid up for them, and not for them only, but for "all them also that love His appearing" (II Tim. iv. 8).

But still they bore in mind and they call upon us to bear in mind always the condition, the only condition of the realization of such a hope. "Every man that hath this hope in him purifieth himself even as He is pure."

Into that city of our God " there shall in no wise enter anything that defileth, neither whatsoever worketh abomination or maketh a lie."

They that are before that throne cease not day nor night crying "Holy, Holy, Holy, Lord God Almighty." If we walk in the light the blood of Jesus Christ cleanseth us from "all sin." Then "our conversation is in heaven, from whence also we look for the Savior, the Lord Jesus Christ, who shall change our vile body, that it may be fashioned like unto His glorious body."

"He that walketh righteously and speaketh uprightly; he that despiseth the gain of oppressions, that shaketh his hands from holding of bribes, that stoppeth his ears from hearing of blood, and shutteth his eyes from seeing evil—thine eyes shall see the King in His beauty"—no more veiled in mortal flesh, no more hidden from us by our own dimness of vision by reason of sin, but as He is, in all the pure glory of His infinite loveliness. "How great is His goodness and how great is His beauty!" And there is something mysterious to the reason, yet self-evident to the spirit, in the effect of such a vision of the perfection of positive beauty by the perfectly clean heart. "We shall be like Him; for we shall see Him as He is." It would seem that the attractiveness and the spiritual power of such a vision will transform the soul, that the pure heart in such a presence shall fear and be enlarged, and as it shall see, shall flow together and, as it were, merge itself in that infinite blessedness, and so repose in the bosom of its Lord forever.

"As for me," saith the sweet singer of Israel, "I shall behold Thy face in righteousness. I shall be satisfied, when I awake, with Thy likeness."

IX.

THE BELIEVER'S REST.

The Believer's Rest.

For we which have believed do enter into rest.

This is the testimony of a believer to the fulfillment of the promise of the Savior; "Come unto me all ye that labor and are heavy laden, and I will give you rest." These are words which have been fulfilling themselves ever since the day when the Savior spoke them. The assurance of the sympathy of Jesus the Christ does of itself breathe through the soul the rest which it promises. It is as, when David played before King Saul, the very music of his harp, even without the words of the song, had power to charm away the evil spirit from the frenzied mind of the king. Even so in the griefs and burdens which fall upon us here, the soul, receiving this assurance of its Lord, does not stop to ask any further question, to inquire what medicine He has for a mind diseased, what strong arm He has to lift its burden. The mere assurance of the Savior's sympathy is in itself healing to the wounded, and strength to the fainting soul.

In that sympathy itself the soul recognizes its strong deliverer, as well as its tender lover. It recognizes these words as the words of God, because it feels them breathing through the depths of the soul, as only He that made the soul could affect it. So instinctively the believer receives the peace and comfort and assured truth of that saying, and the instinct, which receives them and the healing which they bring is the proof of that truth. It brings peace and strength to the heart, as medicine for the body soothes its fever or restores its vigor, by a process which our own study or worry cannot help, but may hinder or destroy.

And yet there is a wisdom of God in it all, which He would have us discern and love. He would have us see by whom and how the burden is lifted from the weary soul.

We recognize this relieving of our burdens as a truly divine office. Isaiah, in the midst of the sublimity of his prophecy, exclaims, "The Lord God hath given me the tongue of the learned, that I should know how to speak a word in season to him that is weary," and the sentiment fills the splendor of his poetry with the warmth of genial life. Blessed, indeed, is that learning which hath such an end! Blessed, beyond all the proud achievements of the human intellect, that word in season to the weary! We will receive it as the word of God.

The Word, which was made flesh, stands before us professing to give this rest to all the weary and the heavy laden.

Let us consider what were and are some of the burdens with which the world was weary when Christ came, and with which it is now weary. And let us try to see whether Christ gives rest from those burdens.

The context seems to suggest what we should perhaps have thought of early in our inquiry, namely,

A BURDEN OF DARKNESS AND DOUBT.

The soul is lost in a wilderness, not knowing God and not knowing itself, doubting whether itself is mortal or immortal, a living soul for the time inhabiting and ruling a frail body, or a mere bundle of fleshy tissues secreting thought as they secrete blood; doubting whether this world and all the stars are mere balls of dead matter reeling through blank space, or whether they all declare the glory of a God.

The mind might answer for itself some of these doubts, and it did answer them. "For the invisible things of Him from the creation of the world are clearly seen, being understood by the things that are made, even His eternal power and Godhead."

But still all this impression of eternal power and Godhead does not give to the soul that light which is the life of men. The presence of this awful power may crush the soul with a new burden, but it does not give it rest. It still groans for another idea of God. And so the world, by its wisdom, still sought for God and found him not. For He was not to be found by the study of the wise.

It seems as if we might have known as much as that; known that of course the mind of man could not grasp the being of the Creator, that whatsoever man could know of God must come in such a shape that it could be discerned by the most ignorant soul that was willing to know God, as well as by the most learned.

And yet we labor with these doubts; not heathen men, alone, but Christian men are oppressed by them. Our minds try to grasp great problems respecting God and man, and when our ambition has attempted something too great for our powers, we reel under the burden, and we fall into doubt or unbelief, and there lies the poor pride of the philosopher, blessing, while it despises, the simple faith of the child or of the slave. In a world thus oppressed with doubt, stands Jesus, as in the passage from which the promise is taken, saying, "I thank Thee, O Father, Lord of heaven and earth, because Thou hast hid these things from the wise and prudent and hast revealed them unto babes; even so, Father, for so it seemed good in Thy sight. All things are delivered unto Me of My Father, and no man knoweth the Son but the Father, neither knoweth any man the Father, save the Son, and he to whomsoever the Son will reveal Him. Come unto Me, all ye that labor and are heavy laden, and I will give you rest. Take My yoke upon you and learn of Me; for

I am meek and lowly in heart; and ye shall find rest unto your souls; for My yoke is easy and My burden is light."

"The heavens declare the glory of God, and the firmament showeth His handiwork." And yet, the evidence of these stupendous works and operations of God is rather overwhelming than satisfying to the mind. Man cannot bear such a pressure of God without him, unless he has a living power of God within him. And so the heathen mind, whether in pagan or Christian lands, "being alienated from the life of God," has never been able to know God, or to escape from the burden, the oppression, of the thought of God, except by a kind of wilful suppression of its own instincts.

A poet of their own has expressed the state of mind of such unbelievers with rare honesty. Horace says: "To wonder at nothing is well nigh the one and only thing which can make or keep you happy. Men there are who can look upon this sun and the stars, and the solemn movements of the heavens, and not be filled with awe and fear." Oh, what pity, that a man with a soul made to be moved by the movements of the heavens should find no way of entering into rest except by stupefying his own nature, so that he can gaze upon all this testimony of God with a stolid unbelief! And then that he should call this stupidity happiness!

And yet, what should a man do? True it is that all this stupendous movement passes over us in the firmament of day and of night; presses around us in the changes of the seasons, and in the strength and life of nature; passes through us in the operation of the laws of our own life; passes like the equipage of a monarch. As our minds view it and feel it, what can we do but fall down and adore? Surely a man, in whom the senses of man are alive, can do nothing less. And yet a man, in whom is the soul of a man, can hardly do that, can hardly worship unless he can do more. It is not life to the body for a Hindoo to fall down and let the car of Juggernaut roll over him. Nor is it life to the soul to prostrate itself under a sense of the overpowering greatness of the God who moves before us in the grandeur of the Lord of heaven and earth. And yet, there is a knowledge of God which is life eternal to the soul. But the soul cannot accept, though it fears to reject, this awful majesty and might as its God. For it needs and must have a God who exists for some other purpose than merely to be wondered at or to be dreaded. It seems a high thing to say that a Being which could fill all the visible heavens and earth might yet be insufficient to fill the soul of man. And yet, the soul of man has been so made, that so high a thing as that is simply true.

Neither does the soul quite feel that it has found its God, when we add the proofs of benevolence with which He has filled His universe. It may be full of awe, and full of admiration, and yet, it does not feel that it knows God.

It is like a poor slave looking upon the state of an earthly emperor. As the splendor of his train goes by, the poor man looks up from his weary labor, with wonder and awe, perhaps with fear. If he knows that the king is good he may admire. But still he does not feel that he knows the king, and his sense of his own burdens is made more oppressive by the sight of the grandeur which is so near him and yet so far from him. Let the poor man know that it is by the wisdom and goodness of the king that he enjoys the security of law and the various blessings, countless, after all, and inestimable, which belong to him, as even a poor subject of a good king, and he comes to feel drawn to the monarch. He has recognized now a greatness and nobility, a kingliness of another sort from that pomp and parade. He recognizes him as a king, indeed, by this token, that with a wise and strong and kind sympathy he relieves the burdens of his people. He feels that the great man is not only king over him, but that he is his king. It is the idea which the French had, when they deposed a "King of France" and installed a "King of the French;" such as old Homer had when he called the king the "Shepherd of the People." When we see these tokens, the kingly power and the kingly care, all know an earthly king of men. We do not demand in him, the earthly king, the capacity to know or to do all things, or to relieve, or even to think of, all our burdens. We accept him with the limitations of humanity, and we give him such respect and love as he may earn.

But the soul must know something more than this before it can know God. It may see and feel His eternal power and Godhead, but as we have seen and felt, all that kind of discernment of God leaves its personal demand for God only more oppressive than before. The God whom man seeks is not so much a power and an intelligence, as a heart and a soul. Might, wisdom, even general administrative justice and benevolence, are all essential attributes of the Godhead, and yet, even by them all, the soul will not and cannot know God—that "true God, to know whom is eternal life."

The soul wants the personal sympathy of God.

That poor man would not think of asking the emperor to leave his splendor and his affairs of state, and to come to his poor hut and inquire after his personal distresses. For an emperor is but a man, and cannot attend to little things and great things at once. All his action is in a little circle. There are countless things too high for him, and countless things too delicate for him. But God must be free from all these limitations, and we can know God only by that proof— by discerning that he is perfectly all which we ask for in a perfect Lord and King. We see the power, the wisdom, the justice, and even the general benevolence, and we fear and admire, but still we do not know Him. God does not yet enter into the circle of our personal acquaintance, and if He is God He must come into that circle. For me, the soul will say, the center of the universe is in the center of my own soul. So God has made me, and my God must be a God who has his throne in the center of my soul and from that center rules all the world. He must be a God who feels all my griefs sooner and more deeply than I can feel them, who will rejoice in my joy, as this poor soul of mine cannot rejoice—one who causeth all things to "work together for good to them that love Him." Nothing less than that can satisfy the soul of man. It is a high demand for a feeble creature. And yet this very feebleness is the energy of the demand. It is the great want of the babe, which is exactly the strongest natural thing on this earth, which God made that he might ordain praise and strength in this lower world.

Philip saith unto Him: "Lord, show us the Father and it sufficeth us." And Philip speaks for us all. Man doubts not so much from want of evidence of the being or of the greatness or goodness of God, but rather because we do not feel and see Him in that near and tender personal relation in which we feel that God must be near to us, if there is a God at all for us. We want one whom we can know as our own Father, as well as our God—as a Father not only nearer to us than any human king, but even than any human father—the Father, the perfection of that ideal which the mind has of fatherly care, yes, one nearer to us and loving us more tenderly, wisely and efficiently than father or mother, one nearer to us than we are to ourselves. That is what we want, in order that we may feel that we know God. "Lord, show us the Father and it sufficeth us."

And what is the answer of the Word to Philip? "He that hath seen Me hath seen the Father." And again (John i. 18): "No man hath seen God at any time; the only begotten

Son, which is in the bosom of the Father, He hath declared Him." And how hath He declared Him? Simply by coming and adding that element to our thought and experience of God which can make all clear and transparent to us.

In Christ, God presents Himself to our personal and individual acquaintance and sympathy. The train of the King of kings stops before the door of the poor man; the chariot of glory is opened, and forth steps He to whom "all power is given in heaven and in earth." He has laid His glory by; He comes in the form of a servant. He takes the hand of the poor man, He looks in his eye, and He saith, "Come unto me all ye that labor and are heavy laden, and I will give you rest; take my yoke upon you and learn of me, for I am meek and lowly in heart, and ye shall find rest unto your souls, for my yoke is easy and my burden is light."

"This," the soul must cry that has come to feel its want of God, "this is God. All that splendor and might was the hiding of God. But this voice which speaks to my inmost soul, this is the voice of God. And so I know there is a God, and God is near me and He loves me; before the foundation of the world He prepared salvation for me, and now, in the person of His Son, he passes before me bearing my cross, and surely it is a light and a blessed thing that I may take His cross and bear it after Him."

And, behold! upon the instant, every burden of all that labor and are heavy laden has become light. Rest has filled the soul; not that negative rest, which is a mere removing of the load from shoulders that are still feeble, and a mind still imbecile, but that positive and living rest, which arises when the strength of God comes and fills the soul, and the doing of His commandments becomes a joyful play of the spirit. As one hath said, I John v. 3,4,5: "This is the love of God, that we keep His commandments, and His commandments are not grievous. For whatsoever is born of God overcometh the world; and this is the victory that overcometh the world, even our faith. Who is he that overcometh the world but he that believeth that Jesus is the Son of God?"

There is the secret of victory over all "the ills that flesh is heir to." It lies in receiving with all the mind and heart the knowledge of God as revealed in Jesus Christ, of God as our God, sympathizing in all our sorrows as well as our joys, and through them all, and through His bearing them all for us, working out a great salvation for us.

" What shall we, then, say to these things? "If God be for us, who can be against us? He that spared not His own Son, but delivered Him up for us all, how shall He not also with Him freely give us all things?" "Who shall separate us from the love of Christ? "

We shall not, however, get the full force of the manifestation of God in the lowly love of Christ unless we observe the dignity of the King of kings as it still appears under the garb of a servant, and come to feel how, as an earthly king puts on splendor to cover his own feebleness, so the heavenly King lays off His splendor to reveal His eternal glory.

The sovereign God is sovereign still, even in the richest freedom of His mercies. "I praise thee, Lord of heaven and earth, because thou has hid these things from the wise and prudent and hast revealed them unto babes. Even so, Father, for so it hath seemed good in thy sight." There is the sovereign bounty of a king. Herod and the Scribes knew not the child Christ, but to the wise men of the East and to the shepherds of Bethlehem He was revealed by the star and the angels. And further on, "Neither knoweth any man the Father save the Son, and he to whom the Son willeth to reveal Him." It is all of His own free grace.

And shall we, therefore, turn away, broken in heart, because this life which has come so near us is, after all, not for us? No, not yet. For hear what it is that He saith:

"Neither knoweth any man the Father save the Son, and he to whomsoever the Son willeth to reveal Him," and he goes right on to say, "Come unto me, all ye that labor and are heavy laden, and I will give you rest." Thus is the publishing of the decree of the Sovereign. If we are weary, if we are heavy laden, then He will give us rest.

If there be any that are not weary or heavy laden, if there be any who, being weary and heavy laden, still will not come to the Savior of mankind, to them He will not give rest.

Who will stay away and bear his burden alone?

Who will come to the Meek and Lowly in heart and find the rest of the soul, the "peace in believing," "the peace of God which passeth all understanding, keeping the heart and mind in Christ Jesus"?

X.

THE COMMUNION OF THE SPIRIT.

The Communion of the Spirit.

And I will pray the Father, and He shall give you another Comforter, that He may abide with you forever.

Here we have the first distinct revelation of the Holy Spirit as a personal helper, coming from the Father, by the prayer of the Son, to comfort the souls of His children. Christ has reserved this revelation for the hour of sorrow when it would be needed. Judas has gone out to betray his Lord. Jesus is alone with the eleven. Bereavement, danger, sore temptation are before them. They know a little of it, and sorrow fills their heart. He knows it all and sympathy fills His heart. And to prepare them not only for what they foresaw, but for what He foresaw, He announces to them that "promise of the Father," that best gift for men, which He was to receive when He had "led captivity captive." That gift should be another and an everlasting Comforter, a Spirit of truth, dwelling with them and being in them.

It is only a clearer statement of a fact in the Divine and human constitution and the Plan of Redemption, which is often recognized in the word of God.

Man was made for spiritual communion. His spirit inclines to seek it, as the hart pants for water brooks. All ancient and heathen polytheism, and all modern and infidel necromancy are tokens, or perversions of this instinct of man which God made in order that the soul might seek for God. God sends us His Word to call us to the one fountain of living waters, to the one spirit of life, to that communion which is opened for us by the death and the prayer of the Son of God.

We have presented to us a most blessed subject for contemplation in the light of God's word,

THE COMMUNION OF THE HOLY GHOST WITH MAN.

These are wonderful words. It is a wonderful thought that the Holy Spirit of God will converse with men; that we, who are but dust and ashes, may speak to God, and that God will hear us. Even when we have sinned we may come to Him and He will give us answers of peace. How blessed that record of Enoch! "Enoch walked with God!" That beautiful and holy companionship, in the midst of those wicked generations of giants! And so, too, even we may walk with Him in white, and we may open to Him the doors of these poor, shattered, impoverished hearts of ours, and He will come in with His riches of love and riches of bounty, and will sup with us as we with Him.

But these thoughts are so rapturous that we are in danger of forgetting to take of those riches of fuller revelation of God's counsels toward us, which lie in His word, still inviting us to feed our minds with them, as the angel urged Elijah again to take meat before he went on to the mount of God. We will study, then, what is the communion of the Holy Ghost to which the Lord calls us.

If we confine ourselves to the clear teachings of the word of God, we must speak of the communion of the Holy Ghost with regenerate men. We do not say that the unregenerate heart stands in no relation to the Spirit. God said before the flood, "My spirit shall not always strive with man." "No man," saith Christ, "can come unto me except the Father which sent me draw him." There is a continual persuasion of the word and works of God; of His providential dealings, and of the conscience which he has implanted, and we know not of what other influence of our Father, to lead us to come to

Christ. But we do not find this called the communion of the Holy Spirit. The Holy Ghost is the most mysterious, secret, and as one might say, delicate, manifestation of Deity. God the Father in the grand and everywhere manifest diguity of His greatness and goodness and truth, sendeth rain on the evil and on the good. He does not leave Himself without witness. Christ saith, "No man can come to me except the Father which hath sent me draw him." God the Son could come and die for us while we were yet sinners, and He says, "No man cometh unto the Father but by me." But the Holy Ghost is that peculiar manifestation of God, which speaks to them that dwell in the secret place of the Almighty.

It would seem that the Spirit stands at the door of the heart, waiting with yearning love for the heart to be opened, waiting till Its holy influence shall be sought, and then, when the doors are opened, coming in and renewing the soul, sometimes pervading it with a sudden and unspeakable joy, or, when It sees that that will be better, diffusing a purifying influence in silent or even sad blessing, like the rain, which clouds weep upon the mown grass and like showers that water the earth.

The communion, then, of the Holy Ghost with the Christian, begins with the act of regeneration.

The soul of man is brought by the drawing of the Father's love to the Son; and then the sympathy of the Son leads it to the Father again, as our Father, and then "the love of God is shed abroad in our hearts by the Holy Ghost which is given unto us;" and we receive the spirit of adoption whereby we cry, Abba, Father. The Spirit itself beareth witness with our Spirit that we are children of God. By a supernatural influence, a new life is created in the heart, a life of holiness, life eternal. "Except a man be born of the Spirit he cannot enter into the kingdom of God." This birth is not an event which our philosophy can comprehend, but its effects we can see and feel, standing still and seeing the salvation of God. It is not " by works of righteousness that we have done, but according to His mercy he saveth us by the washing of regeneration and renewing of the Holy Ghost." It is a curious question of speculation, and a stumbling block of some unregenerate hearts, to ask whether man is not capable of renewing his own heart. But it is not a question which a pious heart raises. Even if it be so, that it could have turned itself from sin to holiness, it is well pleased that such was not the fact in its own history. It is so much sweeter and better for the soul to have thrown itself into the arms of the Holy Spirit of God, and to have been renewed by Its communion, to feel that tie of holy gratitude and love binding us to that blessed Spirit, so that " God may be all in all" and that we may be clothed only in His righteousness.

The work of the Spirit does not end with the new birth. But thenceforth we are sons, dwelling in the house forever; and this Holy Comforter abideth with us forever. Earthly friendships, however sweet, carry with them always an undefined disquiet in the consciousness that they are transient; but the communion with this Holy Friend reaches from the moment of conversion to the end of eternity. He will freely sympathize and aid in every holy thought and right endeavor through all that duration. In every vicissitude of that endless and boundless being He will be the Helper which the soul needs. How dismal it would be, to be an immortal soul doomed to wander without foresight or plan or support through eternity, a soul lost in the great desert expanses of infinite space; but, on the other hand, how happy to be a soul led through such immensity by the life-giving companionship of the Spirit of Holiness which blesses it all; to be children forever of the house of the Lord of this blessedness; and to have the Holy Spirit of our God continually witnessing with our spirits that we are children of God. So forever will this true Spirit abide and walk with us. The new life given at regeneration is but the beginning of blessings which He will impart daily and hourly; it is only the first of those gifts for men, which He, who led captivity captive and ascended up on high, hath received, and which are embraced in that one unspeakable gift of the Comforter, the Spirit of Truth, the Sanctifier. He is a Divine Companion to whom the new-born soul looks up with the trusting love of an infant in the first beginning of its spiritual life, when it looks up also to almost all about it; but it will look up to Him with far more lowly and childlike reverence, as well as with more fervent and clinging love, when it shall have become greater than a seraph; and for every want of the seraph, as well as of the infant soul, will the bounty of that one Spirit more than suffice. Our communion with Him may be like an unending happiness of childhood, led from blessing to blessing with an ever fresh and elastic enjoyment.

But neither can we tarry upon so attractive an anticipation as that of the light-hearted but pure rapture of the young Christian spirit, renewed and made everlasting in that world of spirits made perfect, in whom the joyousness of childhood shall blend forever with the vigor of youth and the wisdom of age, and the communion of the Spirit of God shall be the richness and the glory of them all.

We will inquire further of the offices of the Spirit in this earthly life.

He is the Comforter.

As such Christ continually designates Him in His last conversation with the sorrowing disciples. That we may attain to some idea of the value of His comforting, read the words of Christ, "Because I have said these things unto you, sorrow hath filled your heart. Nevertheless I tell you the truth; it is expedient for you that I go away; for if I go not away, the Comforter will not come unto you; but if I depart, I will send Him unto you." He saith also that this Comforter " shall abide with you forever."

He is forever with us—a Comforter so precious that it was gain, even for those chosen twelve that had of all the race of men enjoyed the personal intimacy of the Son of God, to suffer the sorrow of the loss of their Lord that they might enjoy that comforting. It seems wonderful to us; yet when we remember that their intercourse with Jesus was through the bodily senses, while the communion of the Spirit is an immediate contact and mingling of soul with soul, we may see that it must have a truth beyond all our thoughts. And that same Comforter still continues. "Blessed," saith He that sent the Comforter, "Blessed are they that mourn, for they shall be comforted." There is a happiness, often full and rich and seeming to fill all the capacity of a mortal, in some of the attachments of this earth; and when the object which had so filled the heart is taken away, the void that is left seems incurable. Yet even an earthly friend, coming then, may speak words of comfort; and if the heart has the Holy Spirit for its friend and seeks His consolation, He will come and fill all that void with His divine sympathy ; yea, and enlarge the heart and fill it still with comfort; and in the sense of the presence of so dear a Comforter, we love not less the friend that is gone, but we do love to welcome to the desolate heart the love to which the friend has gone. So tenderly and kindly " as one whom his mother comforteth," doth God comfort His people. But it is not only in the mighty sorrows, which overwhelm the soul and move the sympathy of those about us, that the sympathy of the Spirit sustains us. We may "walk in the comfort of the Holy Ghost." This life is full of little disquietudes, distresses and disappointments, and of those "own bitternesses" which the heart itself knows. These troubles are often of no little weight upon our hearts, but we cannot tell them to other men, or, if we did, perhaps they would despise them. Human spirits are of too coarse a texture to recognize the sense of those small but sometimes sharp griefs, which may be agony in a particular frame of some particular heart. But there is a sympathizing Spirit, which, while it is strong enough to sustain the soul under the most crushing affliction, is still delicate enough to administer the oil of kind consolation in cases where no other sympathy would know how to come. "He knoweth our frame—He remembereth that we are dust." Our greatest sorrows are trivial compared with the greatness of His nature; our least vexations are important in His all-pervading sympathy. So assiduously, by means of all our infantile griefs, does He knit our hearts to His, and when the grief is forgotten the tie abides forever.

The Spirit is not less a comforter that He is not seen. For in this, as in all His operations, He is not confined, as men are, to the cumbrous and imperfect media by which we communicate feeling. But He mingles freely with our emotions themselves, even in their first rising, and almost before ourselves are conscious of them ; as every grief or joy may go down more deeply into the soul, the communion of the Spirit accompanies it, and there abides a happy savor of His presence—a remembrance of rich, peaceful emotions, which He inspired, which will be a perpetual comfort.

The Holy Ghost is also,

THE INSTRUCTOR OF THOSE WITH WHOM HE COMMUNES.

He is the Spirit of truth as well as of comfort. Christ saith: "I will pray the Father and He shall give you another Comforter—even the Spirit of Truth;" and again, "the Comforter, which is the Holy Ghost, whom the Father will send in my name, He shall teach you all things and bring all things to your remembrance, whatsoever I have said unto you;" and still again, "when the Comforter is come, even the Spirit of Truth, He shall testify of me;" and again, "when

He, the Spirit of Truth, is come, He will guide you into all truth; for He shall not speak of Himself, but whatsoever He shall hear, that shall He speak; and He will show things to come."

The Spirit, then, is to be our teacher. But how? Not, as it would seem, by bringing to us new objective facts of the unseen world, but He is to take of the things of Christ and show them unto us; He is to bring all things to our remembrance. His work is in our own minds, to make them clear to discern those things which are spiritually discerned. He is to " open our eyes that we may behold wondrous things out of God's law." The soul enlightened by God's spirit is as one whose eyes are opened, so that he sees and understands God in His works and in His word. In this there is nothing unphilosophical or foreign to the ordinary duty of an instructor. It is but half the duty of a teacher to place the truth before his pupils. He must incite them to desire it; he must, by all means in his power, help them to fix their minds upon it, and to keep and make their minds vigorous and clear for the apprehension of it. But in all the teaching of human minds by human minds this is the most difficult and discouraging part of the process. We may call another mind to go with us in the unfolding of a truth of science, and so we run on, and the principle spreads itself in beautiful harmony before our minds, and we turn to see if our companion is delighted with it as we are; but his eye is like lead— vacancy looking into opacity, and we feel as if we had done a wrong to the bright truth. But the methods by which the Holy Spirit instructs are not so vain and mocking. He can come into the mind and soul itself and remove the incapacity there which excluded the truth. He does not labor all day long to show God to an unclean heart, but He makes the heart pure and then it sees God. And so the Spirit passes on in Its work, continually cleansing the heart and inciting it to long for the sight of God, and God continually reveals Himself, and the cleansed heart rejoices in the sight, and the Spirit rejoices with it, and so with the joy of the Holy Ghost it receives the word of the Lord. The Spirit enlarges the heart and it runs in the way of God's commandments.

Nearly allied to this enlightening and illuminating influence of the Spirit is what we may call,

THE INSPIRATION OF THE HOLY GHOST.

By this we mean that working of the Spirit by which He breathes into us those desires, those aspirations by which the mind is borne aloft to heavenly things. He produces the tempers of mind which are needful for our preparation for the gifts, which God is more ready to give than we to ask them. He shows us the poverty of our spirits, and says "Blessed are the poor in spirit, for theirs is the kingdom of God." He teaches us to be meek, and says "the meek shall inherit the earth." He incites to hunger and thirst after righteousness, and says "blessed are they which do hunger and thirst after righteousness for they shall be filled." Mark that—"filled with righteousness"! they shall be holy even as He is holy! He teaches us to be kind, and says "blessed are the merciful, for they shall obtain mercy," and we shall all need mercy.

But beyond and above all these specific blessings which we can name, we all feel that there is a higher and purer gift —a state of blessedness beyond the sight of the eye or the hearing of the ear, "which God hath prepared for them that love Him." We know not what that glory shall be. But we feel that it is our chief want, and so we groan within ourselves waiting for that full adoption, which shall make us fully "Sons of God." But how shall we ask for it? "We know not what to pray for as we ought." Our desires are ready to sink back again. But here, too, the Spirit helpeth our infirmity, inciting us still to cry unto God and inspiring in us that petition of the poor, hungering and thirsting soul, which knows its want, but does not know its supply, and so it cries to God with inarticulate groans for His own gift, and God, who knoweth the meaning of the Spirit, and what it is that will fill that longing which the Spirit hath inspired, shall supply our want. We "shall awake in His likeness and be satisfied."

But the instruction of the Spirit has a higher aim than the mere imparting of truth.

He is to Sanctify Us through the Truth.

"This is the will of God, even your sanctification." "God hath chosen you to salvation through sanctification of the spirit and belief of the truth." This sanctification, this "perfecting holiness in the fear of the Lord," is the end of all God's work with men. For that end Christ came and shed His blood, that His "blood might cleanse us from all sin," that by that blood of the covenant we might be sanctified. The same is the main use of truth in the mind of man—that through it he may be made true, may be sanctified—and so Christ prays to His Father after the Supper: "Sanctify them through Thy truth, Thy word is truth," and again, "for this cause I sanctify myself that they also might be sanctified through the truth." And this same end of making us holy is the labor of the Spirit in all His communing with us. He is himself called not only the Comforter and the Spirit of Truth, but most especially is He called the "Holy Spirit" the "Holy Ghost," and all His intercourse with us is holy intercourse. If we go into any unhallowed ways He will not go with us. The Holy Spirit is "hidden from us." But in all His operation, if He teaches us, it is that the holy truth may sanctify us; if He incites, it is to holy thoughts and endeavors; if He comforts, it is with holy consolation, telling of that pure abode, where God

Himself shall wipe all tears from their eyes—telling of the Father of the fatherless and the God of the widow. He always suggests holy thoughts, and a holy thought is in itself a thought of instruction and of comfort. For the mind dwelling holily upon holy things, is in the proper action of mind, and that action is its blessedness.

Such is the communion of the Holy Ghost. A Divine Spirit, a person of the Godhead, since Christ has died, abides continually with believers upon this earth, to comfort, to instruct and to sanctify them. He becomes the companion of their joy and of their sorrow, mingling His spirit with theirs, and leading them on with Him in the holy thoughts and emotions of which they may be capable. Wherever there is a single Christian heart, that heart is a dwelling place of the Holy Ghost. The Holy Ghost has been invited to take up His abode there, and has accepted the invitation, with its pledge that that soul will commune with Him. Thus hath He committed Him to that human soul, and come with His riches of spiritual blessing. How does it become men to receive such a guest? How in fact do men receive Him?

Brethren, grieve not the Spirit, that Spirit of Truth, which comes to instruct you, that Comforter, that Holy Spirit, by which ye are sanctified. But seek His companionship; draw near to Him. The communion of the Holy Ghost is the spiritual communion for which men were made. Christ died that we might enjoy it, and if we receive it, it is life from the dead to us; it is the Spirit which giveth life, the life of God. The grace of Jesus Christ and the love of the Father are always with them who believe, but the blessed spiritual presence that is with them is the Holy Spirit.

What a thing it is to be a human soul in this world of probation! The very Spirit of God bends to commune with us. He comes with treasures of blessing; those gifts which

Christ has received for men. He invites us to commune with Him, with Him who is so wise, and so mighty and so holy; and He promises to make us like Him, wise unto salvation, mighty through God, holy as our Father in heaven is holy.

Is it true? May we, who are so feeble, and so ignorant, and so wicked, may we have hourly communion with God's Holy Spirit? Yes, we may; our imagination is staggered at the thought, but so it is. There is none of us so weak or so sinful, that He does not invite us to walk with Him. And He will purify us from sin and fit us to stand before the great white throne. A little while is His presence here. There are a few days that we may enjoy His communion on earth if we have it, and there are a few days that we may seek it if we have it not. Shall not the time past suffice us to have wrought the will of the flesh? Henceforth may we have communion with the Holy Spirit of God. We shall need Him, His communion, His instruction, His comfort, His sanctification; that He may restore our souls, that He may lead in paths of righteousness. Doubt and danger are coming, temptation is coming, bereavement is coming, death is coming, eternity is coming. And we shall need Him. For He saith: "When thou passest through the waters, I will be with thee; and through the rivers, they shall not overflow thee," "Yea," would our soul answer, "Yea, though I walk through the valley of the shadow of death, I will fear no evil; for thou art with me; thy rod and thy staff they comfort me." Yes, there is no human soul but must say when he comes to die, "That, that is what I want, thy rod, thy staff." May it be ours now and forever!

XI.

THE GOOD SHEPHERD.

THE GOOD SHEPHERD.

Preached at the Installation of Rev. Joseph Collie, a first graduate of
Beloit College, in his pastorate of forty years at Delavan, Wis.

John x. 11 and 14.

I am the Good Shepherd.

In these words Jesus expresses the relation between Himself and His people.   They are words full of meaning to us,
but how much more full of meaning to the people of the East,
whom the continual observation and experience of life for
generation after generation, even from the time of righteous
Abel, had instructed in those ideas of pastoral care and lamb-
like trust, which were so fit to train souls for the reception
of the principles of the kingdom of heaven; to the people of
David, the shepherd of Bethlehem Judah, who sang that
song, "The Lord is my shepherd, I shall not want."   We
remember that they were "shepherds watching their flocks
by night," to whom the angel announced the birth of Christ
and who heard the song of the heavenly host.

And now Christ in the Temple announces Himself as the
Good Shepherd.

And thus He had been announced by His prophet of old—
(Isa. xl. 10, 11) "Behold, the Lord God will come with strong
hand, and His arm shall rule for Him; behold, His reward is
with Him and His work before Him.   He shall feed His
flock like a shepherd; He shall gather His lambs with His
arm, and carry them in His bosom, and shall gently lead those
that are with young."

He it was that "led His people like a flock, by the hand
of Moses and Aaron."   And He it is that leads them now by

pastors whom He hath ordained, realizing unto us, so far as we prepare ourselves by turning unto Him, His word by the mouth of His prophet: "Turn, O, backsliding children, and I will give you pastors according to mine own heart, which shall feed you with knowledge and understanding."

Thus, it hath pleased the Good Shepherd, not only to make them that come to Him lambs of His flock, but also to employ them in His own office of leading and feeding the flock.

Let us consider that system of pastors and flocks, which Christ has planned for the saving of the world; and first let us see the estimation in which Christ Himself held the office of the pastor.

"When they had dined, Jesus saith to Simon Peter, 'Simon, son of Jonas, lovest thou Me more than these?' He saith unto Him, 'Yea, Lord, thou knowest that I love Thee.' He saith unto him, 'Feed my lambs.'"

"He saith unto him again the second time, 'Simon, son of Jonas, lovest thou Me?' He saith unto Him, 'Yea, Lord, Thou knowest that I love Thee.' He saith unto him, 'Feed my sheep.'"

"He saith unto him the third time, 'Simon, son of Jonas, lovest thou Me?' Peter was grieved because He said unto him the third time, 'lovest thou Me?' and he said unto Him, 'Lord, Thou knowest all things, Thou knowest that I love Thee.' Jesus saith unto him, 'Feed my sheep.'"

The first, the second and the third duty of the lover of Christ is to feed the flock of Christ.

The true function of the man of God is that of a *pastor*— a shepherd.

It is an office constituted by Christ when He was on earth. It is one prepared by the Word when He made the worlds. The foundation of it is laid in the nature of man. In all ages of the world, in all religions of men, the spiritual guide has held a position of peculiar respect in the community. This respect has been paid to the office itself. The instinct of men clothes it with a sanctity which has been found to attract and to hold the veneration of men, even when they knew that the persons, who bore the sacred office, had nothing in their own character to entitle them to such a distinction; and what is all this but the practical assent of the souls of men to the belief that there is a sanctity and a truth which lies beyond the sphere of our senses, that man is made to receive from the lips of his fellow man the words of God, and needs those words of God, that he may live by them?

Our human nature looks for a shepherd, who may feed it with the bread of life. It recognizes that that bread must come down from heaven, but still it does not look for God to speak out of heaven. The children of Israel under Sinai, spoke only the general instinct of mankind when " they said unto Moses, speak thou with us and we will hear; but let not God speak with us, lest we die." The Lord said, "They have well said all that they have spoken." God did not make man to be awed into obedience by overpowering displays of His awful majesty, but to be gently won by a persuasion addressed to the heart. Therefore that He may win our love rather than conquer our awe, He speaks to our human hearts through human lips. Even when Himself would come, He came in fashion as a man.

Man's nature needs three authorities—the Prophet to teach the word of God, the Priest to offer our prayers acceptably to God, and the Magistrate to preside over the community of mankind. In the perfect state all these authorities reside in Christ alone, our Prophet, Priest and King. Now Christ retains the priesthood for Himself "abiding a priest continually," having once offered up Himself and now standing ever before the throne to present our prayers to God. All the legitimate authorities of civil magistrates are fragments of His kingship, and the prophet work of uttering the word of the Lord devolves upon the men whom He sets to be the pastors of His flock. Their office is distinctly marked in that map of human life which exists in the minds of men, lying aloof from every other occupation, holding the line where humanity borders upon Deity. He is a man of God, the body, mind and spirit of a man, yet if he be a true man of God, he has the Spirit of God dwelling in him, he has the mind of Christ, he is an ambassador of God.

It is indeed an honorable office; that respect in which the heart of man holds it, prevalent and potent as it has been, is, after all, but a faint shadow of the real dignity of the office, as it is measured by the dignity of the God whose ambassador the pastor is, by the worth of the soul to which he is sent, and by the importance of the message which he brings. Yet it is a most hopeful and true feeling in man. It is just and wholesome, so far as it regards and affects the pastor himself. It is a most just and necessary and saving feeling, in its relation and effect respecting members of the flock. As the kingdom of heaven is in its beginning but as the grain of mustard seed, so there is an untold importance in those little things, by which grace first springs and continually grows in the heart.

As Christ, the Shepherd Lamb, hath appointed that His elect be gathered into flocks, and placeth pastors over them, there is no feeling so appropriate to that relation as an affectionate regard on the part of each Christian for his pastor. The mind, which loves to criticise the minister, is in an unhealthful and unchristian attitude, but when you hear one say "our pastor," you recognize a soul in which is the true home feeling of the house of God, a soul which, thus "speaking the truth in love," is in the way of growing "up into Him in all things which is the head, even Christ." There is almost nothing so essential to the health and growth of a church, of a flock of Christ, as that it have a shepherd, a pastor, who shall not be a mere sojourner, but who shall be theirs and they his, bound together by home feelings, by responsibilities and cares mutual and common: that the pastor should be received and welcomed and cherished by the generous love and confidence of the flock, a love and confidence essential to him, but even more essential to them; and that he, feeling the continual pressure of that confidence, should watch over their souls and the souls of their children, as one that must give account. Such an one the apostle exhorts the church to obey, that he may give that account "with joy and not with grief, for that is unprofitable for you."

The office of a pastor is a fearful office. It is an office fearful to assume and an office fearful to refuse. "We are," says Paul, "unto God a sweet savor of Christ, in them that are saved and in them that perish; to the one the savor of death unto death, and to the other the savor of life unto life, and," it is well added by the apostle, "who is sufficient for these things?" What man shall dare to go to men with those words which, if they be not unto life must be unto death? What man? What strongest and wisest of men shall undertake such a commission? Who shall dare to assume it? Let no man so confide in his own strength, as to presume to do the work of God. But who shall dare to refuse it? "We have this treasure in earthen vessels, that the excellency of the power may be of God and not of us." And who shall so magnify the importance of his own weakness, as to presume that it can make void the power of God? Therefore, let every man say humbly, "Lord, what wilt Thou have me to do?" assured that God can cause the lips of a child to be touched with a live coal from off his altar. And have we marked those words of Paul: "We are as a sweet savor unto God in them that are saved and in them that perish." Even in them that perish the faithful minister of Christ is a sweet savor unto God. He hath done his duty. He has spoken the truth in love; and so the work of love is wrought in his own heart. Therefore,

The Office of a Pastor is a Blessed Office.

"If a man desire the office of a bishop he desireth a good work." Every proper employment of men has a blessing in it, in that its ordinary duties may be done as unto God, who is served and honored by the fidelity of men in all the duties and labors of which it has pleased Him to make up the life of man. But to make the saving of souls and their training for heaven, the direct and ordinary business and employment of every-day life, that seems like life. To be the bearer of the messages of an eternal God to immortal souls, is not that an exalted office? To bear to them that sit in darkness the message that God is light, to bring the words of eternal life to souls that were in the shadow of death, is not that a joyful errand? And then to be the pastor of the flock of God, to be His chosen servant in leading them, as He led His people of old, "like a flock, by the hand of Moses and Aaron," is there, or can there be, anything in all the range of human employment, so desirable for a man, who has but one life to live before he passes into the presence of the "Good Shepherd"? For this life, so blessed in its course, is surprisingly blessed in its end; for "when the chief Shepherd shall appear he shall receive a crown of glory that fadeth not away."

If such is the calling of the pastor, so honorable, so blessed, so solemn as is that work of him that watcheth for souls, as one that must give account to God, who made this world for the saving of souls, to Christ that died for souls, account for souls whose eternal life or death is trembling in the balance; if all this is so, "what manner of person ought the pastor to be in all holy conversation and godliness?" How should the man of God flee the snares of this world

" and follow after righteousness, godliness, faith, love, patience, meekness, fighting the good fight of faith, and laying hold on eternal life !"

We have a habit of thinking that such passages are for ministers, that they are the pastors, the shepherds. And certainly the responsibility of the pastor's duty has not been overrated. But is it in truth quite so diverse from the duties of all other men as we sometimes seem to assume? If the pastor does stand upon the line between humanity and Deity, is there, between that line and the position of us who are in other callings, "a great gulf fixed"? I fear that, while we have been more just to him, we have suffered ourselves to fall back from our station. This care of souls devolves upon other men as well as upon the minister of a church, and so that charge of Jesus, " Feed my sheep, feed my lambs," passes on to us.

Some of us are teachers or hold some charge in church or state, and there is not one who has not some influence upon some soul or souls for which he must give account. Some are parents, and each father in his own family is more a representative of Christ than even the pastor of a church, for he holds in some measure the triple office of teacher, of ruler, and even of priest. There is no one in all the community who is not his brother's keeper, and there is no one who is not influenced by his brother. We bear, each one to every other, something of the relation of the pastor and something of the relation of the flock. Therefore it is fit that the " elders feed the flock of God—not as being lords over God's heritage, but being ensamples to the flock; likewise that the younger submit themselves to the elder; yea, that all be subject one to another, and be clothed with humility; for God resisteth the proud but giveth grace to the humble."

So, throughout all the society of man, are these relations

of the flock to the pastor, and of the pastor to the flock, woven back and forth, that so every man may stand in manifold ways in each of the relations, and all should help all, and receive help from all, in the nurture for heaven.

Therefore, to all the intercourse of each one of us with every other one applies that charge of the great Shepherd, " Feed my sheep."

Moreover, when we separate ourselves from our fellowmen we do not escape from the charge of souls. When you go by yourself to your study, to your office, to your counting room, to your field, there goes with you a soul whose shepherd you are—a soul for which Christ died and which He charges you to keep. For that one soul no other man can have such a responsibility as rests upon you. You are to it as prophet to apply to it the words of Christ, as king to direct all its acting, as priest to lay it as a living sacrifice wholly upon the altar of God. Here, in this mysterious but conscious power over ourselves, for good or for evil, lies the real fearfulness and wonderfulness of the nature of man. Great and manifold as is the outer world, all that man sees without him is not more great, more manifold, more marvelous, than the world which is within him; those thronging thoughts, those rushing passions, those emotions, various and many as the winds, those mines of truth, those wastes of ignorance, those gulfs of error, those perils and those hopes, those tempters and those helpers, and among them all there is a soul to be saved, and you are the shepherd of that soul.

Thus, even into the recesses of his own heart, the duty of the pastor and the dependence of the flock goes with every man. As a magnet may be divided into a hundred pieces, and every one shall be a perfect magnet, with its positive and its negative pole, so even in every single human soul, we find still the shepherd and the sheep, and the law of Christ. It is a care which may not be evaded or transferred.

As we follow these thoughts upward, they lead us to a great mystery. We speak concerning Christ and the church. That pastorship which we find so prominent in the pale of an individual soul, is still more perfect in that more perfect One, which is made up of all humanity. Mankind was one. That one was broken by the fall. Christ comes to make us one again. He is our Shepherd. We are " the people of His pasture, and the sheep of His hand." Yet, He is not merely a Shepherd. The " Son of God " becomes " Son of Man." The Shepherd Himself becomes a "Lamb of God." Let us draw nigh and behold this great sight, the Shepherd-Lamb.

We are accustomed to distinguish two uses of the word "lamb" in the scripture; one regarding the lamb as the object of care, and the other as the offering for a sacrifice. Perhaps we ought not so to distinguish them, but each to regard ourselves, in relation to God, at once as objects of His care and as whole burnt offerings upon His altar. So the Son, coming to rescue us, laid hold upon our nature; He became of us, became not so much a man, as Man, identifying Himself with the whole human race, constituting " one new man, one whole of humanity, of which He was the Whole, and each individual that should believe on Him should be a member. Taking, then, our common humanity into His own heart, He that was thus become the whole of ourselves, laid Himself upon the altar of God's justice, " was brought as a Lamb to the slaughter, and as a sheep before her shearers is dumb, so He opened not His mouth." Thus was He " the Lamb of God taking away the sins of the world," and thus did He become " the Author of eternal salvation unto all that obey Him." Thus, even by offering Himself as a Lamb, did He become a Captain of salvation—become the Shepherd of the flock. He is " the Good Shepherd; the Good Shepherd giveth His life for the sheep."

In the Book of the Revelation, the offices of the Lamb and of the Shepherd are blended in forms of such truth to the soul that we never think of any incongruity in the picture, but rather recognize in it the truest truth. We read, "They shall hunger no more, neither thirst any more; neither shall the sun light on them nor any heat; for the Lamb which is in the midst of the throne shall feed them, and shall lead them unto living fountains of water; and God shall wipe away all tears from their eyes." And again, "I looked, and, lo, a Lamb stood on the Mount Sion, and with Him an hundred and forty-four thousand having His Father's name written in their foreheads; these are they which follow the Lamb whithersoever He goeth."

So He is truly "Son of Man," in that He not only comes to be our leader, a guide as a shepherd, but He comes to be as ourselves, He becomes one of the flock, and that not one proud and high in station, but He becomes a Lamb. For truly the Lamb, in all its meekness and dependence, is the proper expression for the true present and the permanent condition and attitude of mankind as a race. Here on this earth, in a little degree and for a little season, one becomes the shepherd of others. But such a shepherd is all the while more a lamb than a shepherd. The greater his duty of care for others, so much the greater is his need of help and guidance and grace for himself, and in a little time all these pastorships shall cease, and all sanctified humanity together will be one as a lamb in the bosom of the Father. So it was meet that He who in Himself represents the whole of humanity should be styled the Lamb.

The Lamb of God says to the Father, "For their sake I sanctify myself, that they all may be sanctified through the truth."

Shall we, led by the word of God, go higher still and consider how, as in all humanity, and as in every soul of man, there is that double character of direction and obedience, of pastor and lamb, of fatherly care and filial dependence, so even in the Godhead itself, in whose image man was made, exists a like mysterious relation. Here we have the Father and the Son, a mystery to us, but not more a mystery than the facts of which we are most familiarly conscious in our own natures.

"The Word was in the beginning with God and the Word was God." "Christ Jesus, being in the form of God, thought it not robbery to be equal with God." And yet He saith, "the Son can do nothing of Himself, but what He seeth the Father do; for what things soever He doeth, these doeth the Son likewise." "I can of mine own self do nothing. As I hear, I judge; and my judgment is just; because I seek not mine own will, but the will of the Father which hath sent me."

So we see that before all creation there existed the type of these earthly ties that are before us to-day. There was a Father and there was a Son, and, so long ago as the foundation of the earth was laid, there was a Lamb, the representative in the Godhead of the new race of babes and sucklings out of whose mouth God was ordaining strength. So long ago, the fall and rising again of that race was present in the Divine mind, and therefore there was in the bosom of the Father "a Lamb slain from the foundation of the world."

In the fulness of time the Lamb came and was slain, for our sakes sanctifying Himself, and praying for all that should believe on Him, that all might be one—"As thou, Father, art in me, and I in thee, that they also may be one in us; and the glory which Thou gavest me, I have given them; that they may be one, even as we are one, I in them, and Thou in me, that they may be made perfect in one, and that the world may know that Thou hast sent me, and hast loved them as Thou hast loved me." There is the fold to which the Good Shepherd by all these earthly pastorships, would lead His flock. When a soul has believed in Christ it is dead, and its life is hid with Christ in God. There it is, one with the Lamb, folded in the bosom of the Father, and "when He who is our life shall appear, then shall it also appear with Him in glory."

There were the souls of all that should believe on Him already present in His thought and in His heart from the beginning, even when "God chose us in Him before the foundation of the world." Even then He loved us and gave Himself for us, first loving us. How the tenderness of that heart, which from the beginning had loved the souls that were to be, beamed forth when Himself was on earth, the tenant of a human heart, clasping those souls closely to His own heart of hearts. Hear Him as He sent forth His twelve disciples to seek the lost sheep. "He that receiveth you receiveth me, and he that receiveth me receiveth Him that sent me. He that receiveth a prophet in the name of a prophet shall receive a prophet's reward; and he that receiveth a righteous man in the name of a righteous man shall receive a righteous man's reward." But now, as He closes, see how the divine tenderness of that soul, that had waited so long, gushes forth—"And whosoever shall give to drink unto one of these little ones a cup of cold water only in the name of a disciple, verily I say unto you, he shall in no wise lose his reward." "These little ones;" men do not love so to be styled; they think themselves experienced and strong and wise. It is the tenderness of Him that was from the beginning, looking with an eternal and an infinite love upon souls that were just commencing that immortality, which they were to spend in Him, in His own everlasting blessedness in the bosom of His Father.

In His love He came and took our nature, and His aim is to raise us to His joy. And what is His joy? It was not enough for Him to rest there in the bosom of the Father, in the peace of a Lamb, forever. It is the joy of a pure spirit to communicate joy. The Lamb must also become a shepherd, and for that joy set before Him He endured the cross. And the like joy He offers, as we have seen, to all His flock—that even the "lambs," His "little ones," may be shepherds also, and may learn how much more blessed it is to give than to receive. So our life is filled with these relations of care and and of dependence, that we may in all things learn to put on Christ. And, in that great judgment day, what shall be the test by which the sheep shall be distinguished from the goats? What else than that they have been found faithful as shepherds? "The righteous shall answer Him saying, 'When saw we Thee a-hungered and fed Thee? or thirsty and gave Thee drink?' And the King shall answer and say unto them, 'Verily, I say unto you, inasmuch as ye have done it unto one of the least of these my brethren, ye have done it unto me.'" Ah! that is the assurance which makes it heaven itself, even here, to feed the lambs of Christ. We are doing it to Him. We are doing it to Christ. Yea, even we, poor lambs of the flock, are permitted to satisfy the longing soul of the good shepherd himself.

So let us learn to follow Christ, and so may "the God of peace that brought again from the dead our Lord Jesus, that great Shepherd of the sheep, through the blood of the everlasting covenant, make you," you that take to-day the solemn office of pastor, and all of us in our little pastorships, "perfect in every good work to do His will; working in you that which is well pleasing in His sight, through Jesus Christ, to whom be glory for ever and ever. Amen."

With what shall we close more fitly than with that injunction with which Jesus closed His charge to Simon Peter: "Follow thou me;" for as the redeemed shall follow the Lamb whithersoever He goeth, even so in this kingdom of heaven begun below, our charge is to "follow the Lamb," follow Him first in being a Lamb and then follow Him in being a shepherd, a pastor. In this world there is a broad line between the master and the servant, the leader and the led. "But it shall not be so among you." "Whosoever of you will be chiefest, shall be servant of all." Here is the fault of all our earthly authorities. No one of them is perfectly a ruler, because no one of them is perfectly a servant. But Jesus is fully a shepherd exactly because He is perfectly a Lamb. Therefore He knoweth His sheep and is known of His and they follow Him, because He is a Lamb as well as a Shepherd. So let each of us, in all our pastorships, be fully a lamb that he may be truly a shepherd, following the Lamb—in His humility, in His love, in His devotion, in His care, as He goeth about doing good, as He Himself sought strength from the Father; and follow Him in His labor, and in His prayers, and in the duty of the lamb and in the care of the shepherd, laying ourselves like Him upon the altar of God, especially realizing like Him at once the devotion of the lamb and the care of the Good Shepherd in that offering Himself to the justice of God for the salvation of man, that so when the Chief Shepherd shall appear, we each may enter into the joy of our Lord.

XII.

THE VICTORY OF FAITH.

THE VICTORY OF FAITH.

(Baccalaureate sermon, given, by request of President Chapin, at the graduation of the class of 1865 from Beloit College.)

I John v. 5.

Who is he that overcometh the world, but he that believeth that Jesus is the Son of God?

Life is commonly represented as a warfare. It is so in the common speech of man; for man sees it and feels it continually about him and within him. It is so in the Word of God; for as the veil is drawn away, the human soul is seen, not only as a field, in which passions are striving with principles, but as an infant, over whose fate mighty spirits of light and of darkness are waging fearful battle.

The parties, as they stand in our text, are the human soul and " the world. " The soul, full of convictions of truth and duty, of law and right and honor, the home of " thoughts which wander through eternity," of aspirations which rise to grandeur and nobility of being; and on the other hand "the world," the general name for all those temptations, without and within, which allure it to forget its immortality and its perfectness, and to sink to meanness, and selfishness or lust.

There are few sights under heaven more full of shining promise than the attitude, the common attitude, of a young man just ready to enter the field of active life. Such high enthusiasms! Such generous resolves! He has spent the time of his education in conversing with the great and the true men of all time. He has stored his mind and his heart with great principles; and he means that his life, whether it be more or less conspicuous, shall be at least a true life. So he goes forth, but he finds a cold and barren world, and hunger comes, and hearts about him are stone; and then the tempter shows him some compliance by which these stones may be made bread, and he yields, and, like Esau, "for a morsel of meat he sells his birthright." Another meets some success, and finds himself upon a pinnacle of the temple, and forgets the steadfast laws of God, and in his pride casts himself forth in forbidden ranges of thought or of act, and so he falls, a shattered mind, a mangled soul, upon the rocks of ruin. A third has been enticed by the charm of power—the glory of kingdoms—and, for political success, his soul has fallen down and worshiped the devil.

So, one after another, we may almost say rank after rank, the young men who commence life, resolved that the one life they have to live shall be worth the living, sink from their heroism. Oh! if we could see a generation, if we could see but one class of young men, who should carry on to the noon and through to the evening of life, the rich promise of the morning! And why may we not? Why should "the world" continually overcome the young men who commenced with the high consciousness of sons of God? Is all this enthusiasm of youth a mockery of some lying spirit? or is there "a path of life" in which a man may go, still upward, still onward, until at the end of his course he shall hear the words "well done," and pass from the tuition of time into the fruition of eternity? Is it necessary that all our goodness should be "like the morning cloud and the early dew"?

Our text and all this glorious word of God declare that "there is a victory which overcometh the world." And the instrument of this victory we are told is "faith." If there be such a victory, and if the instrument of that victory be within the grasp of man, we cannot do better with this hour than to inquire respecting that faith and that victory.

What, then, shall be the faith which can raise man above the power of these temptations and debasements of the passing world? Evidently it must be a strong and living realization that there are things greater and better than these, that there is a sphere of things unseen and eternal, to which the soul belongs more truly than it belongs to this world; that these—our ideas of beauty and purity and glory—are reflections truly cast upon our minds from that better sphere, and that these hopes, which men have cherished so persistently through so many ages of night, are gleams of true light let in from the gates of heaven. The faith which shall give us strength, must be one which will give "substance to things hoped for, and evidence to things not seen."

If, then, the word of God which is in our hands, or the word of God which is in our hearts, be true, there must be certain grand realizations, which, entering into the heart of man, will make him great and strong for victory over the world. What are those "powers of the world to come," (Heb. vi. 5), those great beliefs, through which the Spirit giveth a son of man power to become a son of God? In what shall a man believe?

I. LET US BELIEVE IN GOD.

Let there enter into the depth of our being the persuasion, that there is, pervading all this system of things, a Spiritual Presence and Power, living from eternity; searching, ruling, guiding, judging all; searching and knowing us, our paths, our lying down, and all our ways; a mighty God, a holy God, a true God, a loving God.

Let the mind feed upon so great a thought, and can it be a little mind again? let it feed upon so high a thought, and can it be a low mind again? on so pure a thought, and can it be corrupt again? on so dear a thought, and will it ever hate again? Let God be in all our thoughts.

II.   LET US BELIEVE IN MAN.

Yesterday there was born, upon this lower earth, a child that is not of the earth.   He was born feeble as infancy, but he is a child of God; and to-day he is the emperor of earth.   The beasts of the field, the wind, the water and the fire are his servants.   The awful powers of nature obey him, the sun paints his portrait, and the lightning does his errands over the continent and under the ocean.   Yesterday he knew nothing; to-day his thoughts search the foundations of the earth and walk among the constellations.   He weighs the planets and measures the distances of the stars.   The ray, which left its star a million years before he was born, cannot mock his infancy, for it finds him able to tell the journal of its voyage through space.   Though born in time, he is born into eternity.   And when the heavens shall wax old and be changed as a vesture, he shall continue.   His thoughts, that wander now through eternity, take hold upon the eternity, which his Father inhabits.

And all this science is but the preparation for his wisdom.   The heavens and the earth tell him a knowledge which they themselves know not.   They tell him of God; and when that tuition is passed, they, the teaching earth and heavens, shall pass away, and leave their pupil in the presence, in the wrath, or in the bosom of God.

In this ability of man to read the meaning of God's works, to understand God's thoughts and to respond to His emotion, we discern the true nobility of man.   Nature, though she wear the livery of a monarch, is but a mute servant, bearing in her fragrant bosom a letter from the King to the King's son, and the mind that can read and the soul that can answer that letter, is the son of the King.

And so we come to the third element which makes the system of saving faith complete.   Believing in God, and believing in man, let us believe also,

III.   IN THE COMMUNION OF GOD WITH MAN.

The alliance of the human nature with the Divine, the dwelling of the Divine with the human; the passing of the human into the Divine, and the union of the two in one nature, are matters incomprehensible to our philosophy, just as are the highest forms of all truth.   It would be very miserable if they were not, if we were already, in our infancy, come to the answer to all our questions, to the limit of our knowledge.   If it were so, it would be time to lie down and die.   But, in these great questions, with which God has filled the soul, we have wrapped the promise of an immortality, in which a purified mind shall, in the light of God, mount up with eagle wing into higher, newer, purer, holier truth forever.   And this principle of the original oneness, of the continued conversation, and of the future new at-one-ment of the human and the Divine nature, is a conviction which has always filled the human mind.

Heathen fables represent human heroes as sons of gods, and gods as coming down to walk with men, entering into their wars and their labors, their sorrows and joys, and again they represent men as going to dwell among gods and to be gods; and heathen philosophies conceive that man's nature is a spark from the Divine, shining here for a little time and destined to be lost in the eternal light again.

What shall we say of all this conviction of the soul of man—this clear persuasion, hardly ruffled by the incapacity of the mind to answer the questions which it involves? What can we say less than that here we have the Spirit of God witnessing with the spirit of man, testifying that man is the son of God.

To this son of God, conscious of his birthright and discontented here in the far country, feeding swine, comes the summons of our text, "Who is he that overcometh but he

that believeth that Jesus Christ is the Son of God?" It is
the Messenger of the covenant, saying, "I am the Way."

Man's nature is so made that it never could and never can
be satisfied, with anything less than the recognition of its
sonship to God; and the statement that the "fulness of the God·
head dwelleth bodily in the man Christ Jesus," only presents
before us in definite form, the great hope, which mankind
never would let go, and which has sustained man through
his long debasement, the hope that "the creature itself also
shall be delivered from the bondage of corruption into the
glorious liberty of the children of God."

Jesus Christ knew better than any Epicurean or Sadducee
could know, that the doctrine of the sonship of man involved
questions which man's mind cannot answer, and yet He knew
better than Plato or Gamaliel could know, that that was
the truth by which man must come to God. And so He says,
with that wonderful calm authority, with which He was accustomed to speak out of the heart of God into the heart of man,
"None knoweth who the Son is but the Father, and who the
Father is but the Son, and he to whom the Son will reveal
Him."

The doctrine of the Trinity is presented in the Word of
God, not because man is able to comprehend it, nor yet for
the purpose of perplexing our minds with an enigma, but
because, in that doctrine, necessarily, like all heavenly things,
stretching off beyond our horizon, lies the power which the
Spirit uses to save us.

Our souls, by their very nature, want nothing less than
the communion and the union of man, man like ourselves,
very man of very man, with God, the infinite and the perfect God, very God of very God. When man let go of God
by sin, man fell; and what a fall! How shattered the
nature is, from that day to this. For its salvation it must
come back to the Father again. And how shall it come back

to God? The way, which the perfect wisdom has chosen, is the appearance of God among us as the Son, wearing our nature that he may draw us back to the Father's bosom. Now, what by the felt necessities of our nature must such a mediator be? Let any man ask his own soul if it is not necessary that such a mediator be genuinely, honestly, fully man, otherwise he could not lay hold of our nature. Again let him ask his soul if it is not necessary that such a mediator be genuinely, honestly and fully God, that he may bring us with him "into the bosom of the Father."

That, nothing less than that, can be our glad tidings of great joy, the fellowship of man with the Father and with His Son Jesus Christ, the fulness of the light of God.

To that fact, that Jesus is the Son of God; that union in Christ and through Christ, of man and God, "there are three that bear record in heaven, the Father, the Son and the Holy Ghost." What simple wonders there may be in God; what manifold unity in the Infinite One, we cannot know. Three persons, three manifestations, are revealed to us because immediately concerned in our salvation. Our minds need to know God as the Father from whom come our own beings and all that blesses us, to whom we may kneel in thankfulness and praise and prayer; and we need also to know God as the Son. God is the All in All; His nature is too infinite to be bounded and excluded by our own. If we truly kneel, He not only looks down upon us with a Father's forgiveness and love, but He also kneels with us with a son's affection and contrition, and His prayer goes up with and in ours; not that, but ours in His. Also, we want to know God as the Spirit—a holy, pure and perfect Spirit, mingling with our spirits, shedding the love of God abroad in our hearts, renewing, comforting, instructing and sanctifying us.

In these three aspects of Father, Son, and Spirit is presented the testimony of heaven to the plan of our salvation;

the Fatherly bounty giving us all things and withholding not His own Son for our salvation; the Son taking our nature and dying among us and for us, and the Holy Spirit manifesting His presence in our own souls. And this heavenly testimony is answered by a threefold testimony on earth: " The Spirit and the water and the blood." The spirit of man, feeling the communion of the Spirit of God, feeling its own wants met by this plan of salvation, and rising to newness of life as the Spirit of God applies to it the saving touch of God; and the water, the purifying of the nature of man, under the influence of this sense of salvation by Christ's blood, as applied by the sanctifying Spirit, is a testimony in the heart and life of every true believer, and in the history of mankind, that Jesus is the Son of God, and to the restoration of the fellowship of man with God.

And then the blood; Christ beareth not the cross alone. From the beginning of time till now there has been passing through the history of the world a procession of witnesses who have by their blood set to their seals that God is true in His great and precious promises; to faith as the substance of things hoped for and the evidence of things not seen. How grand and inspiring, as well as pathetic, is the view of that " cloud of witnesses" summoned in the Epistle to the Hebrews. And what witnesses they are!

The first witness is Abel. And what testimony can righteous Abel give to the victory of faith? We see him lying beside the altar of his accepted sacrifice, slain, murdered because his sacrifice was accepted. Is that victory, and will it assure our faith? It would not, it could not, unless there were in our natures a chord answering to the faith of Abel. But because there is such a chord in human nature, we see in his death a higher testimony than that of any earthly success. As one who looks upon the face of a first born son, early at rest, and sees in those features so still, so calm, so purely white, not death but the better life; not trouble and sorrow, but the calm fulness of joy and peace in the bosom of a Father able to comfort, so humanity sees in her righteous Abel, sleeping beside the accepted altar, while the murderer stands haggard and remorseful over him, the testimony that death may be the gate of life and that the true answer to our prayers lieth within the veil, and she assures herself that truth is victory. So the procession passes on; the conquerors, who had tokens of victory here, "who through faith subdued kingdoms, wrought righteousness, obtained promises, stopped the mouths of lions, turned to flight the armies of the aliens;" and the other class, to whom the higher reverence of man has given the name of martyrs, "who were tortured, not accepting deliverance, that they might obtain a better resurrection; who were stoned, sawn asunder, tempted, slain with the sword." These are they that bear witness on earth, "not with water only but with water and blood." "These all, having obtained a good report through faith, received not the promise; God having provided some better thing for us, that they without us should not be made perfect."

For Jesus and the martyrs testify that not only in the coming life, but also in this world, shall the promises of God be fulfilled. All their work and all their testimony is a part of God's fulfilling of great and precious promises for mankind. They testify to suffering and fallen man that his Redeemer liveth, and shall stand in the latter day upon the earth. The work, to which Abel gave his early blood, went on in sorrowful victory till the Apostles saw Him that was "the Desire of all nations." But the Apostles died and left the promises of God promises still. What would they, as well as the prophets and kings of old, have given to see the days that we see? And yet these days of ours, rich as they are in fulfillment, are yet more, far more, rich in promise. We shall see greater things than these. And if His work appears so great about us, how shall His glory appear to our children? Yes, and to all those witnesses also, for they are not dead. The God of Abraham is the God of the living.

" Wherefore seeing we also are compassed about with so great a cloud of witnesses, let us lay aside every weight, and the sin which doth so easily beset us, and run with patience the race that is set before us, looking unto Jesus, the author and the finisher of our faith."

In our own day we have seen a great battle in the war for the law of God and the liberty of man.   Both were trampled upon in our own land, and when the conscience of our nation was moved, the oppressors felt the protest and, in their madness, though no man lifted hand against them, they made war upon their country. They, too, bore a standard of liberty— the liberty of man to enslave his brother; and of law—the law of man's despotism against God's law of liberty. We loved peace and we loved our brethren, and we tried to defend our land without disturbing the old order of things. But that was not God's plan. It was a "great day of the Lord Almighty." And at last we heard the oracle which heaven and earth were telling us, and called forth the chained powers. Casting ourselves upon the eternal laws of God and the rights of man, we proclaimed liberty, and we found that we had great allies. The bondmen rose in armies and proved themselves men; our own souls, resting at last upon firmer ground, grasping at last great truths, were mighty; and God wrought mightily for us. Though the contest, while it was on us, seemed weary and long, now that it is passing away, how swift, as well as how vast it appears. In one hour such greatness brought to naught!

And, now, what a world appears ! We come forth like Noah from the deluge. The nation restored ; slavery swept away ; the sunlight filling all the West ; black clouds rolling away, and such a rainbow on them as the world never saw before. And as that rainbow shines, how the nations break forth into song. Where are the birds that in the day of storm hid themselves timorously among the branches? Where are those that flew screaming away? Where are those that sat upon the left-hand hollow oak, boding disaster? They are joining the hymn. And let them sing. For the victory is for them as well as for us. "While we were yet sinners Christ died for us." "We reap the fruits of the labors and deaths of martyr men and peoples of old, and it shall be blessed if other peoples, too, shall enjoy the blessings of our deliverance."

But what a new earth we have; if henceforward these great powers of liberty and law, these convictions of the rights of God and the rights of man, that have been so at war, shall work together in building up that kingdom, and greatness of the kingdom under the whole heaven, which "is given to the people of the saints of the Most High."

Shall we not, then, accept with reverent hope those proofs that the promises of God are sure, and, as sons of God, press on toward the realization of that great hope, that the creation itself shall be delivered from the bondage of corruption into the liberty of the glory of the children of God?

YOUNG GENTLEMEN OF THE GRADUATING CLASS:

In such a day of great things the Father has given you your education. Into such a day of great things He is ushering you at its close. You are not what you were when you came here, and the world is not what it was. Life is not what it was. God has been teaching you and all men great things, deep things, high things. The great crises, through which nations have passed, have prepared generations for great achievements. What shall be after such a crisis as this, bringing such a nation forth into such a victory? Among

what men are you to stand and work?   What themes shall
fill the minds of your generation?   What great thoughts
of heart shall rise and prevail among them?   What material
and civil and moral greatness shall there be upon this soil
and on all this round world before you are gone.

For many things every day do we bless the good Lord
that hath planted and cherished this College, and among them
not the least is this : that He planted it in such a time and
land as this, so that it may take its place among the instrumentalities for building up the new and better order of things.
As we read the records of Abel and the faithful ones of old,
we remember that there is also a new record like unto these,
of those who willingly offered themselves for the right, and
so are among the bright cloud of witnesses; and we are most
thankful that so many sons of Beloit are among them who
have been true to country, to man, and to God.

Among those witnesses your class is not unrepresented.
More have gone into the field than are with you to-day. Some
have returned, some will return, and some return no more.
You recall especially one who joined you early and was with
you long. Edward Barber came here with an honest heart to prepare for life.   He sought with you the wisdom of this world,
but especially here he learned to look to Jesus as his Author and
Finisher of Faith.   He loved his classmates, he loved his
studies, he loved the College; but he thought that his duty
called him away.   In no fever of excitement or flush of ambition, but in the dark hour, because it was so dark, he felt, as
he wrote, "an imperative call to delay no longer the assistance which friends and brothers, already wearied and almost
discouraged by long and apparently unavailing labors in the
field, needed."   And so he went, that heart so brave and
patient and true—true to do and dare and suffer.   When at
last, worn by long disease, far from classmates and from home,
his mind wandered before it took its flight, he fancied that

he was here again with us.   It was not to be.   His education
was finished.   He was called to the commencement of a higher
life.   But in that higher life, how thankfully does he revisit
these scenes, remembering that here Jesus was to him the
"Author" as he is there the "Finisher of his faith."   And so
he is added to "our cloud of witnesses."   Let it not be in vain
for us that such have lived and died.   But let us, too, lay hold
of that great faith that overcometh the world.   "Jesus Christ
is the Son of God."   "He giveth us power to become sons
of God." Claim the promise and in His strength may you have
the victory.   Our prayer for you is that you may be true to
God, true to man, true to the fellowship of God and men ;
that in that faith ye may overcome the world, and that to
each of you may be fulfilled that promise : "To him that
overcometh, will I grant to sit with me in my throne, even
as I also overcame and am set down with my Father in His
throne

XIII.

THE WORD AND THE SEED.

THE WORD AND THE SEED.

Preached in the First Congregational Church in Beloit, June 30th, 1872, at the time of the twenty-fifth anniversary of the founding of Beloit College.

Mark iv. 26.

And He said, so is the kingdom of God, as if a man should cast seed into the ground.

Christ was in a boat by the beach of the Sea of Galilee. His audience were upon the shore, and His discourse to them repeated and explained the parables, which the shores of the Sea of Galilee had been setting forth to their cultivators, ever since the first "sower went forth to sow" upon them. He pointed to the brown hillsides, on which the sowers were passing to and fro, and He gave them the parable of "the sower," to illustrate the minds that receive the truth; and now this of the seed as committed to the fostering care of the earth, showing how the kingdom of God comes, and how little, and yet how responsible, is the part which man has in the work of God and the coming of His kingdom.

Those men on the shore were looking for the kingdom of God. For had not the old prophet told of a Prince that was to reign in righteousness? And had not John the Baptist lifted up his voice in the wilderness, saying that the kingdom of heaven was at hand? And Jesus, Himself, had come into Galilee preaching the gospel of "the kingdom of God, and saying, The time is fulfilled, and the kingdom of God is at hand." That was His proclamation, and when those men on the bank heard Him say, "so is the kingdom of God," they were intent to hear how it is. "So is the kingdom of God, as if a man should cast seed into the ground, and should sleep and rise, night and day, and the seed should spring and grow up, he knoweth not how." The kingdom of God is to come in every heart and in all the world as the kingdom of summer comes in the land. When the sower went forth to sow, all the fields upon the plain of Gennesaret, and upon the hills which looked over the plain, were brown and bare; but the sower went forth to sow, and returned to his home, leaving the fields still brown; but as he slept there rose from these fields an army, with millions of spears, and now, before the harvest, how the broad fields were waving with the banners of an empire.

Like that, then, shall be the coming of the kingdom, so silent, so hidden, so gentle, so mighty, so victorious, so glorious.

And the secret power of it all lies in something which is, for the world of mind, what the vital seed is for the soil of the field. What is that? Christ tells in another parable: The seed is the word; the field is the world.

A word and a seed; they are the two parallel condensations of power which God has made in His physical and in His moral world. He, Himself, takes the mustard seed as His illustration to those people on the shore of the Galilean sea, and it would almost seem that He had been preparing, from long before, the same illustration for times when the kingdom should have entered a broader field. I might show you a seed not heavier than a mustard seed, which came from a tree that may have been broader than this church and loftier than its spire; a tree which may have been growing on the mountains of California when the Savior was speaking on the Sea of Galilee, and whose parent may have been contemporary with the trees of Eden. And that little seed was the finished result of such a life, and in that seed was the energy which might produce such another monster. Just so, a word is the finished work of a mind, lighter than air, and yet stronger than any other thing in the universe below God; yea, even the creative might of God Himself is called "the Word."

There was the "Word made flesh" upon that boat floating by the shore of the sea; and as the farmer, whom He saw upon the hillside, scattered the living seed upon the soil, so He was casting the words of life upon the minds which were before Him.

A mind, before a word comes to it, is like a soil waiting for seed. As the live seed gathers the dead matter into a living plant, almost so, a living thought will come into an inert or a chaotic mind and, as we say, make a man.

They say that there are little seeds, spores they call them, floating in the air, so minute that we cannot feel them or see them, but we breathe them, and they plant themselves in the tissues of our system and draw our life away, working fevers and physical death in our members. However that may be, we all know how evil words are fatal to the soul, and that there are words whose "entrance giveth light;" "words which are spirit and are life."

Single words in which are condensed great thoughts of men are grand powers which hold and which move the world. They embody living forces, which come in and take possession of intelligent natures, and form them and move them as they will. Man is a creature of motive. He calls himself a free agent, and yet he finds himself to be so the subject of his ruling thoughts and of the motives which come to act upon him, that he is compelled to admit that he is not his own. These ideas, these words, which rule and form us, seem like a race of living creatures. And they have kings among them; and they have their own wars, and in the struggles of these mighty thoughts our minds are traversed or are captured, as the fields or the cities of the earth are by the race of man.

Every year in midsummer our nation holds a festival.

For what? For a victory which, a hundred years ago, one idea gained over another. And before that time, and since, all the land, and all the live world has been throbbing or convulsed with the strife of those thoughts. All the live world, we say. For there runs a clear line among the nations of men, between the living and the dead, or at least between the wakeful and the sleeping—between those which feel the life which was brought into the world by the words of Him who sat in the boat, on the shore of Galilee, and sowed His seeds of thought upon the multitudes on the beach, and those in whom those words have not yet taken root.

Of these mighty words there are orders, as there are of the angels. Some are true and some are false, some are high and some are low, some noble and some mean, some earthly or brutal or beastly, and some humane, angelic or divine. And they come into our human nature and change us into forms, loathsome and noxious, or beautiful and good, according to the character of the seed.

As the sower goeth forth to sow the good seed, the enemy cometh also and soweth tares. Every noble thought has its base counter thought. If from Bethel, "the house of God," there rises an unseen ladder to heaven, from Bethel there also goes down, as every man may see, a steep gorge to the Dead Sea. For against truth and law, and liberty, and love, and heaven, and God, there are hypocrisy, and tyranny, and license, and lust, and the everlasting fire prepared for the devil and his angels.

Perhaps we should also recognize a kind of intermediate class of moral growths, as of plants. We will not call the wild vine and the wild olive noxious, like the nightshade or the upas. They are unfruitful, but yet they perform a certain office in preparing the soil for a better growth. They may even receive an engraft which can change them, as "the engrafted word is able to save the soul." As yet they are earthly, not devilish; selfish, not malignant. The words of Christ, taking effect in minds which are not renewed by the Spirit of God, produce fruits of education, refinement and civilization. So there has grown from those seeds of the kingdom this cultured realm, which even now we call Christendom, the domain of Christ. The organic life of this civilization, such as it is, centers in the words of Christ, especially in that law, "Thou shalt love thy neighbor as thyself."

The great achievements of this civilization show how great a nature this human nature is; and they begin to suggest how great it may become. If so little of the law of Christ as we have, can make the difference between Wisconsin and Dahomey, what will the world become when every man's heart is full of the fellowship of man, and every man shall rise to the greatness of "loving God with all the heart and all the soul and all the mind and all the strength"?

So broadly and so greatly have the words of Christ sprung up in the arid soil of the wilderness world. "Go ye and teach all nations," said He who brought from heaven those seeds of truth. And the teachers whom He sent have gone, scattering them on the good ground, and among the thorns and by the wayside, and even where they have not brought forth fruit unto perfection, "the word has not returned to Him void, but has accomplished that which He pleased and prospered in the thing whereto He sent it." All this humanizing influence of civilization, with its advance in arts and sciences, in institutions of public and private life, in government, in education, in laws and in customs, has been preparing the soil for that Tree of Life which He came to plant.

Of that Tree of Life, He, the Word of God, is the seed upon the earth; and that only is true life, which draws its life from that vital seed.

As the seed falls into the ground and dies, losing its

narrow and secluded life to draw to itself the elements that are around it and to form with them a new body of quick life, and as that new body sends roots far down and far round in the dark and dank earth, that it may gather more and more of the capacity which is there and lift it up, by its own life, into the free air and toward the bright heaven, so, forth from the bosom of the Father came the Word of Life, the Son of God, the seed of heaven, and lived with us and died for us, that we might rise in Him in newness of life.

Here is the secret of the true life of the renewed world. The precepts of the living Savior, like those of Confucius, might change the form of society and the habits of men's thoughts. It is beautiful to say, "Thou shalt love the Lord thy God with all thy heart and thy neighbor as thyself." And such a precept, becoming popular, would put a fine surface upon society. But He who lived and died that doctrine, became a center of death to sin and of life to righteousness for as many as receive Him. He says, "Except a grain of wheat fall into the ground and die it abideth alone, but if it die it bringeth forth much fruit; and I, if I be lifted up from the earth, will draw all men unto me." Upon our earth was shed that precious blood. In the cold ground the Savior lay for us, and for the Father's love and law. That is a Word that means something; a word not of show but of life, and as we look upon it, we feel a secret power drawing us to it. We, or even the masters of Israel, may not understand what that power is. The particle of moisture or of earth does not understand what is the secret attraction of the seed, or the germ or the root, which is drawing it. And yet it is an earthly thing; it is in accordance with the deepest laws which the Son of God fixed in the world when he made the world. He did not make the soil to be forever inert. He did not make the soul to be only an earthly soul. Each was for something higher; for transformations from death to life, and from life to higher life, ceasing not short of the very life of God. This strange attraction which draws the soul to Christ, is the very leading of the Father, the working of the law for which He made the world; and this new moving in the heart to self-sacrifice like that of Christ, to love to God filling and expanding the heart and reaching to lay hold of heart and soul and mind and strength, it is the new "law of the spirit of life in Christ Jesus," making us free from the law of sin and death.

But how can these things be? Is it not all mysticism? We may answer, how can the seed, which dies in the ground, draw dead matter to it, and lift it up in newness of life? Oh, that we could at least have such faith as is in a grain of mustard seed. It does not pause to puzzle itself with the theory. It just falls into the ground and dies and draws, and up springs the plant, and the tree; and the birds rest on its boughs, its cheerful blossoms fill the air, and for one seed in the spring there are thousands in the summer, all full of the same faith. Oh, if we had faith like a grain of mustard seed, how soon the earth would be full of the glory of the Lord! From this power of the seed of life spring, not only individual souls, like annual plants, but institutions, which stand like trees of righteousness to bless the world from age to age. Indeed we may better view the whole salvation as one tree of life, appearing in various forms and bearing twelve manner of fruit, but all from one seed, and from one root.

There is the Church of God, the one fellowship of true believers, which, as it becomes more and more perfect, needs less of form, Jerusalem and Gerizim fading like morning clouds, as the day comes on, when the true worshipers shall worship in spirit and in truth. In the midst of human governments is growing a kingdom of God, ruling by laws written in the hearts of men.

The power which is bringing all this on, is under this charter, " Go ye and teach all nations, baptizing

them in the name of the Father, and of the Son, and of
the Holy Ghost; teaching them to observe all things
whatsoever I have commanded you; and lo, I am with
you alway even unto the end of the world."   Do you observe
what that is, "teaching and baptizing?"   Is it anything else
than what we call "Christian education?"   Perhaps it is, for
He goes on to say, "baptizing them in the name of the
Father, and of the Son, and of the Holy Ghost."   That is, it
is an evangelical Christian education.   That is the Tree of
Life, which the Son of God came to plant.   The first and central trunk of that tree was the little school of Christ; those
twelve disciples, perhaps the happiest number for a class.   He
would not preach fully to the people till those men were fully
prepared to bear the seed of life.   They were His Seminary.
Do you know what the word "Seminary" means?   It comes
from the Latin word "semen"—a seed—and it means a place
for seeds—a nursery; and the system then instituted is one of
the centers of preparation, from which the sowers go with
the word of life.

In Cairo I found myself under a strange tree.   Here and
there, along its branches, come down long and strong shoots,
seeking the ground, and when they find it they grasp it with
new roots and become new centers of the life of the tree.   It
was a Banyan tree, transferred from the banks of the Ganges
to those of the Nile.   I come back to the valley of the Mississippi and find that a tree which sprang from the words
spoken by the Sea of Galilee, and which the Pilgrims planted by
the Atlantic shore two hundred and fifty years ago, that that
tree—the Christian college—has sent a strong arm across
the land toward the setting sun.   Here and there on its way
it has sent down a shoot which has found good soil, but of
them all there is none so dear, or to a perhaps partial eye so
hopeful, as one which we saw, twenty-five years ago, coming
down and striking the soil in our own Beloit.   We did not make

it; it came from above. But we invited it and we promised to cherish it "with sympathies and prayers and contributions according to our means," a pledge of which we have not been altogether unmindful. But how much more faithful has the Father been! The little shoot, then seeking root in the border, how it stands now as a tree in the midst of the land and of the earth! See how its boughs are spreading westward! See the shoot coming down from them and striking gloriously in Minnesota; and that other one in Kansas, fed by martyr blood; and another is just striking the soil in Nebraska; and this year has gone from here the impulse which may produce another in Dakota. Meanwhile the sowers go to the South and the broad North from sea to sea, and over the oceans to England and Japan, to Turkey, China and India.

Great things God hath done for us, whereof we are glad. Dare we remain here and keep the charge which He hath committed to us in behalf of the Tree of Life? But who is sufficient for these things? How shall we enter into such a future? Who is sufficient? Christ is sufficient, and all we have to do is to take into our hearts that seed of life—that "Christ Jesus be formed in our hearts, the hope of glory." "Twenty-five years from now," said, in that day, a voice which is now gone up higher, "twenty-five years from now the Rock River Valley will be one of the most blessed abodes of the earth." Thanks to God for the blessing thus far fulfilled and prayers to Him that He will carry on His promise unto its perfection.

Such were the prayers and hopes in which Beloit College was planted, and in the early fulfillment of which the preceding discourse was given, at its twenty-fifth anniversary. The second quarter-century, now closing, has seen a larger fulfillment.   Men who have gone from here have been engaged in the planting or development of more than twenty-five colleges, and have sown the seed of the word in almost every state and territory of our great nation.

It is moreover a great blessing to the Rock River valley, that from it have gone those who, drinking "of that Spiritual Rock that followed them," have borne the Seed of the Tree of Life to the ends of the earth.   It is thrilling, even now, to trace that line of living green around the world.   We see it close at home among our own Indians; in Eastern and in Western Mexico; in Micronesia and Hawaii; in Japan and China; in Further and in Hither India; till we come to the lands where Eden was and where Enoch and Abraham and Paul walked, and we find the line again in Syria and Assyria, in Armenia, Cilicia, Macedonia and Bulgaria.   There, in that Turkish empire, to-day, angels and men are looking upon the spectacle of a Christian people, slaughtered by Moslems, while in Christian Europe, six "Great Powers" stand by, paralyzed by their own policies ; and almost the only relief is a band of American Missionaries, dispensing the sympathy of Christendom.

Among those missionaries have been eight from our own College, and now there are three Institutions of higher Christian Education, presided over by three sons of Beloit ; one on the Tigris, one on the Euphrates, and one in Tarsus, the city from which the Apostle to the Gentiles came.   There they stand, in their patient energy and their peaceful valor, giving aid and comfort to body, mind and soul.

It is an image of those silent but true influences of the word of life, working not only there but in every land and in every calling, which, as we hope and pray, shall make Hiddekel and Euphrates, and our own Rock River also, "heads" again of the river which "went out of Eden to water the garden. "

www.ingramcontent.com/pod-product-compliance
Lightning Source LLC
Chambersburg PA
CBHW021725110726
47902CB00005B/1349